# Other Novels by S. P. Perone

## Adult Fiction

*The StarSight Project*
*Crisis on Flight 101*
*Einstein's Tunnel*
*Murder Almighty*
*Judgment Day*

## Young Adult Fiction

*Youthanasia*

## Juvenile Fiction

*Star of the Future*

# TURNED ON!

A Young Professor's 1960s Memoir

## S. P. Perone

# TURNED ON!
## A YOUNG PROFESSOR'S 1960S MEMOIR

*iUniverse books may be ordered through booksellers or by contacting:*

*iUniverse LLC*
*1663 Liberty Drive*
*Bloomington, IN 47403*
*www.iuniverse.com*
*1-800-Authors (1-800-288-4677)*

*ISBN: 978-1-4917-4788-9 (sc)*
*ISBN: 978-1-4917-4720-9 (hc)*
*ISBN: 978-1-4917-4394-2 (e)*

*Library of Congress Control Number: 2014915195*

*Printed in the United States of America.*

*iUniverse rev. date:    09/12/2014*

# CONTENTS

Preface.................................................................................xi

Acknowledgments ...........................................................xiii

Prologue............................................................................ xv

    Purdue University, May, 1969 ....................................xvii

## Part 1. Beginnings

    Chapter 1    First Impressions .....................................................3

    Chapter 2    First Meeting .........................................................6

    Chapter 3    The Research Talk .................................................9

    Chapter 4    Negotiations ........................................................13

    Chapter 5    Out of the Frying Pan .........................................17

## Part 2. Getting Into It

    Chapter 6    Back to the Fifties ...............................................25

    Chapter 7    First Lecture.........................................................29

    Chapter 8    MUACC, 1962....................................................33

    Chapter 9    Recruiting............................................................38

    Chapter 10  Into the Fire........................................................43

    Chapter 11  Awakening ..........................................................48

    Chapter 12  Getting Acquainted.............................................54

    Chapter 13  Getting It On.......................................................59

    Chapter 14  Would Things Ever be the Same? .........................65

    Chapter 15  Snowstorm..........................................................69

    Chapter 16  A New Flock of Students .....................................74

## Part 3.  Fighting for Tenure

Chapter 17  The Intrepid J. R. Birk ...............................81
Chapter 18  Relationships ........................................89
Chapter 19  Making Ozone .........................................94
Chapter 20  Wet Dreams ...........................................97
Chapter 21  The Big Bang .........................................102
Chapter 22  'Searching ...........................................106
Chapter 23  Reflections ..........................................113
Chapter 24  Storm Warnings .......................................119
Chapter 25  Mike .................................................124
Chapter 26  Tenure or Not? .......................................126
Chapter 27  Country Time .........................................130
Chapter 28  Choices ..............................................135
Chapter 29  A Conversation .......................................138
Chapter 30  An Exam for the Ages .................................143
Chapter 31  The Day Arrives ......................................152

## Part 4.  California Calling

Chapter 32  Opportunity Knocks ...................................159
Chapter 33  Summer of Love .......................................166
Chapter 34  A Love Affair ........................................169
Chapter 35  All's Fair.... .......................................174
Chapter 36  Play Time ............................................177
Chapter 37  What Have We Wrought? ................................185

## Part 5.  1968

Chapter 38  What Was It about 1968? ..............................189
Chapter 39  A Meeting in San Francisco ...........................198
Chapter 40  Flying Home ..........................................203
Chapter 41  Getting Ready ........................................207
Chapter 42  Pressure Cooker ......................................214

## Part 6.  Things We Did Last Summer

Chapter 43  Computers Anyone? ....................................225

Chapter 44   Selected Photos from Summer Computer
             Course, 1968 – 1974 ..............................230
Chapter 45   Computer Games.................................236
Chapter 46   Welcome Additions..............................239
Chapter 47   Pranks, Incorporated...........................242
Chapter 48   Other Side of Midnight ........................248
Chapter 49   A Happening ....................................260
Chapter 50   Cleaning Solution ..............................263
Chapter 51   Football ........................................267
Chapter 52   Family Affairs..................................271
Chapter 53   End of an Era? ..................................284

## Part 7.   Reaching for the Brass Ring

Chapter 54   What's It All About?............................289
Chapter 55   Playing Games—a Flashback .....................295
Chapter 56   A Bump in the Road..............................300
Chapter 57   Get a Ph.D. and See the World...................307
Chapter 58   Zurich..........................................316
Chapter 59   Options ........................................322
Chapter 60   Finish Line.....................................326

Epilogue.......................................................331
Author's Notes.................................................361
About the Author...............................................363

# DEDICATION

For priceless memories—

Buck, Mike, Dave, Zip, Larry, and J.R.

# PREFACE

No decade before or since witnessed cultural, technical and social change as dramatic as the 1960s.

Kennedy's charm opened the decade, while Nixon's paranoia closed it. Pop culture reflected a transition from the rigid fifties to the permissive seventies. The birth control pill gave rise to the spirit of free love. Women declared themselves "liberated" and burned their bras. During this era before AIDS, sex became as casual as was sharing malts at the corner soda fountain in the 1940s and 1950s.

Lyndon Johnson turned Vietnam into the most powerful negative force of a generation. The increasingly unpopular war spawned protest music, draft card burning, and a hippie counter-culture—prominently displayed in 1967's "summer of love" in San Francisco. Mind-bending drugs like LSD surfaced, especially on campuses. Psychedelic music evolving at the end of the decade emulated a drug-assisted escape from reality.

The "establishment" did not share in this "liberal" movement on campuses. A conservative generation still controlled university administrations, government, law enforcement, and the military. Vietnam catalyzed the spread of student activism, even to conservative Midwestern campuses. Clashes became inevitable. Remember Kent State?

Ah yes, these were turbulent times. The sixties changed us all forever. And nothing reflected these changes more vividly than American campuses.

This memoir provides a portal to that era that will be nostalgic for some, enlightening for others, and hopefully entertaining for all. Based on my experiences as a twenty-three year old professor beginning his university career in 1962, it offers the intriguing perspective of a faculty member who was young enough to run in student circles.

This is not intended to be a literal accounting but is told rather as a collection of personal experiences that characterized that turbulent decade. Some stories are dramatized composites of multiple separate events. But each episode is based on real events and real people. Except for a few incidental characters, no names have been changed.

Taken together, these episodes describe a personal journey toward self-realization in a world that was rapidly changing in fascinating ways. This collection is intended to not only capture the impact on campus life of historical events that defined the 1960s, but also to provide insight to the inner workings of the academic world, in that era and beyond.

S. P. Perone
July, 2014

# ACKNOWLEDGMENTS

I am grateful for the assistance of a small army of reviewers—particularly former Purdue students Bill Kretlow, Vic Evins, John Patterson, Rick Baldwin, Keith Dahnke, Bill Gutknecht, Heinz Stapelfeldt and Bernie Bulkin—who were also the sources for much of the content and photos. The inputs of former colleagues—Jon Amy, Harry Pardue, Betty Hatfield, Jack Harrar, and Walt Selig—are also gratefully acknowledged. Other reviewers included: Sandy (Mrs. Jim) Birk; Carol Carbone; Bonnie Patterson; Maria Espinosa; Mark Machado; Ole and Mary Nordhavn; Dorene and Jerry Donaldson; and Jessica Perone. Their inputs were most welcome. I'm especially grateful for the invaluable contributions of my wife, Sylvia, and of our children—Sammy, Vita, Amy, Renée, Stephanie, and Melanie. I am particularly indebted to Don Ebert for the cover graphics and Mike Burke, Jr. for vintage family photos.

I must acknowledge also the assistance and cooperation of a number of individuals in the Purdue Library Archives Division and the Department of Statistics for securing vintage photos from the 1960s for publication here.

# PROLOGUE

# Purdue University, May, 1969

Alarmed by student protests on campuses in Wisconsin, California, and elsewhere, Hoosier legislators naturally figured they should punish the students of their own state.

The news hit the newspapers over the weekend. The Indiana legislature had imposed a punitive spike in tuition that virtually screamed: *This'll teach you ungrateful long-haired freaks!*

What the hell were they thinking?

By Monday afternoon, thousands of normally conservative Purdue students had converged angrily on the administration building in West Lafayette, Indiana. Fanning the flames of protest was that small core of campus activists opposed to the Vietnam War.

*Student protest outside executive building, May, 1969. [Courtesy of Purdue University Statistics Department, 1950s – 60s Gallery, www.stat.purdue.edu, copyright, Lillian Cote, used with permission.]*

That was when I got the call.

The youthful male voice was raspy. "Dr. Perone, you need to cancel the exam in the Hall of Music tomorrow night."

"What? Who is this?" I asked.

He ignored the question. "We're shutting down the campus."

"It's the last mid-term *exam*," I protested. "People have—"

"We don't care," the angry voice interrupted. "Everything gets shut down."

"I can't do that."

The voice remained silent for a few moments. Then it hissed. "Dr. Perone, you really don't want to be *responsible*. People are going to get hurt."

There was a click. And the voice was gone.

A million thoughts swirled in my head. Who were these protestors? What would they do? Could they be stopped?

The chilling vision of sixteen hundred students—trapped in the debris of the cavernous Hall of Music—flashed before my eyes. I caught my breath.

Surely the campus police could maintain order. Couldn't they?

I recalled the televised spectacle of Chicago police mauling anti-war demonstrators at the 1968 Democratic convention. Student protests had only gotten bolder and more violent since then.

Then the irony hit me.

A few years earlier I might have been right in the thick of it—occupying the administration building along with the students.

But here I was now, thirty years old, on track to become the youngest ever to make full professor in Purdue's chemistry department. Against all odds, I had become part of the "establishment."

"Don't trust anyone over thirty" was the catch phrase of the day. And I was now on the wrong side.

It hadn't always been that way, of course.

Seven years earlier I had been a neophyte professor, painfully naïve, more comfortable running with students than faculty.

Those youthful adventures had taken me into uncharted territory. It had been the sixties, after all. Everything was getting a fresh look.

My thoughts wandered back to the very beginning....

# PART 1
## Beginnings

# CHAPTER 1

## First Impressions

If there were a more dreadful vista than northern Indiana in 1962, I hadn't lived long enough to see it.

From the foul stench of ugly refineries around East Chicago to the flat featureless cornfields stretching from Ohio to Illinois, the Hoosier state welcomed my first drive-through with a thousand reasons never to return.

For added enjoyment on this Sunday in early April, it had taken most of the day over many two-lane highways to drive 250 miles from Madison, Wisconsin to West Lafayette, Indiana.

I was hungry and nearly *late*. Late for perhaps the most important date of my life—a cocktail-dinner meeting with Purdue University faculty that would size me up for a job as assistant professor of analytical chemistry.

I guided the green '59 Chevy Biscayne past the city limits sign of West Lafayette, thankful for the pleasant change of scenery. There were trees and hills and the Wabash River Valley up ahead.

But I cursed the timing. There was no way I could check into the Union Club, shower, change, and still make it to the home of Professor L. B. (Buck) Rogers in time for the five o'clock engagement.

I could see all the professors sitting in Buck Rogers' front room, looking at their watches and wagging their heads.

That disturbing vision provoked a consoling thought. *Hell*, I said to myself, *I've already* got *a job offer. From Wayne State. A damn good offer. And another thing*—

Then something strange happened.

3

Following a downward curving Northwestern Avenue past Ross-Ade football stadium, I cruised slowly past the main quadrangle of Purdue University. There, on the right, across a broad green field was a large fountain. Behind that was the administration building and the magnificent 6000-seat Hall of Music—the one people compared to Radio City.

It wasn't the sight of the fountain, the mall, or the massive red brick buildings that struck me. After all, Wisconsin's campus, with its lakeside setting, was pretty impressive. No, it was the fact that everything was *green*.

The grass was green; the trees had green leaves and colorful blossoms. Male students scurried about the vast grassy mall—in shorts and tank tops—tossing Frisbees or footballs. Co-eds were lounging about in short shorts and halter-tops, sunning themselves. It was *spring*.

When I had left Madison that morning, it had been *winter*. Trees were bare; grass was brown; skies were gray; Lake Mendota was frozen; students were bundled up. It was *winter* there but spring, glorious *spring* here.

Only someone who has endured a long, harsh Wisconsin winter can understand what a beautiful sight that was.

Strangely, this pleasant vision jogged a perverse flashback to my very first interview trip—to the University of Minnesota in mid-February. I had abandoned my car in a raging snowstorm and switched to a passenger train that eventually made it to Minneapolis a dozen hours later. The morning of my interview, I had awakened to twelve inches of new snow and a sunny 25 degrees below zero.

The Interview Gods weren't smiling on me. It was February 20, 1962. John Glenn's first space orbit in Friendship 7, the Mercury capsule, overshadowed everything that day, as the entire nation huddled around radios and TVs during the historic five-hour flight.

And I didn't help myself by delivering a shaky research talk.

The Minnesota faculty were very cordial. But they turned me down. I wasn't a good fit, they suggested tactfully. Too much overlap with another electrochemist there, Stanley Bruckenstein. Stan had phoned my major professor at Wisconsin, Irv Shain, with that message, adding that I might want to sharpen up my research talk.

The second interview, just one week before the Purdue trip, was to another wintry spot: Wayne State University in Detroit. With the humbling Minnesota experience to motivate me, this interview went spectacularly well. At the end of the day, the department head invited me to his office, mixed a couple martinis, and offered me a job right on the spot—assistant professor at 7500 dollars a year.

I floated back to Chicago O'Hare on one of those American Airlines Electra propjets—the ones whose wings had been falling off—and didn't even worry about it.

Wayne State had a good reputation, especially in my field. It would be a good place to start a career. The only problem was I really didn't want to live in *Detroit*.

Nevertheless, the plain truth was that Wayne State *wanted* me. They had called my major professor to apply gentle pressure and the hint of more money.

God it was nice to have that job offer in my pocket. *So what if my tardiness turns off the professors at Purdue*, I thought. *Detroit wouldn't be that bad a place to live, would it?*

Then I looked out the window to my right at the green, the flying footballs, and the co-eds in short shorts.

Suddenly, unexpectedly, I felt an overwhelming sense of kinship with this place. It was a compelling emotion I hadn't previously experienced.

Strangely, at that moment, I knew I wanted to be at Purdue.

Then, as if I had just entered a black hole, an eerie hollowness pulled at my chest.

What if they didn't want *me?*

# CHAPTER 2

## First Meeting

The gas station restroom was small and grimy. I splashed water on my face and wiped it off with a handkerchief. Shedding my grubby jeans and sweatshirt, I slipped quickly into the suit and shoes. I wet my hands and ran them over my black crew-cut hair.

Looking into the scratched-up mirror, I saw peering back a tired face needing a shave.

Grabbing the pile of cast-off clothing, I shot out of the restroom, avoiding the glare of the service station attendant. *How many times has he witnessed this kind of scene?* I wondered.

The '59 Chevy carried me toward the residential area east of campus. Professor Rogers had given me good directions, describing vividly the old two-story bungalow.

It was a charming old place, nestled among large established trees and flanked by similar homes. It was still daylight as I pulled into a parking spot on the street. I glanced at my wristwatch. The snap decision to pass up the Union Club had gotten me there on time—smelly, perhaps, but not tardy. For an instant I wondered which was worse.

Oh well, it was too late now.

Stepping out on the front porch was a tall, slender man in a grayish suit and narrow tie. He saw me getting out of the Chevy and waved. I took in my first sight of the famous Professor Lockhart B. Rogers—"Buck" Rogers to everyone.

My hasty research on Buck Rogers quickly came to mind. Purdue had hired him away from M.I.T. the previous year. In his mid-forties,

Buck was a well-known, powerful force in the world of analytical chemistry. Of most concern to me, though, was Buck's early career research that overlapped with my own.

I didn't want to be "Bruckensteined" at Purdue as I had at Minnesota.

Apprehensions aside, Buck's warm greeting outside his home in West Lafayette was memorable. I hadn't been prepared for his stature. Tall and lanky with crew-cut graying black hair, a narrow, pinched face, and large, piercing gray eyes, he wore a drab gray linen suit that hung on his slender frame. The only colorful item was a narrow knit tie with sprinkled patches of orange and black. (*School colors?* I wondered.)

Buck ushered me into the foyer. To my right was the front room with a seated circle of formally attired males—the hiring committee. He introduced me to them and to his wife, Eleanor—a lovely lady, tall, dark-haired, and slender like her husband. Eleanor excused herself to the kitchen where she was preparing dinner.

Buck's introduction of me to his guests had been followed quickly with an offer of a drink. "Scotch, bourbon, gin, or vodka?" he asked in that deep authoritative voice.

I hadn't eaten anything but chips and pretzels on the road and probably should have insisted on something soft. But that wasn't being offered. "Bourbon," I replied, assuming he would dilute it with 7-Up or Coke or something.

Buck spun around and disappeared into the kitchen, and I was drawn into a conversation with a young, good-looking, sandy-haired organic professor by the name of Dick Sneen. I soon learned that Dick was an associate professor and the only bachelor at the party. He was filling me in on local eateries when Buck showed up with a twelve-ounce tumbler filled to the brim with an amber liquid and two or three ice cubes.

"Thanks," I said, as Buck turned away. I took a deep sip, hoping to soothe my parched throat. In return, the bourbon lit a fire in my gullet. I barely avoided gasping aloud. He had put 7-Up in the drink, but not much.

Dick Sneen saw my red face. He winked, leaned closer, and explained, "Buck's trademark—big strong drinks—so he doesn't have to waste time getting refills."

Before dinner was served an eternity later, my tall glass of bourbon and my brain had both been sucked dry as I tried to respond to engaging questions from all directions.

I do recall one strange thing, however. In response to some unremembered question from one of the analytical faculty, Dale Margerum, I had jokingly *slapped* my own face. Even the next day I couldn't remember why. It was a dumb thing; and it made a loud sound.

Who could have missed it?

I could only imagine the hiring committee gathering together in a few days and clucking their tongues.

What a dumb way to kick off an interview.

# CHAPTER 3

## The Research Talk

Buck took the steps two-at-a-time, hesitating briefly at each landing to be sure that he wasn't leaving me too far behind. Someone had mentioned that Buck had been a track star in college. He certainly didn't waste time getting from place to place. I couldn't match his long-legged stride or the spring in his step.

I panted my way to the third floor classroom where I would deliver the all-critical research talk, if I survived the journey.

About fifteen rows of desks rose stadium style toward the back of the long, narrow room. Toward the rear were two slide projectors—one for bulky lantern slides, the other for smaller two-by-two-inch slides. Graduate students already occupied a handful of the desks. Someone had written my name and the title of the talk on the black board—*Cyclic Voltammetry of Benzophenone*. The four thirty seminar was ten minutes away.

I wondered which faculty would be there. Would they be joking about the kid who had gotten tipsy at Buck's house the previous evening?

Standing at the front of the classroom was one of Buck's grad students, waiting for my slides.

"Lantern or two-by-two?" he asked.

"Lantern," I replied, as I showed him the sturdy cardboard box containing my twenty-four homemade slides. "But I might not use them."

I looked at Buck, half expecting his protest.

9

He threw me a puzzled glance and changed the subject, as if to dismiss my remark. I only half listened to what he was saying. The student was still there, waiting for my decision.

I had tussled with that decision all day.

Lantern slides were three-by-four inches and fabricated with large, heavy glass plates. Mine were poorly crafted by a dexterity-challenged draftsman—*me*. Good thing I hadn't decided to become a brain surgeon.

I had used my slides at the Minnesota interview. We know what happened there. I had used the same slides at Wayne State. They had jammed the projector. I finished my Wayne State lecture as a "chalk talk." They offered me a job.

It didn't take a rocket scientist to figure this one out. I decided to give a "chalk talk" at Purdue.

I knew what Buck would think. A professional-level talk with slides was expected. I had gotten away without slides at Wayne State because mine had killed the projector. Now, at Purdue, I was about to tell them that I *chose* not to use slides.

I told Buck.

For the first—but not the last—time I got "the look"—the *I-disapprove-but-OK-whatever-you-say* stare, with Buck's large steely eyes peering down that narrow aquiline nose.

I braced myself and gave him my *I-may-not-be-as-smart-as-you-but-I-know-what-I'm-doing* look. He shrugged and dismissed his grad student. Then he went on to show me the electrical controls on the stone-topped desk at the front of the room.

The classroom filled up, and the noise level rose. Some of the students joked and laughed. Many stared at me, sizing me up. *Will this guy be on the faculty here next year?* they wondered.

A dozen faculty were easy to pick out—all wearing coats and ties. Some of the hiring committee encroached on the front rows. By this time I knew them well.

Dale Margerum, a tenured analytical chemist in his early thirties, would ask curious, sharply-honed science questions. Harry Pardue, a second-year analytical chemist from West Virginia—with his own grueling job interview fresh in mind—would toss softballs. Bob Grimley, a young physical chemist nearing a tenure decision, would attack like a pit bull.

I had no idea what kind of questions Buck would ask. His agenda was still a mystery to me.

Buck and I were standing together at the front of the room, nodding to arriving faculty, when the bell rang signaling the four thirty hour. Buck asked me to take a seat in the front row while he introduced me to the audience. In his hand was a sheet with the title of my talk and a short bio.

Buck decided to wait a minute to let stragglers get seated. I used these moments to ponder my opening words: *Thank you, Professor Rogers. I'm delighted to be here ... blah, blah, blah.* Then I did a quick mental checklist of the talk outline.

Irv Shain—my major professor at Wisconsin—had given me good advice for organizing my talk: the first twenty-five minutes should be tutorial, followed by fifteen minutes describing my research, five minutes to summarize, and the rest for questions.

Shain practiced this approach to perfection. He used *slides*, however.

And I had never given my talk from the top *without* slides. My last thought before hearing Buck loudly clear his throat was the impossibility of chalk-talking the content of all twenty-four slides—without chalk dust spewing over the first three rows.

The sound of Buck clearing his throat brought a curtain of silence down over the classroom. Pavlov was right.

Then something quite unexpected happened.

Through the front door walked a gentleman dressed in a dark tailored suit, starched white shirt, blue silk tie, smartly shined shoes, and impeccably styled light brown hair. The man was average height, sixtyish, and fit. Everything about him, including the professionally dyed hair and sunlamp tan, screamed power and wealth. I had met the man briefly that morning and would spend a half-hour with him the following day.

It was Earl (E. T.) McBee—the department head—one of the most powerful figures I would ever meet.

I looked at Buck. He was obviously surprised. I had heard that McBee rarely attended these seminars. He was much too busy ruling the department with an iron fist or making money through his company, Great Lakes Chemical.

My heart leapt into my throat as I watched the department head take a seat in the front row. I didn't know what I had done to deserve a personal visit by the infamous E. T. McBee—but it had to be either very good, or very bad.

And here I was, giving a *chalk talk*.

# Chapter 4

## Negotiations

It wasn't until the following morning, when I met with Buck Rogers for breakfast, that I got the verdict about my research talk.

"That was a hell of a talk yesterday," he commented, while munching on a piece of toast. "Damn good chalk talk. Earl McBee told me that later." He wiped the corner of his mouth and gave me a half-smile.

I beamed. "Thank you, Buck." (He had insisted from the beginning that I call him "Buck.") "I *was* a bit concerned," I admitted.

Inwardly, I thanked *Lady Luck* once again. If my slides hadn't killed the Wayne State projector the previous week....

Buck continued, "Well, it worked. Purdue folks believe professors ought to be good teachers as well as good researchers. You showed some good stuff yesterday. Derek Davenport called and told me that later."

There was a question mark on my face.

"Derek's the head of the general chemistry division. Publishes in the *Journal of Chemical Education*. His endorsement goes a long way."

I nodded and returned my attention to pushing the scrambled eggs around my plate. I was much too excited to eat.

"Look," Buck continued, "just between you and me, there's a good chance we're going to offer you the job."

I blushed. Truly, I was speechless. Getting a faculty job at a Big Ten school had been my dream. I couldn't believe it might really happen. He did say "a chance," I reminded myself. *Just a chance.*

Buck kept talking. "I've been wanting to get someone here doing modern electrochemistry, like what you and Shain are doing at

Wisconsin. This cyclic voltammetry stuff you talked about yesterday is really exciting."

Suddenly Professor Buck Rogers turned into salesman Buck Rogers. He was actually trying to convince me that I should choose Purdue. I didn't know what was coming next, but I didn't have to wait long.

"Would you feel uncomfortable telling me about your other job interviews?" he probed, peering at me tentatively.

"No," I replied quickly. "I've got an offer from Wayne State. I'm scheduled to visit Ohio State later this month."

Buck nodded. His eyes turned away discreetly. I knew what he was thinking. Ohio State had already hired somebody. I knew it. He knew it. My interview there would be a meaningless formality.

Buck began to probe further. "I'm sure Wayne State's offer is competitive; it's a good school." He arched an eyebrow. "I'll bet they don't have an instrumentation support group like we do."

Hell, I didn't know. Each school claimed they had instrumentation support. I had dealt with "support" staff at Wisconsin—glassblowing, machining, anything mechanical. *Electronics* support? Shain's group had learned how to be self-reliant.

Purdue had a *real* instrumentation group, led by Jon Amy, a former Purdue Chemistry Ph.D. graduate. I had done the tour. It was first class. Amy didn't think professors should build or repair their own electronics. He had put together a skilled staff to back him up. Buck really didn't have to sell me on it.

However, I did see an opportunity here to squeeze something out of him.

"You're right," I responded finally. "Jon Amy's operation is pretty impressive. But...." I paused. "I'm concerned about a couple other things."

Buck's eyes widened slightly while he waited for me to continue.

I revealed my concern that my research interests might overlap with his. Shain had warned me that if I had to compete with Buck for research students, or if there were any perception that he was influencing my work, it would be utterly fatal to my chances for tenure.

"Don't worry about that," he declared. "I've given up electrochemistry research. Nobody's going to think I'm the brain behind your work. If they do, I'll set them straight."

I nodded slowly. I could only take Buck at his word. But there were other, more subtle, issues, and I mentioned one. "At Wisconsin, two new analytical professors recently got hired at nearly the same time. The word is only one will get tenure. Is that what I would be walking into here? With Harry Pardue and myself?"

Buck dropped back a bit. Although my bluntness surprised him, he wasn't deterred. "You know, we had a situation like that back at Tech," he began. (I would later learn that whenever Buck urged his Purdue colleagues to take a fresh look at something, he referred to things from his days at M.I.T.—"back at Tech," as he put it.)

"You know what happened?" he continued. "The guy that came in one year after the first had a terrific advantage. He watched everything his predecessor did, and did him one better. Motivated the two of them like hell. In the end, we promoted them both." He gave me that soon-to-be-familiar half-smile once again.

I thought about it. I didn't know if I could ever do Harry Pardue "one better" on anything. However, I was just insecure enough to like the idea of having someone pave the way for me.

I didn't know then what a nightmare that might become later.

My final concern was the most pressing. Screwing up my courage, I blurted, "What if something happens and I haven't finished my thesis work by September?"

Buck's eyes widened again, and he backed away ever so slightly. "Is there a problem?" he queried.

"Oh, no. No," I replied too quickly. "But, you know...." I hesitated.

Buck picked up the thought. "Yeah, I know. Research is never a sure thing." His face inched a bit closer, and his eyes bored into mine. "How much experimental work do you have left?"

I sketched out my exit plan from Wisconsin. Three months to write the thesis, preceded by a month of final experiments, should get me out by mid-August. "There's one big potential monkey wrench," I added. "We—that is, Shain's group—will move all our research labs to the new chemistry building in June."

Buck's eyes went blank while his mind chewed on the problem. Then his eyes caught mine again and he said, "Well, if you're writing your thesis, the move shouldn't hold you up."

Apparently he didn't like the pained expression on my face. He added, "Oh, I see. What happens if your experiments aren't finished?"

It was a rhetorical question. We both knew the answer—*disaster*.

I remained silent—hoping Buck would provide an encouraging answer to his own question.

And he did.

"Look, Sam, everyone around here knows that Ph.D.s can slip a bit. Not that it's going to happen to you. However, if it did…."

He paused, and I held my breath.

"Well," he continued, "I'm sure we could cover your teaching assignments for a while."

I broke into a grin. "Gosh, that's great. I hope it won't be necessary."

Neither of us realized then the depths of hell that this issue would eventually put us through.

# CHAPTER 5

## Out of the Frying Pan

I sat outside Irv Shain's office in the new UW chemistry building. After working through the long August night, collecting what I hoped were the final data for my Ph.D. thesis, I had left my lab and traipsed down the hall to wait for Shain's arrival.

As I anticipated nervously his usual nine o'clock appearance, a number of other grad students poked their heads into Shain's outer office. I scowled, and they left. Nobody was going to see Shain today before I did.

I was supposed to show up at Purdue on September 1—barely one week away. Completing my thesis by then was impossible. A couple weeks earlier I had reluctantly informed Buck Rogers of the problem. Buck had repeated his commitment to cover my teaching assignment. He told me to stay at Wisconsin until the thesis was done.

Buck had won my unabated worship.

And I had been working around the clock—determined that Buck would not be strung out too long.

Unfortunately, during the preceding week Buck had called to say that some faculty at Purdue had "pitched a bitch"—his words not mine. They insisted that I honor my contract. Buck claimed to have been caught by surprise. "Back at Tech," he had proclaimed, "people were more reasonable."

I didn't know who had objected to Buck's plan. Maybe the senior faculty were growing weary of Buck's "back at Tech" contrariness. Putting him in a bind would provide perverse satisfaction.

Or perhaps the junior faculty were objecting to Buck's pressure on them to pitch in and cover for me. Not that I could blame them. The new faculty members at Wisconsin had assured me that no good deed ever went unpunished, especially if it got in the way of the prime directive—publishing lots of papers and bringing in lots of grants.

So, regardless of who was screaming back at Purdue, Buck had been betrayed. Now I would pay the price.

I pondered the gravity of my situation. A Ph.D. degree depends primarily on the thesis research project. Time of completion is very unpredictable, and the major professor has complete autocratic control.

Nevertheless, my thesis project had progressed well enough at the beginning of 1962 that my major professor, Irv Shain, had allowed me to apply for academic openings. It had been a calculated risk. Why take the risk? Because academic openings are normally filled only at the beginning of the fall semester. If you miss that target, you wait—and spend a year in professional limbo until new jobs open up.

Added to the dilemma was the unpredictability of academic openings. My goal was to be a professor at a Big Ten university. In 1962 there were only *three* of these openings in my field, with dozens of potential applicants.

If I were forced to wait a year, there might not be *any* desirable openings.

These somber thoughts were interrupted by the sound of Shain's lumbering footsteps in the hallway. He turned the corner into the outer office, and the tall, dark-haired figure came into view. There was no surprise on his face, just a pained look.

He was not looking forward to this conversation any more than I was.


Shain looked at the graph I had placed on his desk. It was crude but convincing. I had finally produced a credible theoretical treatment that fit the data—a goal we had pursued for months.

He raised his eyes, and I inquired hesitantly, "I think I can start writing now, don't you?"

I held my breath as Shain sat back in his chair and gazed out the office window. It was a familiar pose. The squinting eyes focused on some faraway object. The brow furrowed beneath the short tightly curled black hair.

Finally, he turned away from the window. The dark eyes bored into me. "You think you're done?"

"Well ... yes," I mumbled. Then I sucked up some courage. "We've nailed down the benzophenone mechanism; and gotten kinetics, too. I ... I'd like to start writing it up."

He nodded blankly. "Your data *do* seem to fit." Then he shot a skeptical glance at me. "But you're using *approximate* theory."

"True," I conceded. "No one has rigorous second-order theory. We're years away from that. Nicholson is only now looking at first-order stuff."

Shain remained silent. He leaned back and propped his long legs up on the desk, gazing at the ceiling for a few moments. Then he looked back at me and said, "You want to get out of here, don't you?"

"You know the situation, Dr. Shain. I'm really in a bind."

"You know me, Sam," he drawled. "I don't give a *damn* that Purdue is putting pressure on you ... or on me."

"I ... I do understand," I replied.

"Christ!" he exclaimed. "You've only been here three years. I've got people that were here before you, and they'll be here long after you've left."

"I know," I admitted. Shain had graduated a handful of Ph.D.s. None had taken fewer than four years. There were some that would take much longer. "But I've been on fellowships the whole time," I reminded him. "I've gotten a lot of research done in three years."

Shain turned his head slightly and asked, "How old are you now? Twenty-four? Twenty-five?"

I shook my head sheepishly. "Twenty-three." I knew how extraordinary that was. Hell, Ken Martin had been thirty when he finished.

Shain wagged his head and looked away. "Buck asked me to let you go if you only needed to finish the writing. Did you know that?"

"Yuh ... yes," I stammered. "He mentioned it to me."

He snapped his gaze back to me. "Is that what you want to do?"

"If I don't show up, I'll lose the job."

"That wouldn't be the end of the world." He didn't add what he was thinking: *You could look for a job again next year.*

19

I didn't reply. What could I say? Shain knew that an opportunity like Purdue might never come my way again.

Shain continued, "You know how difficult it is to get your thesis written somewhere else? Hell, you saw what Ken Martin went through, right here."

I nodded slowly. Ken had been a close friend. I had watched Shain put him through hell. No shrinking violet, Ken had struggled to get Shain to read thesis drafts. When he had succeeded, Shain had demanded numerous rewrites and additional data. It had been a nightmare. I could only imagine the difficulty of writing my thesis *in absentia*.

Shain added, "I've never allowed a student to leave without finishing the thesis first. It's bad policy. In most cases the thesis never gets done. That's a fact."

"I think you know me, Dr. Shain. I'll get it done."

He shook his head, a sour expression on his face. Some internal argument was raging. Finally, he opened up. "I'm *pissed off* with Purdue for putting me in this position. And they're not thinking of *your* best interests." He paused for a long moment to engage my gaze and then said slowly, "But I *will* let you go."

I digested his reluctant words, and a sense of relief rushed through me. "You ... you mean no more experiments?" I croaked.

His eyes narrowed. "We'll have to see."

"I ... well ... thank you," I stammered. I wanted to say more, but Shain's harsh gaze cut me off.

He placed his feet back on the floor and leaned forward. His eyes locked with mine. "You have no idea what's ahead, Sam. Teaching; research; writing your thesis. They're setting you up to fail."

"I can do it," I insisted.

"Really?" He wagged his head slowly. "I'll give you six months to have that Ph.D. in your pocket, or you'll be *finished* at Purdue."

Within a week I had moved my wife and two little girls to Lafayette, Indiana. I had shown up for work on time, and my first year at Purdue had begun.

Would it be the nightmare that Shain had predicted? Would it be my *last* year at Purdue, let go ignominiously for lack of a Ph.D.?

Or would this first year draw me into a whole new world—the exciting academic arena of a major research university?

Mind-blowing journey or abject failure? My first year at Purdue would be the gateway to one or the other.

# PART 2
# Getting Into It

# CHAPTER 6

## Back to the Fifties

I was not your typical entry-level assistant professor when I arrived at Purdue. First of all, I didn't have a Ph.D. I was also uncommonly young—twenty-three—and had never done any teaching.

These factors were only part of the story, however. Much more weighty personal baggage would impact navigation through the world-changing events of the following decade. So, before getting into the misadventures of my first year at Purdue, I'll detour briefly back to an earlier time

I was the product of an Italian-Catholic culture in blue-collar Rockford, Illinois. I had received all the traditional "benefits" of a Catholic school education—*fear and guilt*. In 1951, after completing seventh and eighth grades in one year, I entered St. Thomas high school—a Catholic boys' school—at age twelve. Physically, I had matured early. Nevertheless, girls needed only one date to figure out that I was basically clueless.

Not that it was always a problem. Some girls seemed to like dating a kid who couldn't find second base with a map and a compass. Never mind that I really *wanted* to find it.

My parents didn't help. Permissive they were not. They instilled a work ethic that compelled me to take on steady part-time work from the day I began high school until the day I completed college. While my classmates cavorted after school and on weekends, I shined shoes for tips and later learned the shoe repair trade.

Don't get me wrong. I was far from unique in having to work through school. But considering that I was *already* socially-challenged, well, I never did get to run with the "in crowd."

Give my parents credit for pushing me toward college from the day I climbed out of the crib. Frank and Celia (Parrinello) Perone were second-generation Italian-Americans, who lived through the Great Depression and World War II. My father left school at the ninth grade to help support his parents and eight siblings. He supported us with manual labor and small independent business ventures (grocery, restaurant, real estate). His constant advice to me was "Make a living with your brain, not your back."

Except for my Uncle Nick (my mother's brother, Nick Parrinello) no family member had ever gone to college. My grandparents could not have paid for his education. His opportunity came through the intercession of one of his high school teachers to get him into a co-op industrial program. My parents cast Uncle Nick as my role model, and like my parents, he urged me to attend college.

*Left to Right. Uncle Nick Parrinello, Celia (Parrinello) Perone (Mother), Frank Perone (Father). Ca. 1940. [Copyright, S. P. Perone]*

Though my parents understood that college would be my ticket to a better life, they were unable to help financially. My earliest dream had been to attend Notre Dame University. By high school, the dream had scaled back to Marquette. It soon became clear, however, that living expenses alone would make *any* university too expensive. And community colleges were virtually unheard of in 1955 Illinois.

I applied for a scholarship to St. Thomas College in Minnesota, to no avail. I considered entering the military. But I was too young, scheduled to graduate high school at age sixteen.

It was then that one of many, many fortuitous events occurred in my life.

During my senior year of high school, the small, highly-regarded, local women's school, Rockford College, announced that they would begin accepting male students. They founded a coordinated college, called "Rockford Men's College," that would occupy the same campus. I applied, and the college awarded a scholarship for half my tuition. My parents provided free lodging.

My problems were solved! It was a miracle. Frankly, I don't know what path my life would have taken if Rockford College hadn't opened its doors to men in 1955.

*Sam Perone, age 16, 1955. [Copyright, S. P. Perone]*

Attending Rockford College was an incredible adventure. Try to imagine a socially challenged, naïve, sixteen-year-old, Catholic-school-educated young man's first taste of *secular* education. Imagine his amazement to learn that others did not share his literal concepts of creation, heaven, hell or salvation. Imagine his discovering political, social, and ethical viewpoints that hadn't been dictated by the *Catholic Voice.* Imagine his first encounter with liberated, free-thinking females!

It was a mind-blowing experience.

Clearly, Rockford College was my intellectual and spiritual awakening. Unfortunately, it did little to rectify my social immaturity. When I wasn't attending classes at the college, I continued to live in a world far removed and very different from the small college campus.

There was one overriding factor, however, that affected my social evolution during college. I was married at the age of *seventeen*.

You have to understand the mind-set of a Midwestern Italian-Catholic culture in the 1950s, particularly in a working class town like Rockford. You were expected to marry early, get a steady job, have children, and raise a family.

My new wife, Anita, was eighteen and had just graduated from high school. I was seventeen, but going into my sophomore year of college. It was not a marriage of necessity, but everything about our culture had funneled us to that point.

We lived with my parents until I finished college. In 1959, when I entered graduate school at Wisconsin-Madison, we moved into a one-bedroom apartment in a brand new graduate student housing development called Eagle Heights. Our first child, Vita, was born on Christmas day that year.

Anita would give us four wonderful children—three daughters and a son. She supported my quest for higher education and a professional career. And she was a good wife and wonderful mother to our children.

Nevertheless, some would say it was predictable that our marriage would fall apart. So many young marriages of the 1950s did. Ours would have had to endure the strain of entering a world dramatically different from that of our youth. It didn't. The drift apart was inevitable and painful.

Although I will occasionally allude to family matters in the chapters ahead, the focus of this memoir will be on *campus life*—the interactions, conflicts, struggles, victories and defeats of a young professor in an academic, social, and cultural environment undergoing dramatic changes. I hope this brief trip back to the 1950s will help the reader understand better the episodes that follow.

# CHAPTER 7

## First Lecture

I arrived at Purdue in fall, 1962, without having done any university teaching. Most graduate students do *some* teaching—supervising labs or conducting recitation classes. Some even present lectures.

I had done none of that at Wisconsin.

So, naturally, the Purdue Chemistry Department decided that my first assignment should be to teach the intermediate graduate analytical chemistry course.

I was *so* unprepared.

Don't get me wrong. The department had a perfect right to expect me to do some teaching. In fact, they had made a point of insisting that I show up at Purdue that September—rather than put the finishing touches on my Wisconsin Ph.D.—presumably because only *my* warm body could plug some otherwise unfixable gap in the teaching assignments.

Nevertheless, it was customary at research universities to give a new assistant professor some lightweight assignment—like assisting one of the senior professors in teaching a course. That would be a more typical assignment for a new guy who was busting his hump to get a research program off the ground.

Well, the department *did* give me that kind of assignment, *in addition to* the responsibility for the graduate lecture course.

I sucked it up and looked into the course I would be expected to teach. Chem. 521 was a three-credit survey course open to advanced undergraduates or "deficient" graduate students. Mostly graduate students took the course. And these students were pretty darned sharp. They simply hadn't been taught much analytical chemistry as undergraduates.

I sought Buck Rogers' advice. He recommended a syllabus that had me starting off the course with a segment on elementary statistics. This was the sort of material normally taught in sophomore analytical courses, and I should have been prepared. Unfortunately, I wasn't. Somehow, the statistics segment had eluded my undergraduate course.

So I got out my trusty copy of Laitinen's advanced text, *Chemical Analysis*, and resolved that I would quickly learn whatever I was supposed to teach.

You might expect that someone who had (nearly) completed the requirements for a chemistry Ph.D. should be knowledgeable about all things in his field, particularly in his chosen specialty, analytical chemistry.

Not so.

The Ph.D. is a *research* degree. Besides the all-important thesis research, some graduate chemistry programs require no more than competency tests on core topics. A Ph.D. candidate might only take courses supporting the thesis research problem—often in other fields like mathematics, biology, electronics, computations, etc.

The University of Wisconsin, where I did my doctoral work in the early sixties, had minimal course requirements. Purdue's doctoral program, on the other hand, had perhaps the largest course requirements of any in this country.

My entry to university graduate teaching couldn't have been a greater *mismatch*.

It took me a week to construct notes for my first lecture. I walked into the classroom and saw about fifty first-year graduate students, most of them my age, practically all of them more mature and knowledgeable about *everything*.

I had practiced the lecture and was putting on a good face, despite the butterflies in my stomach. Inexperience, however, led me into some fundamental errors in judgment.

One of these was to pose questions to the class and wait for a response.

My simple inquiries were met with deafening, unnerving silence. The sweat poured down my back as I answered my own questions.

This little Socratic self-dialogue did accomplish one thing. It encouraged the students to ply *me* with questions. It soon became quite clear that I was in for a real struggle that semester—trying to keep one step ahead.

One student in class that day stood out from the rest. Seated near the back of the tiered classroom was a tall, bespectacled young man. He asked questions in a deep, crisp New York City accent. His tone was respectful, but the confident knowledge behind each question intimidated the hell out of me.

Later, I would learn that my inquisitor's name was Bernie Bulkin and that he was a physical chemistry major. We were destined to become good friends. Nevertheless, for the duration of that first lecture, his polite questioning caused me to manufacture sweat in record quantities.

Somehow I plowed through my lecture notes to the very end. Then I checked out the clock at the back of the room.

Over *twenty minutes* still remained.

But the tank had run dry. I hadn't prepared anything more. I had nothing left to say.

I panicked, searching my brain for something—*anything*—that I might discuss for twenty minutes. Was there something tucked away in my mind that could be relevant in any possible way?

I seized on the *only* thing on my mind at that time—my thesis research. Now *there* was something I could talk about at the drop of a hat.

Following this brief pause in my lecture, I introduced the new topic. "To emphasize the importance of statistical analysis of data, let me give you an example from my thesis research...." The research I described easily. The statistical analysis was all bullshit.

Because I had nothing to write on the blackboard, I faced the class and examined their faces. I caught the curious gaze from Bernie Bulkin at the rear of the room. I prayed to God that he wouldn't ask a question.

Unfortunately, God wasn't listening. Bernie raised his hand. I nodded at him and held my breath.

Very politely, in that deep voice, he asked, "This is all very interesting, Dr. Perone, but what does it have to do with the price of tea in China?"

I froze. Bernie was challenging me directly. But—*Damn it!*— he was right. I made a snap decision.

I shrugged and forced a smile. "Not a damn thing," I replied. Then I managed a chuckle. "I just like to talk about my research."

Bernie hesitated for a moment. Then he beamed and chuckled too, a deep throaty guffaw that spread to the rest of the class. It was a good-hearted laugh. They were laughing *with* me, not at me.

Then I did something I eventually learned to do really well, acting as though I had planned to let the class out early—giving them a break on the first day. I can still see Bernie's puzzled look from the back of the room. Then the puzzled look turned to a knowing grin. I hadn't fooled him.

Bernie and I had a continuing dialogue during that semester. His questions were always curious and polite, though with that deep, knowing, New York voice he could have massacred me. He didn't. I returned the favor. I 'fessed up to the class that I was also just learning a lot of this stuff. I urged them to "keep me honest."

Bernie had already figured that out the first day. Much later he told me so.

By the end of the semester a bond had been forged with the members of that first class of mine—the class of '62— that I valued for many years.

That was the *good* news.

The bad news was very bad. Not only was my thesis unfinished, it had hardly begun. A copy of the one-page outline jotted down for Irv Shain five months earlier was still sitting in my briefcase, unembellished.

That six-month deadline Shain had set for me was looking more unrealistic every day.

# Chapter 8

## MUACC, 1962

The bell sounded, and my Chem. 521 students fled the room. The lecture had been pretty dry. It was a beautiful late fall afternoon, and there were better things to do.

I hastened down the third floor corridor toward my office-lab. The experiment running in my lab was on my mind. The activity at the end of the hall escaped my attention.

Buck stood outside his office down the hall from mine. Performing his daily ritual—when he was in town—he buttonholed each of his students in adjoining labs for research up-dates. His back was to me, and he stood, hands in pockets, grilling Don Guran just outside the corner lab.

I tried to slip by them unnoticed. Buck sensed the movement, however, and reached out an arm. "Hold up," he commanded. "I need to talk to you."

I forced a smile and paused. He broke away from Don and indicated he would walk with me to my office. I hoped this wouldn't take long. I had to wrap up an experiment. The ninety-minute electrolysis time was nearly finished.

"You know about the MUACC meeting?" he asked, as we reached my door. He pulled up, plainly intending to have this conversation in the hallway.

I nodded. Harry had mentioned it, an annual informal gathering of analytical chemistry professors from Midwestern schools—hence, the name, "Midwestern University Analytical Chemistry Conference." The idea was to meet sometime in the fall semester over a Friday-Saturday.

33

It was a social gathering, but each participant was expected to give a brief informal talk on his or her current research. Cocktails on Thursday evening and a banquet/entertainment on Friday were traditional highlights.

"You're planning to go, aren't you?" asked Buck. It wasn't really a question.

It was the furthest thing from my mind. Struggling to prepare lectures for the Chem. 521 course, I had been unable to get my thesis written. Needing desperately to get my first publications out, I was also doing all I could to get my fledgling research program underway.

"Well ... no," I stammered. "I ... I'm really pushing to collect experimental data. I don't think—"

"Believe me," he interrupted, "nothing's more important right now than letting people know who you are and what you're doing."

"I ... I'm not sure...." I paused. Did I really want to admit that I hadn't completed enough work to present a talk?

"Nobody talks about stuff they've published at these meetings," he offered, reading my mind. "This is where people talk about work they're *thinking* about doing. It's understood things will be sketchy." He nailed me with those wide piercing eyes.

"Yeah, well ... maybe...." I mumbled.

"Good!" He clapped me on the shoulder. "Next weekend. It's in Columbus this year. We're taking a university van. G. F. Smith is the host."

He pulled back as if to walk away and then added, "My secretary's making all the arrangements—lodging, registration. We'll drive up Thursday and come back Saturday afternoon."

Then he whirled around and strode away. "See you later," he called over his shoulder.

I had to admit, it was fascinating to mix with the established scientists in my field: Phil Elving, the well-known Michigan electrochemist; Herb Laitinen of Illinois, the author of the most widely-used graduate-level textbook in analytical chemistry; and the renowned G. Frederick Smith, Illinois professor and founder of the chemical company that was hosting the event. I also re-acquainted myself with Stan Bruckenstein of Minnesota and met a number of younger analytical chemists from other Midwestern schools.

Technical meetings were held in a small, crowded hotel conference room. In keeping with the spirit of the conference, no slides were allowed. A small blackboard was available for hand-drawn chalk diagrams.

I really didn't want to give a talk. I tried to keep a low profile. I listened to the others speak. Elving, in a nasal Eastern twang that surprised me, talked about extending the pioneering work he had done on organic electrode mechanisms. Laitinen talked about novel potentiometric concepts. Buck discussed some interesting ideas he had for fluorescence measurements. Harry Pardue described his current work with kinetic methods of analysis.

Harry's presentation had been clear, meaty, and promising. His talk meshed well with those of the more established chemists.

I hunkered down a little further in my corner of the conference room.

Buck—God bless him—was still determined to throw me out there. He rose from his seat after Harry's talk. "In case you haven't already met him, I'd like to introduce the newest member of the analytical faculty at Purdue—Sam Perone," he announced.

As all eyes turned to me, I managed a crooked smile and a nod while Buck added, "Sam's not on the schedule, but I know he's eager to talk to us about his research."

That was a lie. But I wasn't about to argue the point. I had prepared myself with a few notes jotted down on index cards.

I rose and walked to the chalkboard. I pulled the notes from my jacket pocket and gazed around the room. Somehow it seemed even smaller than before. Elving, Laitinen, Buck and all the rest had infringed on my comfort zone. They looked at me expectantly. So I began.

I was thankful for the lecturing I had done in my graduate course that semester. Overcoming my jitters, I laid out the premise of my initial study at Purdue—trace analysis of silver using stripping voltammetry from graphite electrodes. It was an extension of work I had published at Wisconsin—not very exciting. Nevertheless, the graphite electrode angle was new and publishable, and I had collected data to talk about.

Then I made a mistake. I tried to jazz up my talk by mentioning that my next study would involve detection of trace organic substances using surface adsorption on graphite electrodes. Now that was something exciting to talk about—novel and very useful, if it worked.

Problem was it was all pure speculation.

Now that's what awakened Laitinen and Elving—two giants in electrochemical research, who had literally written the books on the subject. Elving expressed skepticism but thought it was an idea worth pursuing. Thank you, Phil.

Laitinen, however, decided to take me to task regarding the fundamentals. "How do you propose to adsorb organic redox compounds without electrolyzing them?" he asked.

"That shouldn't be difficult," I replied. "Reactant adsorption can occur at electrode potentials less negative than the standard reduction potential."

Laitinen screwed up his face and stroked his chin. "You have that backwards," he declared. "Reactant adsorption occurs at *more negative* potentials."

I froze for a moment. Beads of sweat grew on my forehead. My literature studies told me I was correct, but here was the acknowledged analytical chemistry guru of the era telling me I had made a mistake. The chances of my shooting him down were very remote. Yet I didn't feel I could back away.

"There are many studies," I responded, "that describe adsorption of organic molecules prior to electro-reduction."

Then, in a dismissive voice, he said, "Well, I'm sure that Professor Elving will tell you that reactant adsorption *always* occurs more negative than the standard reduction potential." He looked at Elving who nodded solemnly.

The sweat was literally drenching my shirt now. I couldn't believe what I was hearing. I had been researching the literature on this subject for over a year. Surely I couldn't be wrong.

What should I do? Go for the head-to-head confrontation, or back down? It was like arriving first of four cars at a four-way stop. When the last arrival begins to pull out just as you do, should you charge ahead? Be right and get crunched?

"Well, it looks like I'll have to take another look at the literature," I offered meekly. Then I did what others had done when they wanted to get off the hook—I said to the audience, "Thank you all for listening." They applauded politely, and I walked quietly to my seat in the corner.

I took my seat, hoping that my face wasn't too red. I was furious inside. Nevertheless, the last thing I wanted at that time was to do battle with the most powerful figure in my field. Later, I would realize that we had misunderstood one another—a matter of terminology. Perhaps we could have straightened that out if I had stood my ground. But I doubt it. Laitinen wasn't in the mood to spar with such an unworthy opponent.

Some battles can't be won. And winning some battles can cost you the war. I thought this was one of them.

As it was, Laitinen would quickly forget the youngster who had given his first MUACC talk. During the next couple decades, however, when he would serve as the editor of the prestigious journal, *Analytical Chemistry*, he would get to know me as someone who was publishing five or six solid papers a year in that journal.

Oh, and by the way, a little over a year later, I published in *Analytical Chemistry* the article on adsorption-dependent stripping voltammetry—with results just as I had predicted at that 1962 MUACC meeting.

# CHAPTER 9
## Recruiting

Throughout my first year at Purdue I had let students and faculty call me "Doctor Perone" or "Professor" or simply "Doc," without revealing the technicality that, in fact, I *had not yet earned a Ph.D.* After all, I reasoned, the thesis would be done well before the end of the school year, right? So, why allude to a minor issue like my temporary *illegitimate* status?

In fact, Buck had recommended that I conduct myself in every activity as if indeed I really *was* "Doctor" Perone; and I happily obliged.

One of those activities unfolded in spring, 1963—interviewing and recruiting first-year graduate students. Of course, if there were any doubt that I would make it to a second year at Purdue, such recruiting would have been highly questionable.

But I was very good at suppressing such doubts.

I turned on all my charm and took advantage of my similar age and recent grad student status to gain familiarity with a number of new students. One of these, Chris Frings, an affable recruit from Alabama, seemed interested in my research. We also discovered a mutual appreciation for jazz.

I took the bold step of inviting Chris and a couple advanced grad students I had befriended, all with similar tastes, to my home for an evening of "music appreciation." I had checked this out with Buck first, to make sure I wasn't crossing over some line in the student recruiting game. (I had heard stories of the "old days" when faculty would meet new grad students at the train, wine and dine them, and lock them into their research groups.)

Buck had given me his blessing for the social event at my home, noting that most of the invitees were advanced students who were already working for other professors.

The "music appreciation" night turned out well. Though we never discussed it, I was convinced that Chris would choose me as his major professor after the spring "rush" week. This was a week when all first-year graduate students were required to interview every professor in their selected specialty area. After a specific date, each student could declare his or her professor of choice.

A professor could decline a student, but technically could not accept a student until it was clear that students would distribute pretty evenly among the research faculty in the division.

This was a great idea for faculty, but not so good for students.

Many students apply to a particular graduate school with the intention of working for a specific professor. Perhaps their undergraduate advisor directs them. Or perhaps they know the professor by reputation. The choice of the graduate school is often a secondary consideration.

The preliminary "quota" for each analytical faculty person in spring, 1963, was two. No faculty person could accept more until each had picked up two students.

Sounds simple, doesn't it.

Not really. At Purdue, for example, Buck Rogers was by far the best known of the analytical faculty. That year, it seemed half of the new analytical students came to Purdue wanting to work for Buck. None of them were planning to work with a fledgling like me.

Well, not quite true. There was one student that showed up in my office and delighted me by relating his decision to work with me.

No, it wasn't Chris Frings. Chris did show up at my office. He sheepishly informed me that he had come to Purdue to work for Harry Pardue. He found my research very exciting, but he was really interested in clinical chemistry.

So much for recruiting.

On the other hand, when Bill Kretlow, a new student from the Chicago area, informed me that he wanted to work with me, I couldn't have been more surprised or more pleased.

"Doc," he began, as he stood just inside the door to my office-lab, "can I talk to you about research?"

The deadline had long passed for initial decisions. All analytical faculty had picked up their quota except for me. I knew that all the students had not yet chosen professors, but I hadn't even had a nibble. Mentally, I was resigned to working on my own for another year.

Then, when Bill asked to talk about my research, following up on our initial required interview, I was ecstatic. Not that I showed it. I just replied, "Sure, come on in and sit down."

Bill took a seat and got right to the point. "Doc, I'm really interested in your research."

I beamed.

"But," he continued, "I understand that you've got a problem."

My heart sank. "What problem?" I asked apprehensively.

Bill cleared his throat. As I had already observed, Bill always chose his words carefully. Always neatly groomed, this handsome young man had impressed me from the start. He was one of the "class of '62" that I had bonded with in my very first lecture class the previous fall. I waited expectantly for his response.

With a sideways gaze, as if he didn't really want to take responsibility for his words, he said, "The rumor is that you don't have your Ph.D. And ... well ... that you might be let go early."

There was a profound silence for a few moments.

Buck had promised that *no* students would be told that I hadn't yet finished my Ph.D. thesis. I had naïvely clung to this fantasy—not realizing how impossible it would be for the entire group of thirty-some chemistry professors to keep their mouths shut.

Bill had done me the favor of bursting the bubble. He knew. Others knew. Everyone knew. I had just learned a valuable lesson, *don't trust anybody*.

Deciding to level with him, I said, "That's right, Bill. I'm still writing up my thesis."

"Does that mean—" There was a pained expression on his face. "I mean ... you know ... that you're still up for tenure?"

I was beginning to wonder.

If grad students had spread rumors that I was going to be "let go," those rumors must have started somewhere, undoubtedly with one of the faculty. *Oh, yeah. Perone's history. Idiot came in without a Ph.D.*

In a confident tone that belied my inner fears, I replied, "Of course I'm still being considered for tenure. I'll have my degree before the fall semester." I didn't mention that my major professor had been MIA since I had sent my most recent thesis draft.

Bill gave me a shy smile. "I'm sorry, Doc, for bringing this up, but could you explain this 'tenure' thing? I hope you understand. I think it … it would be a disaster to pick a major professor who might leave before I finish the Ph.D."

I nodded solemnly. No wonder all the new students had stayed away from my door.

"Simply stated, *tenure* means you can't be fired without cause," I began. "I was hired on a 'tenure-track' contract. That means they have to give me tenure if they keep me here more than five years. I have five years to prove myself."

"You're saying that you'll be here for at least five years?"

"That's the plan," I replied casually. "I'm expecting to have tenure after that." I was beginning to speculate, though, about those little "escape clauses" in my contract.

"So they really can't let you go once you get tenure?" he asked. "Seems like a good deal."

"It's all about academic freedom," I remarked. "It allows professors—once they've proven themselves—to do whatever research they want, even if they never publish another paper."

Bill frowned. "Seems like they'd want to get rid of people who turn to 'dead wood'."

"Well, let's say an assistant professor makes his mark. Publishes good research papers right off. Five years pass, and he gets promoted to associate professor—tenured. Then he doesn't publish another paper until thirty years later. But *that* paper describes the cure for cancer."

Bill's puzzled frown slowly gave way to a big grin. "Oh, I get it!"

I nodded. "That's right. That *tenured* professor was able to keep his job while tackling a problem that took an entire career to solve."

Bill nodded approvingly and said, "I don't know about your long-range plans, Doc. But I am interested in the research you described to me." He cleared his throat and flashed that pained smile I had seen before. "Anyway, Doc, I'd really like to work for you, if you'll have me."

I tried to control the emotion in my voice. "Sounds like a deal," I croaked, and reached out my hand.

To my surprise, Bill's face lit up. He seemed genuinely excited.

I had to know. What had persuaded Bill, when all the others had shunned me? Had Buck Rogers put pressure on him?

I asked him.

Again he got that shy look and looked away for a moment. "Nobody pressured me, Doc. I think I'm gonna like working for a young professor with time for personal attention. I mean, look at Rogers. He's got ten students and a postdoc. And he's always on the road. When would he have time for me?"

I smiled and nodded. "That's a good point. I expect we *will* be working closely." Then I chuckled. "Hope you don't regret it."

Bill sighed. He seemed relieved. Then he said something I would never forget. For many students I would have passed it off as bullshit. But it was something that Bill would repeat many times, even after graduation.

"Doc, when I met you, I knew I wanted to be your *first* student. For better or worse, that's something no one else will ever be able to say."

I couldn't reply. Bill's words had moved me.

Silently, though, I worried, *would he also be my* last *student?*

# CHAPTER 10

## Into the Fire

Picking up my first research student during the spring semester of 1963 provided a huge morale boost. I needed it badly. Not that things were going poorly. I had squeezed in some laboratory time, and my first independent research paper was ready to submit to the leading journal in my field, *Analytical Chemistry*.

But I hadn't gotten my Ph.D. thesis done.

Not that I hadn't tried.

Finding time to write the thesis had been nearly impossible during the first semester. My major professor, Irv Shain, had predicted as much. Christmas and semester breaks had allowed me to complete the rough draft, however. I had mailed it to Shain at Wisconsin by the end of January.

After six weeks with no response, I called Shain. He admitted he hadn't had a chance to get to the draft, but he promised a response in a couple weeks.

A month later I called again. This time he was more honest. He wouldn't be reading it before *summer*.

I was devastated.

I informed my division head, Buck Rogers, about the problem. He clucked in dismay and offered to call Shain to apply pressure. I said no. Buck gave me that "look" again—the *I-disapprove-but-OK-whatever-you-say* stare.

I suspect that within this exchange with Buck was the origin of the "rumor" that I was not long for Purdue—the rumor that had nearly steered all the first-year graduate students away from my research group.

Buck did give me some good advice though. He told me to go to Madison and "camp out" at Shain's office door until he read the thesis.

That's exactly what I did, just as soon as the spring semester ended at Purdue.

Summer 1963 found me working 'round the clock in Madison, with an occasional sixty-mile freshening-up trip to Anita's parents' home in Rockford, where she and our two young girls would stay for the duration.

Not surprisingly, freshening up was the thought on my mind as I stretched out on the conference table in the darkened room. It was three o'clock on a Sunday morning. The new chemistry building on the Wisconsin campus was dark and quiet. Only the hum of the central air conditioning disturbed the solitude. My body was dead tired, but my mind refused to sleep.

If my eyes hadn't protested, refusing to focus, I would still be typing my thesis.

This was the *final* draft—typed on 24-pound bond paper that eventually would be bound as the university's library copy. There could be no erasures. No white-out. Only perfectly-typed pages were acceptable.

Most graduate students hired professional typists. I didn't have that luxury. It wasn't just the money. My typed copy required instantaneous turnaround. It had been that way for weeks now.

I chuckled to myself, thinking about how skilled I had become at typing, and at operating the department's new Xerox machine. Shain had given me his account number, and I had learned to operate the beast. I had wrangled a key so that I could access the copy room at odd hours of the night.

But there would be no copying tonight. Someone at the main library would have to examine and approve my final copy of the thesis. I hoped they wouldn't find my erasures. Replacing a few flawed pages would be fine, but I couldn't bear the thought of re-typing the entire thesis.

Silently, these thoughts turned over in my mind as I shifted positions on the hard table. I wished for a pillow and a blanket and a fresh change of clothes.

Suddenly, my thoughts were interrupted by the sound of a key scratching its way into the conference room door. Startled, I raised my head. Through the frosted glass of the door, against the dim light of the corridor, I detected the outline of someone attempting to enter the room.

The door opened inward, and I glimpsed the face of the intruder. It was John Lewinson, another of Shain's graduate students. I was stunned. I hadn't figured my hard bed would ever be sought by anyone else.

John's eyes caught mine. He seemed just as surprised as I. He started to turn around.

"John," I called out, "do you need something?" I propped myself up on one elbow.

He broke off his exit and turned to face me. "I'm sorry. Didn't know you were in here. I've got a long experiment running. I thought I could...." He hesitated.

"Yeah, I know, great place to catch some Z's."

He nodded and took a step back into the room. "How's the writing going?"

"I'm done. Shain approved the final yesterday ... Friday, I should say."

"When's your oral?"

"Set for next Friday. I'm typing the final draft. Have to get copies to my exam committee before Tuesday."

John walked into the room now and pulled up a chair. "How the hell did you get Shain to read it?"

"I'd hand him a fresh draft every morning and wouldn't leave until he read it. You saw me there. I did all my typing in his outer office."

He shook his head. "Shain's very distracted these days. Nicholson's work is all he wants to hear about. I'm surprised you got his attention."

"I'm a big sore on his butt right now. He just wants me to go away."

John snickered. "You can say that again. Tells us he won't ever let someone leave early again."

We chatted for a few minutes before John left to find another bivouac. But my thoughts remained stuck on something he had said. Shain *had* been preoccupied all year. A very talented graduate student, Dick Nicholson, was working on something that was destined to revolutionize electrochemistry. The names "Shain and Nicholson" would soon become part of the lexicon.

Lewinson's work, my work, the work of others in Shain's group, all of it was passé. Part of what had been, not what was to be. I realized at that moment that my thesis work would never be published—a fact that could torpedo a person's chances to land an academic job.

I thanked *Lady Luck* once again. I had left Wisconsin under a cloud one year earlier. That situation had tortured me throughout my first year at Purdue. Fortunately, Shain had allowed me to *take* the job a year earlier—black cloud notwithstanding. Now I was on the verge of putting that darkness out of my life forever.

It didn't matter that my thesis work was so outdated now that Shain, justifiably, would never publish it. My career would be made or broken by whatever I might accomplish at *Purdue*.

I just had to get Wisconsin behind me.


My eyelids drooped, and I stuffed several potato chips into my mouth. Jaws and teeth worked at attacking the crunchy treat, providing just enough stimulation to keep me awake.

I glanced to my right as the fence posts flew by at sixty miles per hour. Up ahead about a half-mile was the spot where it had happened.

Not that I could remember it. That's the funny thing about falling asleep at the wheel.

The county road that I traveled between Madison and Rockford connected the two cities by a nearly perfect straight line. It followed the contour of the land, providing a roller coaster ride. The road also followed farm property lines. Any deviations in the route tended to be right angle turns.

Two weeks earlier, I had missed one of those turns.

That was before I discovered that eating crunchy snacks could keep me awake at the wheel.

Two fortunate things had combined to save my life. One was that I had insisted on the installation of front seat lap belts when we bought the used '59 Chevy. Very few autos of that vintage came with seat belts.

The other thing was that the incident occurred at a drop-off into a drainage plain. The soft earth slowed the car down before it plowed into a cattle fence. There had been little damage to the fence or the car. Surprisingly, I drove away from the incident with just bumps and bruises.

That event had occurred when I had been at the very pinnacle of sleep-deprived thesis writing.

Thankfully, that saga was over now. I glanced over at the briefcase containing copies of the papers signed by my thesis committee. I smiled and then flicked my gaze back to the road ahead just as I came over a ridge and spied that fateful right angle turn to the left.

I saw the mud tracks that the Chevy had made and the distended fencing that the grille had battered. I slowed to take the turn safely, took one hand off the wheel, and waved at the small cluster of cattle grazing just inside the fence. *Are they white with black spots, or black with white?* I mused.

"So long!" I cried. I didn't plan on coming back.

# CHAPTER 11

## Awakening

Professionally, my first year at Purdue had been surreal. Thrown into the middle of an academic rat race for which I was ill prepared and *illegitimate,* I had lived a nightmare. The promise that no one would find out that I was a "professor-without-credentials" was just so much crap. It had been the worst kept secret in the world.

But somehow, by the summer of 1963, two graduate students—Bill Kretlow and Tom Oyster—had decided to work with me. They never wavered, even when other students did their best to persuade them that I would be let go and that their careers would suffer.

The only thing that had saved me was the desperate summertime ploy of camping outside the door of my major professor's office at Wisconsin. That day in late July, 1963, when I passed my Ph.D. final oral exam was the real beginning of my academic life.

I was excited to begin *enjoying* my time at Purdue.

Nothing spelled *enjoyment* at Purdue more than football weekends in the fall. Part of the Big Ten conference with perennial national contenders—Michigan and Ohio State—the Purdue Boilermakers always fielded a competitive team. Never a Rose Bowl invitation, but always an exciting season. The rivalry game each year with in-state independent, Notre Dame, routinely garnered national attention, as the Boilermakers upset that powerhouse with surprising regularity.

Football at Purdue in the 1960s was particularly exciting as they fielded winning teams and finally achieved a Rose Bowl invitation for January, 1967, with Bob Griese—the future leader of the Miami Dolphins' unique undefeated season—at quarterback. Faculty tickets for home games were less than ten dollars a game, and even with our tight budget, we made sure we had two season passes.

In fact, most students and a large fraction of faculty members attended home games. Football season in a small Midwestern university town is the social highlight of the year. There were parties before the game, after the game, and during the game. Everyone knew the players by name. And everyone had an opinion on the play selections, the performances, and who should be the next coach. The game time weather could be in the upper nineties and sunny in September and below zero with a foot of snow in November. Nevertheless, the stands were always filled.

Shortly after the fall 1963 semester began, my wife and I were invited to two faculty parties celebrating the first home football game. One was a pre-game gathering, while the other was a post-game party.

My student, Bill Kretlow, was sitting in my office-lab, chatting with me about his research project when I received the phone call from my wife about the party invitations. As I hung up the phone, Bill put that crooked smile on his face and said, "Sounds like you might have a social life this year."

I nodded. "Got my credentials now."

He looked down for a moment, as if debating his next words. "You know, we're having a party over at Sheetz Street Saturday."

"Sheetz Street" was the shorthand reference to the two-story flat that had been taken over by a half-dozen chemistry grad students, including Bill. The street and the flat were located in the heart of "the village," just south of campus. Their game day parties were notorious, beginning in the early morning and continuing throughout the game and well into the night and wee hours. I hadn't yet been to one of their parties. Few, if any, faculty had.

I spied Bill quizzically. "You inviting us?"

He nodded. "I talked to the guys. They'd like for you to come."

I knew this was a big deal. Guys got shit-faced at these parties. They didn't want any faculty there. I decided to play dumb and probe.

"When should we come?"

"Any time. The party goes all day and all night."

"When will *you* be there?"

"All the time."

"You're not going to the game?"

"Somebody's got to make sure the place doesn't burn down. Anyway, it's Ball State. I'm going to the Notre Dame game next week."

"Can we bring anything?"

"There'll be a keg. Everybody chips in. Bring your own hard stuff; or talk to Oyster."

"What?"

"Tom can get you a deal." The crooked grin reappeared. "So, how about it?"

I hesitated, feeling a frown tightening my brow. "Any other chemistry profs coming?" I asked.

"Nope. The other guys all work for organickers. Old farts."

My head nodded absently several times. "I'd really like to come. But we're already committed before and after the game."

"That's OK. Come over for breakfast. Or drop in real late."

I shook my head. "How can I refuse?"


"Hey, Doc!" I heard a familiar deep voice calling as I headed toward the stairway. "Got a sec?"

I turned to see Tom Oyster, striding purposefully toward me in shorts, tee shirt, and sandaled feet. The broad grin dimpled his deeply tanned handsome face.

He reached me and blurted, "My buddies are having a pre-game party. They'd like you to come."

"Who's that?" I asked, marveling once more at my newfound popularity.

"You know. Steve and Barney. Benkeser's group."

I did know Steve and Barney. We had met when Tom dragged me down to Harry's "Chocolate Shop" for a beer. *Harry's* was the only "wet" spot in West Lafayette, grandfathered in some time in the distant past. It was only a block off campus, immensely popular, and a thorn in the side of the straight-laced university administration.

"Where's it gonna be?" I asked.

"They got a new place—the Williamsburg Apartments, down on the Wabash. Can you make it?"

Not wanting to go through the same conversation I had had with Bill, I quickly replied, "We'd love to."

Somehow we'd squeeze them all in.

We were the first to leave the faculty pre-game party. "Got to see the band march in," I lied as we rushed out the door.

We showed up around twelve-thirty at Steve and Barney's second-floor apartment that overlooked the Wabash River. There were about twenty people crowded into the kitchen/dining/living room. Most were male chemistry grad students. A few young females were there. I recognized a department secretary. The males were in jeans or shorts and cotton shirts, appropriate for the warm September day. The females were in skirts and blouses.

The stereo was cranked up and flooding the apartment with the sounds of Johnny Cash. Tom Oyster and his friend Steve greeted us promptly at the door with two drinks in clear plastic cups. "Here. Vodka gimlets. You got some catching up to do," warned Tom. The trademarked broad smile was there. If he were feeling the effects of the liquor, he didn't show it.

"You guys are living pretty high on the hog for grad students," I commented, "serving vodka instead of beer."

"Oh, I don't know," Tom drawled. He winked, then grabbed Anita's arm and took her off to meet some of the other ladies.

I took a sip of my drink and turned to Steve. "What's in this?" I asked.

"Vodka and lime juice. Heavy on the vodka."

"What kind of vodka?" I asked, as if I knew what I was talking about.

"Oh, it's *Purdue Reserve.*"

"What's that?"

Steve grinned. "Talk to Oyster. He can fix you up."

I turned to look for Tom just as he pulled up to my side. "Hey, Tom, what's this Purdue Reserve I'm drinking?"

"You like it?" he replied. "I can get you some."

I shook my head. "I don't want any. But what's Purdue doing in the liquor business?"

Tom and Steve burst out laughing. I looked from one to the other. As usual, I was on the outside looking in. "What's so funny?"

"It's just a *name*, Doc," Tom replied, still grinning. "I'll get you some."

"How much is it?"

Tom shrugged. "Pretty cheap. You check a liter of alcohol out of the stockroom; and I'll get you a liter of vodka."

I shot back a puzzled frown.

Tom leaned closer and whispered, "Don't ask questions, Doc."

I stared back. "Don't get cute. Did you forget I'm a chemist, too? I know what vodka is."

Tom grinned. "Pretty good deal, huh? A fifth of *Stoly* is six bucks. Lab alcohol's twenty cents a liter."

"What do you do? Cut the lab alcohol with water and use it for vodka?"

"Not that simple, Doc. But basically, yeah, that's right. Gin's more complicated."

"Gin? You make that, too?"

He nodded enthusiastically. "Tastes just as good as *Beefeater's*. I got the recipe from a textbook."

I shook my head. "What do you put in it?" I wasn't at all sure I wanted to drink the rest of my gimlet.

"Distilled water and a little glycerin to make it smooth. Gin requires a juniper berry. That's the hardest part."

I stared at him. "Is that what you use for all your parties? Lab alcohol?"

Tom chuckled. "Where have you been, Doc? How do you think chemists survived Prohibition?"

His words struck me. I was so out of touch. We used alcohol for lab experiments. The university got it tax-free for research. I had used plenty of it for research purposes at Wisconsin.

I'm embarrassed to admit that using lab alcohol for booze had never occurred to me. Perhaps that was because beer was twenty-five cents a quart in Wisconsin—not exactly your premium brew, but good enough for grad students.

I looked at Tom. "You return a liter of booze for a liter of alcohol? How long does it take?"

"Next day for vodka. Takes a while for gin. I use the ninety-five percent stuff, you know, that's 190 proof."

I thought about it. Simple math told me that Tom got to keep one bottle of ninety-five proof booze for every one he delivered.

I never provided any raw materials to Tom. Nevertheless, a small portion of the alcohol solvent procured by my group for research showed up in my liquor cabinet as one-liter reagent bottles labeled "gin" and "vodka."

I returned the favor by throwing frequent parties at my home.

I didn't ask what happened to the rest of the alcohol. Surely, Tom and his partying friends could not consume it all.

I may have gotten my answer one day, just as students were leaving for Christmas vacation. As I walked to the parking garage, I happened to spy Tom, navigating his blue Volkswagen bug toward the city limits on Northwestern Avenue. He was headed to his home in Wisconsin. Strapped to the top of the Volkswagen was a large ten-gallon glass carboy filled with a clear liquid.

Of course, it could have been just water. Nevertheless, I had to believe that Christmas in Wisconsin for the Oyster family might be very merry indeed.

# CHAPTER 12

## Getting Acquainted

One of the first things you learn as a young assistant professor is that you don't have anyone to talk to.

Tenured professors don't know you and don't want to know you. Non-tenured professors, like you, are struggling to make the grade, and, rightly or wrongly, there's a sense of competition. It's hard to root for a colleague's success when that might highlight your own deficiencies. So, friendships with other assistant professors come with a certain amount of unease and apprehension.

Almost immediately I found that I had more in common with the graduate students than with other faculty. Why? Age, for one thing. When I started at Purdue, I was twenty-three, turning twenty-four. Most chemistry grad students were about the same age; many were older. In addition, grad students were going through a process that I had freshly experienced at Wisconsin—courses, prelim exams, research, theses, orals—and generally navigating the treacherous waters of graduate school.

Most young faculty avoided social ties with graduate students. Understandably, young faculty wanted to separate themselves from their recent lowly status. Older, established faculty already had a hard time distinguishing between new young faculty and graduate students. Why hang out with students and make it that more difficult to be recognized?

Apparently, however, I was uncomfortable enough, socially, as an assistant professor, that, during my early years at Purdue, *my* comfort zone encompassed mostly graduate students.

Because the office-lab that I called home in those early years was located in the middle of a suite of labs occupied by Buck Rogers' graduate students, I became an adopted member of Buck's group, at least socially.

Through daily conversations, occasional invitations to parties, and frequent trips to watering holes, I gained invaluable insight to the Purdue faculty—through students' eyes that pierced the façades.

It was four o'clock in the afternoon, and I had just completed my Chem. 521 lecture. Upon returning to my office-lab, three of Buck's students greeted me at the door.

"What's up?" I asked.

The tall, heavy-set, Jack Heveran answered for the group. "Buck gets back in town tomorrow, and we're headed for The Pub. You want to join us?"

"Yeah," added Don Guran, in his laconic Ukrainian accent. "Buck's expecting our … ahh … progress reports."

I laughed. "You looking for data at *The Pub*?"

He grinned. "Maybe."

Phil Bowman added, "We've got data. It's just…." He paused.

Jack finished the thought. "It's just that Buck ain't gonna like the data."

"That bad?" I asked.

"That bad," Don proclaimed in his deep bass voice. Then he clapped me on the shoulder. "Come on. Maybe you can give some advice."

Don was kidding of course. He kidded me a lot. He and his pretty blonde wife, Tamara, had taken a liking to my wife, Anita, and me from the very first faculty-student social. The feelings were mutual. A bit older and wiser, they had taken us under their wings.

I laughed. "Well, I'm awful thirsty right now."

The Pub was just across the river at the corner of Union and Fourth Streets. From the back door you could see, hear and feel the *Monon* trains that rattled down the middle of Fifth Street. Yes, that's right. The train ran down the middle of the street that also cut through the center

55

of downtown Lafayette. Businesses and residences lined both sides of that throughway.

The inside of The Pub was 1950s crude —neon signs, wood panels, low ceilings, dartboard and pinball machine. Waitresses were fortyish and friendly. The favored spots for locals were at the bar that ran the length of one wall, with the usual mirrored display of liquor bottles. Groups of students often commandeered one or more of the tables. For larger parties, back rooms were available.

Several beers were on tap, all domestic. Budweiser was what we had ordered today—a pitcher and four tall mugs.

We had nearly finished the pitcher before the discussion turned to the most frequent topic of these outings—Buck.

Don turned to me and droned, "Do you have any idea how ... ahh ... frustrating it is to do research when your major professor is always away?"

I nodded. "Yeah, my major professor at Wisconsin—Shain—spent a month at Idaho Nuclear Lab, just as I was finishing my thesis research. Bummer."

"Hell," remarked Jack, "Buck is out of town all year round—meetings, panels, consulting, lectures—not to mention he spends most of the summer at the Cape."

"The Cape?" I asked.

"Yeah," Jack replied, "they've got a house on Cape Cod."

"Yes," Don interjected, "he tells us to 'come visit' him and Eleanor at the Cape." Then he grinned and added in his slow, bass drawl, "I don't think so."

I hadn't yet gotten to know Buck very well. But I already knew that if he and Eleanor extended an invitation, they meant it. I was about to say so, when our middle-aged, bosomy waitress, Sherry, interrupted us.

"You boys want another pitcher?" she asked, picking up the empty one. She arched one eyebrow and looked poised to hustle away.

We looked at one another, and Jack took a mental vote. "Sure. Another Bud," he proclaimed.

Sherry winked and headed back to the bar, stopping at another table along the way.

I turned to Don and voiced the question on my mind. "How does Buck keep up with your projects if he's away so much?"

Don laughed—a deep guttural guffaw. "Buck has … umm … E.S.P. or something—knows when we're not in the lab, even half-way 'round the world."

I shook my head. "Right now, I can't imagine being out of town for anything. Too much to do."

Don drained the last of his beer and set the mug down hard on the tabletop. "Listen, Sam," he began. (Don and Tamara always called me "Sam," while all the other students and wives called me "Doc" or "Doctor Perone.") "In five, six years," he continued, "maybe sooner, you'll be doing same as Buck—spending half your time traveling."

I laughed. "I don't think so."

"You wait," he declared. "When you start publishing all those papers, you'll get out on the lecture circuit, and your students will be back here." He patted my arm. "Trust me."

Jack chimed in. "That's what happens when you're a famous professor. You're always somewhere else."

"Well, I've got a long way to go before worrying about that," I declared. "What about you guys? How do you manage?"

Jack and Don turned to Phil. "Why don't *you* tell him?" Jack urged. "You're the expert."

I threw Phil a puzzled glance.

"I was a student here before Buck came to Purdue," he began. "My major professor left for a better job at Kansas State."

"What did you do?" I asked.

"Well, I could have gone with him. But I decided to stay here, and Buck took me on. New project and everything. Like starting over."

"You went from one absent professor to another," I remarked.

Phil shrugged, while Don said, "Phil knows that Buck can … ahh … open doors better than anyone. Besides, Buck will be providing extra help."

"What help?" I inquired.

"Didn't you hear?" asked Don. "He has a postdoc coming. From Princeton. Jerry Fitzgerald."

"Will he be in charge when Buck's gone?"

"That's the idea," Jack affirmed.

"Yeah, a *stupid* one," said Don. "He'll be doing his own research. And … you know … looking for a job. Why would he want to hold our hands?"

"Because that's his job," Jack pronounced.

"Yeah, we'll see," Don groused.

Just then, Sherry whisked by, slapped the second pitcher on the table, and hustled away.

Jack poured the beers while we remained silent with our thoughts. I was excited to hear that another fresh Ph.D. would be joining the analytical division at Purdue—someone that wouldn't be competing for tenure.

I was looking forward to meeting the new kid on the block.

# CHAPTER 13

## Getting It On

Nothing could sink my career more quickly than the failure to establish a flourishing research program at Purdue.

Most research universities adhered to the principle that tenure-track assistant professors would either be promoted (i.e., tenured) or terminated within five years of starting. I was diligently attacking my teaching assignments and conscientiously fulfilling my committee obligations during those first years. However, great *teachers* with *no* publications don't get tenure; and working on every single faculty committee might get you a "thank you" as they wave good bye.

The only thing that matters when the promotions committee meets to decide your fate is the number and quality of your research publications.

Sounds harsh. And it is. But it's fair, because every new professor knows exactly where he or she stands. The old cliché, *publish or perish*, is extremely accurate.

Producing scientific publications doesn't just happen, however. First of all, you need the technical background and experience. Of course, if you've earned a Ph.D., that should be a given.

Then you need research facilities. That's the university's responsibility—to give you laboratory space and start-up money for equipment and supplies.

Assuming you have these things—and I did—the rest is up to you.

I had a plan. It was pretty simple. First, do some straightforward research projects—extensions of things I had done in graduate school. Stuff I might be uniquely qualified to do—stuff that would be easy to publish because I had prior publications. I hoped to crank out half-a-dozen papers based on these research sequels in the first few years to pad my publications' list.

The second thing was to begin work on a totally new research area—one that differed from my previous work. Doing novel stuff; stuff that pushes the envelope—"going where no man has gone before."

Although the first part—simple extensions—was a pretty clear-cut strategy, there were no guarantees. Applying principles and techniques that had worked for one study might not work for another, no matter how closely related they might seem.

The second part was exciting, but very risky. The nature of the next major leap in any field of science might be obvious, but getting there is something else. You might be wading into totally uncharted waters. Sinking is much more likely than swimming. You might go down many blind alleys before finding the right one. Or you might never find it. If you do succeed, you might have a tough time publishing your results, as reviewers and journal editors are reluctant to accept dramatically new papers from unknown authors.

One Saturday morning during my second year at Purdue, while working in my laboratory, I had a conversation with Buck's new postdoc, Jerry Fitzgerald, about this very subject.

"Knock, knock," he cried out, as he pushed open the door to my office-lab. "Can I come in?"

I looked up from the graphic recorder on my Sargent FS Polarograph and saw Jerry's bespectacled, grinning face peering around the door.

"Sure," I responded, "come on in. I'm just getting in some runs before seminar."

Jerry closed the door behind and slid past the large chemical hood that stood to his right. He shuffled down the middle of the narrow lab until he reached my desk at the very end.

Pulling up a chair, he sat on it backwards, placing his forearms on the chair back. "You doing parts per trillion yet?" he asked. The crooked grin wasn't necessary. I knew he wasn't serious.

Perched on my desk with my feet on the wooden seat of my chair, I was still gazing intently at the pen excursions of the instrument's recorder on the nearby lab bench. I reached over—lifting the chart paper as it streamed out of the recorder—and examined the record of the most recent stripping run. Distractedly, I responded to Jerry's taunt. "You think this looks like a 'clean lab'?"

Jerry chuckled and ran a hand through his curly brown hair. "Shit, I'm surprised you can do parts per *thousand*, much less *trace analysis* in this crap lab."

He looked at the chart I held in my hands and observed, "Looks like you've got *two* peaks there. You doing mixtures now?"

I shook my head. "Nope. That's the silver stripping peak."

"Two peaks? I didn't know silver had *two* standard potentials," he scoffed.

"That's 'cause you're a spectroscopist," I shot back. "You don't know anything about the *real* world."

He slipped me a wry smile. "Inform me."

I pointed to the chart. "That's the stripping peak—peaks, that is—after three minutes of plating silver onto graphite from a part per billion solution. Two different stripping processes—silver from silver, and silver from graphite."

A light went off in his eyes. "Oh, I get it. Two different binding energies...." He paused. "Two different potentials!" he added excitedly.

"That's what it looks like."

"How do you get analytical results?"

"Have to integrate the area under *both* peaks."

"Really? That works?"

"You want to see the tables?"

He put out a palm. "Hey. I believe you. But isn't this new territory for stripping analysis?"

"That's the whole idea—although people *have* seen these double peaks *before*."

"Like who?"

"Would you believe your boss—Buck?"

"No shit!"

"Years ago, when he was working at Oak Ridge. They reported plating 'underpotentials' for silver on platinum—basically the same thing I'm seeing with graphite."

"Christ!" he bellowed. "Buck has done everything before everybody."

I chuckled. "That's what he keeps telling us. Fortunately, he didn't look at the analytical possibilities."

"Getting serious, now," he said, "how close are you to writing this up?"

"I've got all the data down to a part per billion, but I need to push it to a hundred parts per trillion or lower. That takes fifty-, sixty-minute plating times, or longer. Hopefully, I'll fill in the missing data in the next week or two."

"How long to write it up?"

"Pretty quick. I can use the paper I published with Shain as a model."

"Think you can get it published before the end of the year?"

"That's the plan."

"What else is in the pipeline?"

"What pipeline?"

Jerry screwed up his face. "The pipeline that gets you *tenure*, that's what. You'd better have a dozen of these studies published before, oh, let's see...." He pretended to count on his fingers. "The *next three years.*"

I shrugged. "Kretlow's working on mercury stripping. Oyster's looking at adsorption-dependent stripping analysis."

Jerry counted an exaggerated three on his fingers. "And then?"

"You want to hear my entire research plan?" I asked.

"Go ahead. I'm open-minded," he declared. I could never tell when he was serious.

"Well," I began, "I've got Oyster building a general purpose voltammetry system with op amp components. When that's done, we're going to look at derivative voltammetry."

"What the hell is that?"

"You take first- and second-derivatives electronically and get an improved signal-to-background ratio. Should improve detection limits by at least an order of magnitude."

"Taking derivatives? What the hell's novel about that?"

"More than you think. Voltammetry is time-dependent—not like spectroscopy. I've been talking to Ted Mueller at Oak Ridge about theory. Scan rate will have a big effect."

Jerry gave an acknowledging nod and remained silent for a moment. Then he pretended to tick off three more publications on his fingers. "Now you're up to about six. What else you got?"

"Kretlow doesn't know it yet, but he's going to be looking at ultra-fast electrode reactions."

"What's 'ultra-fast'?"

"Electro-oxidation of ascorbic acid—vitamin C. Nobody's been able to detect intermediates. We're talking about half-lives of microseconds."

"Whoa!" he exclaimed. "That's a whole new ball game."

"We're looking at new technology—solid state op amps with 100 megacycle bandwidth."

Jerry whistled. "What's that gonna do for you?"

"In my thesis work with benzophenone, I used vacuum tube electronics and couldn't detect free radical half-lives less than hundreds of microseconds."

With a smirk, he ticked off two more publications. "OK. You're up to eight. What else you got?"

I laughed. "Christ! You working for the promotions committee now?"

He shrugged. "I'm just trying to paint your picture."

I nodded. "Yeah, I know that picture."

"So, whatcha got?"

I took a deep breath. "The long shot. I'm going to try something that's really far out."

Jerry raised his eyebrows.

"It's something I've been thinking about ever since I heard George Porter at the Chicago A.C.S. Meeting in '61. You know who I'm talking about, don't you?"

"Sure. They're talking Nobel Prize for that work. Flash photolysis. That's right up my alley."

"He talked about flash photolysis studies of benzophenone."

"Benzophenone? Where did I hear that?" He gave me a mock surprise look. "Oh! Your Ph.D. thesis."

"All right, smart-ass. Fact is, I saw the same free radical intermediates electrolytically as he did photochemically. Same products, too."

"What's your plan?"

"Simple. Porter used spectroscopy to detect transient radicals. I'm going to use electrodes to do the same thing."

Jerry's eyes widened. For once he appeared speechless.

"Of course," I added, "we have no idea how difficult it'll be. Discharging thousands of volts through a flash lamp next to a high-speed electrochemical device might blow it to hell. Who knows?"

"Yeah," he drawled, thinking to himself, "but if it works, it's a whole new technique for transient measurements. Like … " He thought some more. " … like maybe transients that can't be detected spectroscopically." His face lit up. "Hey, Perone, you might just have something."

# CHAPTER 14

## Would Things Ever be the Same?

Friday afternoon is a terrible time to meet a class, especially a freshman chem. recitation section dealing with ponderous problem sets.

The mid-term exam scheduled for the following Tuesday, just before the Thanksgiving break of the 1963 fall semester, was the main reason everyone had shown up and remained awake. When the closing bell rang and students fled, I hoped I had gotten them prepared.

From the second-floor classroom on the northwest end of the chemistry building, I found the corner stairwell and headed up to my office in the far southeast corner. Having been at Purdue over a year, I had wrangled a two-man lab for my students near my own office-lab. Buck had relinquished the space to my only research students, Bill Kretlow and Tom Oyster.

I sauntered down the long hallway, passing by the lengthy segment dedicated to the chemistry library. The halls were empty—not surprising for a Friday afternoon. But I spied Bill standing just outside his lab. As usual, the lab door was open to the hallway.

He caught my eye as I approached my office door. From about fifty feet away, I detected his sideways nod calling to me. I continued toward him as sounds from his radio filtered out into the hallway.

As I approached, I realized Bill wasn't smiling. His face was somber. Something was wrong.

He greeted my grinning arrival with a blunt, "Doc, he's dead. The president's dead."

"Wh … what?" I asked, thinking I had misunderstood.

"President Kennedy. They shot him. In Dallas."

I gazed at him dumbfounded. Crazy images swept through my mind. My first thought was of that ominous feeling I had experienced when first hearing of Kennedy's planned trip to Dallas. Civil rights rhetoric had been heated, and according to many in the South, the President was on the wrong side of that equation.

"What happened?" I asked.

"He was in a convertible. A motorcade. Going through Dallas. I think they got the shooter. It's all been on the radio." He nodded toward the radio on a shelf inside his lab.

For the first time, I paid attention to the sounds—doleful voices repeating over and over the tragic news that the president was dead … shot in Dallas … Governor Connally shot, too … shots came from the School Book Depository … the shooter has been caught … Vice President Johnson sworn in … here is an eyewitness account from someone along the motorcade route....

I turned to Bill. He was wiping tears away.

"I have to call home," I said.

I phoned as soon as I reached my office.

"Did you hear?" Anita cried.

"Just now," I replied. "I was in class."

"Can you come home?"

"I'm on my way."

After a drive through eerily quiet traffic across the Wabash River to our rental home on the north end of Lafayette, I walked in to find my wife and three-year-old daughter, Vita-Marie, cuddling on the sofa in front of the sixteen-inch black-and-white Philco TV. Anita had been crying. Vita looked bewildered and hurt. Walter Cronkite was on the screen.

I sat next to them on the sofa. Vita crawled on my lap and clung. I could see our one-year old, Amy, seated around the corner in the kitchen, in her high chair, munching cheerios.

We sat there in front of the TV set—as did the entire nation—while the painful drama unfolded over that entire weekend. Lee Harvey Oswald, Jack Ruby—names we had never heard before took over our lives. In a noble effort to lift the spirits of the people, NFL commissioner, Pete Rozelle, decided that all the football games would go on as scheduled that Sunday. It was a decision he would later regret.

The heart-wrenching tragedy kept unfolding on television over the weekend and following days. Lyndon B. Johnson is sworn in. We get glimpses of the dazed former first lady. The president's body returns to Washington. The family gathers. The coffin is moved to the Capitol. Eulogies; testimonies; funeral procession drama; somber LBJ; serious Jackie; stoic Bobby and Teddy; bewildered Caroline; John-John's final salute; Walter Cronkite's commentary. It all played out on our tiny black-and-white TV.

It was real-life drama, the likes of which our generation had never seen.

Kennedy's death wasn't a political event so much as it was a national calamity. Yes, there were those few extremists that greeted his passing with insensitive words. But by and large, the country grieved in unison throughout the week following his death, regardless of individuals' political outlooks.

Kennedy's death had consequences that profoundly impacted university campuses. No one knows how Kennedy would have dealt with Vietnam. After all, he had approved the dispatch of military "advisors" to South Vietnam during his administration.

Johnson, however, would turn Vietnam into a war. On August 4, 1964, North Vietnamese torpedo boats in the Gulf of Tonkin allegedly would make an unprovoked attack on U.S. destroyers. President Johnson would retaliate immediately with air attacks and ask Congress for a military mandate. On August 7, Congress would pass the "Tonkin Gulf" resolution, bringing us to a virtual state of war in Southeast Asia.

Thirty years later, many questions would surface about the Gulf of Tonkin incident. Apparently, even Johnson had doubts at the time that the event occurred as was reported.

Would Kennedy have reacted differently? We don't know; we only know what Johnson did.

Kennedy had assigned a few thousands of military "advisors" to Vietnam. But Johnson would eventually escalate the conflict to engage over half-a-million of our military. By 1968, the war would become a quagmire with tens of thousands of U.S. fatalities and the source of escalating tensions between the youth of America and the establishment.

Student draft deferments would become the singular motivation for many youths to remain in college and attend graduate school. A youthful counter-culture would emerge. Campuses would become hotbeds of student protests. In graduate schools like Purdue's, we would see an influx of large numbers of talented but under-motivated graduate students.

In 1963, students were career-driven, exhibiting scientific curiosity and thirst for knowledge. Later it would become clear that many were in graduate school simply to avoid the draft. They would do what was necessary to maintain their deferred status, but, for many, the scientific drive would not be there.

How would everything play out? Even when it was not directly implicated, the Vietnam War would form the backdrop for everything that was happening in America—and especially what evolved on university campuses during the late sixties and early seventies.

None of us knew at the time how the events of that day—November 22, 1963—would change our futures. We just knew that the Kennedy era—the era that many called "Camelot"—had come to a premature, violent, and tragic end.

# CHAPTER 15

## Snowstorm

$7500 a year!

That was a $300 raise over my first year. And I had obtained research funds to pay summer salary, too.

It was time to think about different housing.

Our Lafayette rental was small (900 sq. ft.). "Central heating" was a tiny furnace blowing hot air down the hallway. Air conditioning was a wet dream.

We looked at West Lafayette properties. There was a cluster of university-owned faculty homes in West Lafayette near the Wabash River and Happy Hollow Dr. These were rentals, and there were no openings.

We looked at building a home in a new West Lafayette development called Bayberry. Most of the homes were upscale pre-fabricated structures produced by a local company called National Homes that had several developments in Lafayette and West Lafayette. Not surprisingly, the Lafayette developments were more affordable.

Long story short, we found a model that we liked in a new development at the far south end of Lafayette. It was a three-bedroom bi-level home with about 1500 sq. ft. of living space including a 500 sq. ft. recreation room downstairs. Priced at $18,000, we could get it with $500 down and $115 per month.

We moved in during January, 1964.

With the university on semester break, I had time to put some finishing touches on the interior. I wasn't very handy, but I did know how to hang wallpaper. So I decorated a few of the walls to add some life to the otherwise monotonously white drywalls.

I was especially pleased with the wallpapering job in the downstairs rec. room. Applied only to the walls near the stairway was a sexy red paper with raised black designs. It would make quite a statement as the backdrop for the bottomless vodka-laced punch bowl for our first student party a week later.

The new rec. room and punch bowl were great hits.

Everyone seemed to approve of the wallpapering job I had done throughout the house, but particularly the sexy red wallpaper in the rec. room.


It was a few weeks later when our new home got buried in the big snowstorm of 1964 that rolled through central Indiana. It dumped over a foot of snow on Lafayette and West Lafayette, with an abundance of impassable snowdrifts.

The cities were not completely unprepared. There were barrels of sand strategically placed along the many hilly streets. Worked great for a light dusting—but with a foot of snow and drifts?

Snowplows were as scarce as palm trees in central Indiana.

We awoke to the news that roads were closed, schooldays and workdays had been cancelled, and Purdue had shut down. It took only one glance outdoors to realize the roads had disappeared under a blanket of white. We weren't going anywhere.

So we settled into a cozy day of family fun. Bundled up so that they could barely move, the girls rolled around in the backyard snow. Then I swirled them around on a snow disk, each time launching them into a snow bank—laughing and screaming.


After cavorting in the snow, we came in and thawed out with hot baths. Then I retired to the downstairs rec. room, where I intended to work on a paper and listen to the stereo.

That's when I heard a knock at the front door. I glanced up at the foyer but couldn't make out who it was. I climbed up the half-flight of stairs and opened the front door.

Standing there, with a light coat, scarf and galoshes, was Tom Oyster—grinning and red-faced. Behind him, looking quite cold, were his two friends—Steve and Barney.

I looked over their shoulders for Tom's VW Beetle. It wasn't there. There wasn't a car to be seen on the snow-filled street. "How did you get here?" were my first words.

"Walked," declared Tom, the word escaping in a white cloud. "Can we come in?"

Too dumbfounded to speak, I stood aside and motioned them into the house. I couldn't believe these guys had just trudged five miles through tons of snow.

While they removed galoshes and coats, Anita greeted the new arrivals from the upper level. She offered to round up drinks and snacks, and we headed down into the rec. room.

"What in the world were you thinking?" I asked. "Walking over here in this weather?"

"Hell, Doc," bellowed Tom, "this is just a light dusting back in Wisconsin."

Steve reached into a package he was carrying and pulled out an album. "This is what got us out today, Doc," he explained. "Just got it."

I read the cover of the album—Johnny Cash, *Ring of Fire*.

"Thought you might want to hear it," added Tom.

"You came all the way over here to play that album?" I asked.

Steve nodded. "Can I put it on?"

Once again I was at a loss for words. I simply nodded toward the stereo system that was set up on a table against the wall.

I didn't have a great stereo system at that time. But it was pretty good, and had a pretty healthy output. Tom had helped me build a set of speakers that could blast when we needed it.

While we took seats, Steve pulled the vinyl platter from its sheath and placed it on the turntable. He placed the stylus on the rotating platter, cranked up the volume, and we listened to the great Johnny Cash.

Anita brought down the chips and dip and filled Tom's request for hot, black coffee. I retrieved cold beers for the rest of us from the chilled case in the adjacent storage room.

That set the stage for a day of music appreciation.

Tom and his friends had better-developed taste in music than I did, but we liked a lot of the same things. I had a pre-British-invasion eclectic collection of pop music of the fifties and early sixties—from Elvis and the Beach Boys to Dean Martin, Judy Garland and Broadway musicals. They introduced me to great *new* sounds—from Herb Alpert to Patsy Cline—that I hadn't enjoyed before.

This was my first listen to the Johnny Cash *Ring of Fire* album, and I knew I had to have it.

After listening to both sides of the album and moving on to Patsy Cline, I decided to show the guys the newest toy I had ordered from the Allied Radio catalog.

I slid the box out from under the stereo table, "Here's my next project," I announced. I took the manual out and passed it around.

"Whoa, Doc!" exclaimed Tom. "You plan on putting this together?"

He was looking at the manual for the Eico 100-watt stereo receiver I had ordered. It was state-of-the-art vacuum tube technology, delivered in pieces. It would require a lot of wiring and soldering to put it together. "Yup," I replied. "I want something to really push those speakers we built."

He laughed. "Hope you solder better than you wallpaper."

I grew a puzzled frown.

"You don't know what I'm talking about, do you?" he declared.

I shook my head.

He chuckled. "Did you ever take a close look at that red wallpaper?"

Now they were all chuckling. I looked over at the stairway where I had hung the sexy red wallpaper. I had no idea what was so funny.

Sensing my confusion, Tom rose and motioned me to join him by the stairway.

"Take a close look, Doc," he suggested, running his hand over the raised black images on the wallpaper. "You see these designs?"

I nodded.

"They're upside-down."

Steve and Barney couldn't contain themselves and burst out laughing.

I leaned closer to the wallpaper. Suddenly, it became clear. Those black images that I found so sexy were a stylized representation of flowerpots; and they were *upside-down*. I had hung the wallpaper without ever realizing I had the pattern *wrong*.

"I don't believe it!" I moaned loudly.

Turning to Tom, I asked, "How long have you known about this?"

He made a silly face, like a little kid trying to avoid admitting he'd spilled the milk. He couldn't hold it in. He snickered and replied, "The party."

"Oh, crap! Why didn't you tell me?"

He kept chuckling. "You were so goddam *proud*. What could I say? You gonna take it down?"

Steve shouted at us. "Hey, don't worry, Doc. It still looks great."

Barney chimed in. "Keep the lights low and the punch bowl full. Nobody will know."

I turned to them. "So, Tom told *you* about the wallpaper?" I looked at Tom. "Anybody else?"

He kept a big grin but shook his head.

"All right. Let's just keep it to ourselves and see if anyone else notices."

Tom chuckled. "No one's gonna tell you, Doc."

"*You* did."

He could barely contain himself, but stifled a chuckle. "That's 'cause I don't give a shit," he proclaimed.

"That's pretty clear," I noted dryly.


As much as he wanted everyone to think the opposite, Tom really did care—about many things—very much. Nothing demonstrated that more than his relationship with me. Whether it was recruiting new graduate students, building something for the lab, volunteering home improvement projects, or even babysitting—Tom always seemed to be there.

Oh, we had good days and bad days; and memorable days. The day of the great snowstorm was one of the memorable ones. There were many more to come.

# CHAPTER 16

## A New Flock of Students

I was thrilled beyond words to pick up *three* new graduate students in the spring of 1964.

I would like to take credit for it. But I can't.

After all, my research program was practically nonexistent. My first Purdue publication had come out the previous December; the second in January. Both publications were in *Analytical Chemistry*. The first was my work; the second was the work of Tom Oyster (the study that Herb Laitinen had challenged at the 1962 MUACC meeting).

Both publications were extensions of a research area I had explored at Wisconsin—not exactly earth-shaking. The next publication was not on the radar yet.

I certainly had exciting projects planned. However, that wasn't why three students chose me. It was the *sales job* done by my first two students, Bill Kretlow and Tom Oyster.

What the hell had they said?

It took me a while to find out. Eventually, each of my new students confided they had been persuaded that I was "more accessible and social" than other faculty members.

But I learned that one other trait had been bandied about—one that probably made the difference. Bill and Tom suggested that I was willing to give students a greater degree of freedom in conducting their research.

Frankly, I hadn't consciously adopted *any* philosophy. However, I *had* recognized that the secret to academic success was attracting talented graduate assistants. I wanted to create a casual atmosphere that allowed these talented people to blossom. I didn't want to be a *boss*. I had observed academic autocrats in action. I didn't want to be one of them.

I had been very fortunate to get Bill and Tom in my first year. They had already developed into productive researchers. And I had learned something new and valuable—the best salesmen for recruiting new students are your existing students.

Now—thanks to Bill and Tom—I had three more very talented students working with me.

Jim Birk had come to Purdue from Iowa State University; Heinz Stapelfeldt from the University of Wisconsin-Milwaukee; Vic Evins from M.I.T.

Each of these new students made colorful contributions to the early lore of the Perone research group, but Jim Birk kicked things off.

Jim was the first to inform me of his choice. The others took another week or so to make up their minds, while he had decided early in the two-week "rush" period.

Jim was a tall, bespectacled, bright young man. I perceived him as a polite, quiet, unspoiled lad from the Iowa cornfields. Unfortunately, this perception presented an unexpected dilemma.

When Jim asked to join my group, I accepted him, of course. That wasn't the dilemma. It was the party planned that weekend for my existing grad students, as well as some of Buck's students, spouses, friends and dates. Tom Oyster had provided a liberal supply of lab vodka and would debut the new *Beatles* album. I anticipated a raucous event. I looked forward to it.

Yet I was very apprehensive about inviting Jim—the "unspoiled" kid from Iowa—into this "fast" crowd of wild parties, free-flowing booze and loud music. How could I be responsible for tarnishing this sweet fellow?

After agonizing for a couple days, I finally decided to call Jim into my office and invite him to the party—carefully warning him that it was not one of those polite "socials" that other professors organized for their students. This one could get pretty crazy. He was under no obligation to show up if he felt uncomfortable.

I remember that Jim just kind of looked at me blankly, thanked me for the invitation, and said he'd like to come. Then he turned around and left my office.

I was very, very concerned.

The night of the party, Jim didn't show, not at first. The party was well under way. Loud music rocked the lower-level rec. room. No one could get enough of *I Wanna Hold Your Hand; Please, Please Me;* or *Twist and Shout.* Dancers gyrated in the center—fueled by the bottomless punch bowl of cranberry juice, ginger ale and vodka.

Jim came to the door by himself. He had no car, and we were over five miles from his West Lafayette lodging. Later, I concluded that he must have walked.

No one heard his knock, so he just walked into the midlevel landing. I saw him immediately and rushed to show him in, wondering how the loud craziness emanating from the rec. room might strike him.

Jim didn't show any reaction. He simply flashed that warm, enthusiastic smile that I had first seen during our interview. I led him down the open half-flight of stairs and introduced him to the guests—shouting into people's ears over the din of rock and roll. I left Jim in the company of a couple students, kept an eye on him for a while, and then lost track.

It was some time later that I noticed Jim had discovered the bottomless punch bowl. He had also discovered that he could dance—awkwardly but enthusiastically. It seemed he was enjoying himself. I relaxed and returned to other social responsibilities—like intervening in the squabbles around the stereo regarding which cut got played.

There was a wide range of musical tastes, and students tended to bring their own favorite albums to these parties. There was a heavy dose of the early Beatles, but we fought over what else to play—like the Byrds, Beach Boys, Four Tops, Johnny Cash, Elvis, Buddy Holly, and even some big band stuff. (I would slip in Glenn Miller's "In the Mood.")

I lost track of Jim again. Didn't realize how much fun he was having until much later. That was when I realized that Jim had become the "life of the party." This Iowa "farm boy" had acclimated and graduated to the big league, perhaps a little too quickly. Jim had evidently been dipping into the punch bowl quite a bit.

Some of the older grad students took Jim under their wings. I'm not quite sure how it happened, but the downstairs shower stall—that Tom Oyster had just completed that week—got its first customer.

Two of the more sober party guests made sure that Jim got home safely. Before he left, however, it became pretty clear that Jim had been totally accepted into this little social group. We didn't know if the Purdue party scene had been a step up or a step down for him, but it no longer mattered.

That night, James R. Birk became "J.R." to me and to all his new friends at Purdue. He had reciprocated—in his ebullient state—by beginning to call me "S.P."

Those names stuck. Years later, you might not find any but Jim's old acquaintances from Purdue who called him "J.R." But Jim and I became "J.R." and "S.P." forever more on that one spring night in Indiana.

# PART 3

# Fighting for Tenure

# CHAPTER 17

## The Intrepid J. R. Birk

After a traumatic first year—where my unfinished Ph.D. tainted any glimmer of positivity—my second year at Purdue seemed upbeat in every way. We enjoyed the social whirl, from fall football weekends to springtime picnics and parties, forged strong friendships in both student and faculty circles, and began to put down roots in the Lafayette community.

We bought a new home. We bought a new car. I even sprang for a new suit to wear to my lectures.

*S.P., with new 1964 Chevelle Malibu Super Sport, and a new suit. New home on Arapahoe Drive, Lafayette, Spring, 1964. [Copyright, S. P. Perone]*

And yes, I had even developed a little *swagger* at the university—a bit prematurely, I soon realized. My good mentor, Buck Rogers, subtly pointed out at every opportunity that *assistant professors* weren't permanent fixtures. Yes, very soon I realized that I should be devoting my full energy to the primary obsession of every young professor— *getting tenure.*

By the spring of 1964 I had five graduate students working with me and would soon add two undergraduate research students (two very bright, affable and attractive sophomore women who would work with me for two years). I had enough research ideas to keep them all busy, while I continued working on personal lab projects.

One would think that publications would be flying out like confetti on New Year's Eve. In fact, some papers got published pretty quickly— especially those that were simple extensions of work begun at Wisconsin.

But I knew that the promotions committee would cast a jaded eye on publications that smelled too much like my early work. I could hear the dreaded question: "Doesn't Perone have any *new* ideas?"

One new area of research had occurred to me after Tom Oyster joined my group. I had asked him to enhance the operational-amplifier equipment that the instrument shop had built for me.

One of the pre-built modules was an electronic integrator. Tom wondered why we hadn't built an electronic *differentiator* (a module that would produce at its output a voltage proportional to the time-derivative of the input voltage).

Tom's question caused me to think, *Why not?* That led me down a pathway of questions that culminated in a whole new area of investigation.

It turned out that there were numerous potential advantages to working with the time-derivatives of an electrochemical voltammetric signal. I discovered that there was at least one other researcher—Ted Mueller at Oak Ridge National Lab—looking into this same question. We hooked up and began to work together. This led to a number of joint and independent publications.

But the "derivative voltammetry" project that Jim Birk took on was the most memorable.

The tall shadow cast against the frosted glass told me that it was Jim rapping on my office-lab door.

"Come in," I shouted from my desk.

"S.P.," he said as he slid into the room. "T. J. says you want to see me."

Jim called me *S.P.* or *Doc.* Tom Oyster and Jim were *T.J.* and *J.R.* within our group. Tom called me whatever suited him—*Doc, Sam, or S.P.* I never told any of my students what they *should* call me.

"Hey, J.R.," I called out, motioning him closer. "I need to talk to you about summer research." This would be our first chance to define his initial research project.

Jim sauntered to my desk at the back of the lab and took the chair next to it. He sat down, crossed one leg over the other, and leaned back. He gazed at me expectantly over the top of black horn-rimmed glasses. The familiar friendly smile—sort of a half-smirk—was there.

"You know about the work that Bill and I did with stripping analysis at graphite electrodes, don't you?" I began.

He nodded. "I read the papers. I've seen what T.J.'s been doing, too."

"Good. I'd like to have you look at something similar, but with a new twist."

His eyebrows arched, and he tilted his head to listen.

"I believe we can get much better sensitivity," I continued, "by using a derivative technique."

"You mean lower detection limits?" he asked. "Lower than parts per billion?"

I nodded. "Much lower, I think—two orders of magnitude."

Jim understood the implications. It would be like dissolving a microscopic grain of lead, dispersing it throughout an Olympic-sized swimming pool, taking a one-ounce sample, and accurately detecting the amount of lead—a formidable task.

He whistled. "Parts per trillion? Whoa! Wait till the 'ultra-trace' people hear about this."

I laughed. It was a private joke. My group had published papers describing trace analysis of heavy metals below parts per *billion*, while some workers had touted "*ultra*-trace methods" that detected metals just under parts per *million*.

"You know how we're going to do it?" I asked, not expecting an answer.

He flashed a wide grin. "That instrument that T.J.'s building?"

"I hope so," I replied. "Did he tell you about it? He nodded. "It takes derivatives. You think it'll work for voltammetry?"

"Theoretically, yes. But there's a problem."

Jim sat back and threw me a puzzled look. Then his eyes flashed. "You mean the *noise* problem?"

I nodded. "The differentiator increases signal-to-background, but it *decreases* signal-to-noise. We'll have to figure out how to optimize."

He nodded pensively.

"It gets worse," I added. "We don't even know if we can prepare standards. It's tough enough to do 100 parts per billion. Parts per trillion could be a nightmare."

Jim looked around my office-lab. His lab—two doors away—was identical, except that it housed two (and sometimes three or four) research students. "I bet there's enough lead and mercury in the air of these old labs to contaminate our solutions."

I nodded. "It won't be easy." Our eyes re-connected. "Are you up for it?"

He thought for a moment. "You're not talking about a *Ph.D.* project?"

I shook my head. "This is a *starter* project. To get you familiar with lab research and writing a paper. Not an *easy* project, but you won't be breaking completely new ground."

He nodded. "I understand that, Doc. I just wanted to make sure." He paused. "Do you think I could get this project done this summer?"

I shrugged. "You can never tell. But if it turns out to be too difficult, I'll pull the plug."

He pursed his lips before forming the next question. "You remember when we talked about how long it takes to get a Ph.D.?"

I chuckled. "Don't worry. My goal is to get you out of here in three or four years, with a bunch of publications under your belt."

That eager half-smirk flashed again. "All right, S.P., let's do it."


The first time Jim examined metal solutions below one part per billion, he called me in to look at the recorder trace.

"Look at this, S.P.," he offered, pointing to the chart paper. "This looks just like what we would expect. But it's too large."

"Is this a duplicate?" I asked.

He nodded. "It's the second run on the same solution."

"No, I mean—"

"Yeah, I know," he interrupted, "this is the second sample—made up exactly the same as the first. And I got the same results."

He flipped out his research notebook and showed me the calculations. I could see that the calculated levels of cadmium were about double what he would expect for the amount added.

I knew immediately what the problem was. But this was Jim's first encounter with the frustrating world of trace analysis. I had been fighting these battles since my days at Wisconsin.

"There's nothing wrong with your measurements," I declared. "It's your standard solutions that are messed up."

Jim's eyebrows furrowed. "Come on, S.P., I know how to do dilutions."

I laughed. "How are you treating the glassware?"

There was a flash of anger. "Repeated rinses with double-distilled water."

I pushed out a hand, palm first. "I know. I know. But trace amounts of cadmium stick to the glassware. You have to *leach* it out—with pure water—over and over again."

His eyes widened. "Oh," he mumbled.

I slapped him on the back. "Most people don't believe it until they see it."

He shook his head. "What next?"

"Glad you asked," I replied. "The *leaching* causes another problem."

His face became a question mark.

"When you have ultra-clean glassware, the first time you put trace metal solution in it, the stuff disappears onto the walls of the vessel."

His face clouded for a moment and then cleared. "Oh, I see. Then we'll get results that are too *low.*"

"Exactly. Now, do you see what you'll need to do?"

Jim stared off into space for a few moments. Then that crazy grin re-appeared. "Yeah, I'll have to equilibrate each new vessel with the standard it's going to hold. Like, repeat the same dilution in the same vessel three or four times."

There was a big smile on my face. "You got it. Lots of fun, huh?"

Jim gave me periodic updates after that.

Like everything he did, he dived enthusiastically into this project—never taking half measures.

These kinds of analyses are routinely done today, of course. But this was 1964. We weren't working in a "clean room." Far from it. The lab Jim worked in wasn't even air-conditioned. And he did this work in the *heat and humidity* of the Indiana summer.

Jim quickly discovered that he couldn't work with the lab windows open, as the trace amount of heavy metal in outside air was enough to contaminate solutions above the levels we wanted to detect. He couldn't run a circulating fan, because the dirt and dust packed into the crevices of those old labs contained heavy metals that would totally destroy our experiments.

The water he used had to be deionized and then doubly-distilled. The vessels that held his solutions had to be leached and equilibrated repeatedly, first with pure water and then with solutions that contained trace amounts of the metal in his standard solutions. Even the commercial so-called "pure" solids he used had to be re-purified to remove the trace heavy metal contaminants.

It was mid-August when he hit the stone wall—unable to obtain results for the lowest levels of metals, around five parts per trillion. Everything we knew about the instrument and the calibrations convinced us it was possible, but Jim's repeated attempts netted nothing.

That was when he disappeared.

I hadn't seen him in the lab for a few days when I queried Tom Oyster.

"Stop by tonight," suggested Tom, "about eleven."

"What? He's working nights?"

"Correction," said Tom. "Working *all* night."

I shook my head. "Why?"

He gave me a whimsical smile. "J.R. doesn't like people around. Kicks up too much dust."

I showed up that night and found Jim working in his lab.

"S.P.!" he exclaimed as I walked through the door. The astonished look told me he hadn't gotten any warning. I hadn't made a habit of coming in nights.

"Hey," I replied, "I hear you're working the night shift."

He flashed a sheepish grin. "Yeah, it's cooler. And nobody's around to stir up dust."

The lab was still hot and stuffy—but perhaps slightly less uncomfortable than during the daytime.

"You stay here all night?" I asked.

"Each run takes a one-hour electrolysis. I catch naps." He nodded at the lab bench next to his desk. I could see where he had cleared out space for his six foot two frame and made a "pillow" of a pile of books.

I shook my head. "Is it working?"

He grinned and reached for his research notebook. Turning to the last few pages, he opened it on his desk. "Here it is, Doc."

I saw a recorder trace pasted into the book that looked like an anthill sitting on the side of a mountain. Beneath the anthill, he had sketched in an extrapolated baseline to measure the height of the anthill.

Jim pointed to the anthill. "See this stripping peak?"

"Peak?" I exclaimed. "That's a stretch."

His grin faded for a moment and then reappeared. "That peak corresponds to five parts per trillion cadmium, S.P.—after a *one-hour* electrolysis."


Well, it took a little back and forth discussion and a look at duplicate results. But, finally, I agreed. Jim had done it.

His data clearly showed that we could detect heavy metals at the parts per trillion level—two or three orders of magnitude improvement over anything that had ever been done electrochemically. Other scientists would refer to his publication for many years to come.

I don't know anyone else who would have been able to achieve this under the extraordinarily difficult conditions he had to work. By sheer determination, it seemed, Jim accomplished things that most people wouldn't even attempt.

This was the first—but not the last—of my observations of the "intrepid J. R. Birk" in action. Later on, he would be my first student to explore the world of flash photolysis— persistently discharging thousands of volts through flammable solutions....

But, well, that's another story.

# CHAPTER 18

## Relationships

My first two undergraduate research students were also the first two women in my group. Kendra Davenport and Ann Brumfield asked to do research with me at the end of their sophomore year. At the time, I had five graduate students—Kretlow, Oyster, Birk, Evins and Stapelfeldt. I asked Oyster and Kretlow to guide the new undergraduate students because the women would be following up on the guys' earlier work with graphite electrodes. So the guys made room for the women in their respective labs.

I thought Kendra and Tom Oyster would work well. Both were athletic, attractive and out-going. But Tom and Kendra agreed on very little and seemed to enjoy nothing more than mutual verbal assaults. Still, the state of war that pervaded their lab was good-natured and harmless, if not downright entertaining at times.

I thought I saw Kendra's eyes light up for Tom. But I learned later that she had beaten up on him out on the tennis courts. She must have been very good, as Tom was no slouch. On the other hand, beating Tom in tennis was probably not the pathway to his heart. For Kendra, the score was: *Tennis*, one. *Amore*, zero.

Pairing Ann with Bill Kretlow, I thought, was a pretty wise thing. Ann was petite, dark-haired, and pretty, but serious and quiet—a personality much like Bill's. I thought they would get along well. Because Bill had a girl back in Chicago, I didn't expect any romance to blossom. In fact, I was most concerned about Al Moreland, Buck's student, who resided in the lab adjoining Bill's, but spent much of his time hanging out with my students.

Al was a suave, handsome, Princeton graduate. He made no secret that he had an eye for the co-eds. His lab door opened up to the corridor corner that met the stairwell. He left the door open and set up his desk just inside the doorway so that he was able to take in the sights during class changes. It was not unusual for a number of different young ladies to stop by his lab during the day. Occasionally, Al would bring one of these women to a party. But there never seemed to be that someone special in his life.

Well, my concerns regarding Al were unfounded. But I'm not so sure that sparks didn't begin to fly between Ann and *Bill*. I do know that he stopped talking about his girl back in Chicago.

Regardless of the relationships that did or did not arise when these two young women joined my group, Kendra and Ann certainly did a fine job with their research. Each published a paper with me before graduating and going off to graduate school. They worked within my group for two years and were delightful both socially and technically.

But there was one added fringe benefit that was totally unexpected.

One day during Ann's first year working for me, she came into my office and asked if I would like to meet her father. I agreed of course. She said he would be stopping by her lab late that day after a meeting.

I stopped by her lab at the appointed hour and found only Ann and Bill.

"Am I too early?" I asked.

"No," Ann replied, "my dad should be here any minute."

I walked into the lab and leaned against the lab bench. "Your dad has business here?" I asked.

She cleared her throat. "He's on the board of trustees."

I stood up straight. "What? Your father's—"

"On the Board, yes," Bill filled in.

I shook my head. "I had no idea."

"I don't tell people," Ann explained. "Kinda scares them."

Just then there was a light knock on the lab door and in walked a well-dressed, slender, gray-haired man, slightly shorter than Bill or I. On his face was a big smile. He opened his arms, and Ann greeted him warmly.

She introduced Bill and me, and Mr. Brumfield volunteered that Ann had been telling him good things about us and about her work.

I was at a loss for words. I hadn't ever rubbed elbows with anyone higher in the university than our department head. "I ... I'm glad Ann's talked to you about ... about our work. She's doing a ... fine job," I stammered.

Mercifully, the chit-chat was cut short when Ann announced they had to leave for a dinner engagement—but not before her father insisted, "If there's ever anything I can do...."

How many times do you hear someone say those very words, and it means nothing? Well, not this time.

When Bill and I were left alone, I asked, "What does Ann's father do?"

"Doesn't the name mean anything to you, Doc?"

I thought for a second. "Come on. Are you kidding? He's not *that* Brumfield?"

Bill nodded. "Yup. *Potter and Brumfield, Inc.* Relays. Switches. You name it."

"Oh my God! We use their relays."

Bill threw me a puzzled look.

"For flash photolysis. J.R. is trying to set up a time-delayed switching circuit."

"You're using relays?"

"Have to. But they don't make what we need—way too slow or too unstable."

"You ordered them from Potter and Brumfield?"

I nodded. "We've looked at dozens of spec sheets and tested a lot."

"Maybe you should talk to Mr. Brumfield," Bill suggested.

I shook my head. "What we're looking for is so far out...."

"He'll be here a couple more days."

I blinked. "Really?"

Jim Birk and I got our heads together quickly. It seemed like such a long shot, but what the hell.

Ann left Mr. Brumfield in my office the following day. He took a seat and got right to the point.

"Dr. Perone, Ann tells me you wanted to talk about one of our products."

I nodded. "It's kind of a weird switching application—low currents, low voltages, short very-precise time delays."

He pursed his lips. "Not the kind of thing we usually deal with. Can you tell me what you're trying to do?"

I described the flash photolysis experiments with electrochemical monitoring. Then I added, "We need to electrically isolate the monitoring electrode for a variable length of time after flashing the solution."

"We don't have the right kind of time-delay relay for you?"

"The reed relays have the right specs but create noise. The contacts bounce half-a-dozen times before settling down."

He chuckled. "Have you tried mercury-wetted relays?"

I nodded. "No bounce, but too slow."

"So, what you need is—rapid switching times and no bounce." He scratched his chin. "What kinds of time delays and switching times?"

"A few milliseconds to ten-second time delays, accurate to microseconds. Switching times less than a hundred microseconds."

He chuckled. "No wonder you haven't found anything." Then he looked away into space for a few seconds. "You'd have to do it with two relays. For the longer-time relay we can modify one we already produce. The shorter time? Let me work on that."


A month later, I received both relays in the mail—two of each. Two had a model number. The other two had no markings. Mr. Brumfield had given the task to one of his engineers, and—*voila*—the product had appeared.

The short-time-delay relay was a thing of beauty—one of a kind—exactly what we needed to do the unique kind of flash photolysis studies we had in mind.

We offered Ann and Mr. Brumfield our profound thanks, and Jim Birk got to work. Regardless of the science, we knew for sure that no one else in the world could collect the data that we were collecting.

Things looked great. The Research Gods had smiled on us—at least for a while.

But then, life never moved forward without a few bumps in the road—as we were about to find out.

# CHAPTER 19

## Making Ozone

*Craaack!*

The sound reverberated like a gunshot down the third floor hallway of the old wing of the chemistry building. With none of the labs or offices air conditioned, doors and windows were wide open on this warm spring day in 1964. The shattering noise flushed occupants out into the hallway.

I beat a path to Tom Oyster's lab, fearing what I might find.

I rounded the corner and stood at the doorway, taking in the scene.

In his white lab coat, Tom had backed away from the large bank of capacitors on the lab bench. His arms were outstretched and his eyes bugged out as if he were backing away from a rattlesnake. In his right hand was a heavy twelve-inch screwdriver whose tip had turned black.

"What happened?" I cried, slowing down and scanning the entire lab.

He shook his head roughly—as if he were trying to get water out of his ears. "I was just proving Faraday's Law," he joked, forcing a grin. His eyes remained focused on the capacitor bank on the bench top.

I followed his gaze and noticed a large blackened area around one terminal of one of the capacitor cans. Tiny trails of smoke hung in the air. A whiff of ozone hit me.

"What did you do?" I asked.

Tom moved cautiously back toward the lab bench. "I couldn't get the flash lamp to discharge," he remarked absently, moving still closer. He bent over to inspect more carefully the blackened capacitor can.

"Be careful," I warned. "What's the voltage?"

Tom nodded at the voltage meter sitting on the shelf behind the bank of capacitors. The needle was fixed at "zero."

"The bank was charged to a thousand volts," he explained. "The flash lamp wouldn't fire, so I had to find another way to discharge the bank." He held up the screwdriver with the blackened tip and grinned at me.

"Are you crazy?" I cried. "That's what? A thousand volts and one hundred microfarads? Discharged in a few microseconds?"

"Yeah, I know. Ten thousand amps. Big jolt."

Then I noticed a number of black marks on the water pipe behind the capacitor bank. "You've done this before, haven't you?"

Tom grew a sly grin. "Once or twice."

I wagged my head. "We talked about this."

In fact, we had discussed it in great detail. Tom had chosen not to go on for a Ph.D. He was working for me as a lab technician after completing his Masters thesis. I had asked him to build a power source to fire flash lamps for Jim Birk's flash photolysis studies. Dealing with high voltages and very high currents demanded that we consider safety aspects.

The plan was to wire together a two-hundred-microfarad capacitor bank. When charged to a few thousand volts and discharged in ten microseconds across a xenon-filled

*Early flash photolysis capacitor bank. [Copyright, S. P. Perone]*

flash lamp, intense pulses of light were produced. The entire power source was to be enclosed in a wooden box lined with a grounded wire cage. Opening the door to the box would cause the bank to discharge safely through a heavy-duty resistor.

Unfortunately, the capacitor bank and discharge electronics were being constructed outside the box.

"I don't want you doing this again," I insisted.

"You know a better way?"

"Use the discharge resistor."

He nodded slowly. "Sure. But think about it, S.P. I charge up the capacitor bank; throw the discharge switch; and nothing happens. What would you do? I can't just leave the bank charged up."

"The resistor discharge didn't work?"

"Nothing ever works the first time."

He was right, of course. I searched for words. "Have you gotten jolted?"

He chuckled. "Why do you think I began to carry this screwdriver?"

"How bad was it?"

"Just a couple times, when the capacitors weren't fully charged. It stings like a wasp. Arm tingles for quite a while. I wouldn't want the full dose."

I wagged my head. "Christ, T.J.! I don't want to have to scrape you off the ceiling."

"It's OK," he declared. "I'm putting everything in the box today."

This was the 1960s. OSHA didn't exist. The chemistry department had a safety committee that worried about chemical handling and such. But safety regarding custom-built electronics? Nobody was paying attention yet.

And that was a potential recipe for disaster. We were pushing hard into a brand new area of research. I felt under tremendous pressure to produce something with the flash photolysis experiments. To me, this was the key to attaining scientific credibility needed for promotion and tenure.

The clock was ticking. I had, at most, two more years to prove myself. The research would have to bear fruit. Then we would have to get it reviewed and published before that promotions committee met to decide my fate sometime within the next two years.

That was the dilemma. Safety first? Or full speed ahead?

"All right, T.J.," I said finally. "Finish the box. But I don't want you testing these electronics again unless I'm here."

"Day or night?" he inquired skeptically.

I nodded. "Any time."

"All right. You got it."

Of course, I didn't know then what Tom had in store for me next.

# CHAPTER 20

## Wet Dreams

The rude *brriinnng ... brriinnng ... brriinnng* of the bedroom phone jolted me upright. I reached in the dark for the nightstand and found the receiver.

"Hell-o," I croaked, squinting at the fluorescent dial of the wristwatch on the nightstand: *two-twenty.*

"Dr. Perone?" asked a strange male voice.

"Yes."

"This is the university police. Is your lab Room 306 in the chemistry building?"

I was wide-awake now. "Yes. What's wrong?" I had a fleeting vision of Tom Oyster's smoking body crumpled over the flash photolysis hardware.

"Well, we've got a situation here, Dr. Perone. There's water pouring down from your lab into the lab below. You need to get down here right away."

By this time I was already out of bed, reaching for my discarded clothes. "What happened?" I asked.

"Not sure. We turned off the water, but there's a bit of a mess. We'll meet you at your lab. Say half-an-hour?"

"I'll be right there."


I was afraid I knew what had happened. I hadn't liked the idea. But it had worked just as Tom had predicted. So I had let it go.

Indiana summers were miserably hot and humid. And our labs weren't air conditioned. Yet, we were trying to do trace analysis and construct precision electronics. Needless to say, our technical goals and the environment were incompatible.

The department was slowly air conditioning the old part of the chemistry building where I resided—one small lab at a time. My suite of labs wouldn't be air conditioned for at least another year. Consequently, when Tom came up with the idea of constructing his own air conditioner, I had listened....

"Here it is, S.P."

Tom reached behind his desk and lifted the huge metal object as if it were a loaf of bread.

"That looks like a car radiator," I observed.

"Yup, picked it up for five bucks. Checked it out. No leaks. What do you think?"

"I'm afraid to ask."

"That's the rest of it over there." He nodded toward the large chemical hood at the front of the lab, underneath which sat a large sixteen-inch fan. "Run cold water through the radiator and stick the fan behind it."

"That's gonna use a lot of water."

"It's free, isn't it?"

"Somebody's got to pay for it."

Tom smirked. "Maybe that'll hurry up the air conditioning project."

I shook my head. "I don't know. Sounds a little flaky."

"Hey, listen, boss. I could be up at my folks' cabin on Lake Ripon, sipping a gin and tonic. But instead I'm down here in a steam bath, building your flash box."

I stared back at his devilish grin. "All Right. But let me take a look at it."

I had to admit, the makeshift "air conditioner" did cool down the lab. Tom had set it up at the front of the lab, just in front of the chemical hood, blowing cool air toward the rear. Sturdy rubber hoses were clamped to the radiator and the cold water tap in the hood, with the exhaust hose shoved down the large floor drain. By the time he called me in to look it over, the system had been running for an hour.

"It'll get cooler," Tom declared. "I'll keep the doors and windows closed."

"What happens if you spring a leak?"

He shrugged. "I'll turn it off."

"Yeah, if you're here."

"Hey, S.P., I'm *always* here. When I leave, I'll turn off the water."

I thought it over. "All right. But this contraption only runs when someone is in the lab, OK?"

Tom scowled. "You worry too much, S.P." Then the scowl turned to his familiar grin. "But it's a deal."

I nodded and left the lab. I had a queasy feeling about it. But what the hell, it *did* work.


On the night of the spill, memories of that exchange with Tom raced through my mind. I motored across town to the university. The more I thought, the angrier I got.

The makeshift "air conditioner" had been working just fine for the past few weeks—with much-appreciated relief. Tom's handiwork might have spread to other labs. I didn't know for sure whether other disasters might not already be in the making.

In my anger, I tried to re-construct in my mind what must have happened. Had Tom simply forgotten to turn off the water? Or, lulled by the few weeks of uneventful operation, had he opted to leave the "cooler" running overnight?

I reached a decision. I wasn't going to the lab alone.


I didn't have Tom's new phone number. He had abandoned his apartment when his sister—an instructor in another department—had left for the summer. He had moved into her apartment, and I knew where that was.

Like so many older homes near the university, this two-story flat was broken up into three or four apartments. Tom's was on the upper floor. I pulled up in front, parked, and bounded up the wooden steps of the front porch. I punched the buzzer for Tom's apartment. I punched it several times.

I heard a window open above the porch. "S.P.? Is that you?" It was Tom's sleepy, irritated voice.

I skipped down the steps onto the front sidewalk. That's when I realized Tom must have seen my dark blue '64 Chevelle (with the new car sticker still on the rear window) parked under the street light.

I turned and looked up. Tom was leaning out the window. "What's going on?" he asked in a loud whisper.

"There's a problem in your lab," I replied. "Water leak."

The pained look on his face revealed everything. "I'll be right down," he said.

Disappearing, and then reappearing at the front door dressed in shorts, tee shirt and sandals, Tom shot down the steps and jumped into the car with me. "Let's go!" he croaked.


The Super Sport V-8 lurched away from the curb and streaked out into the empty West Lafayette streets. Nothing but a couple of uncooperative stoplights would keep us from getting there in two minutes.

But that left time for a grilling.

"You want to tell me what happened?" I asked.

"Don't know until we see it," he replied.

I turned to him. "You leave the water running?"

He shrugged. "I guess."

I returned my eyes to the road. "Don't you know?"

"What I mean is, I don't understand what happened. It's been running continuously now for a week."

I shifted my gaze back and glared at him briefly. "That wasn't what we agreed."

"But it was working fine, boss. I checked all the connections. I don't see how it could have leaked."

I shook my head and heaved a melodramatic sigh. "Well, I guess we'll find out soon."

As promised, two university police were waiting for us in Tom's lab. They had roused someone from physical plant that had delivered pails, mops and rags.

Water covered the lab floor, but that wasn't the problem. The police led us to the lab below. It was a mess.

Then there was the lab below that.

Tom and I spent the rest of the night sopping up the water. Some residents of the lower labs showed up and helped out.

We were extremely fortunate. No electronic equipment got rained on. No chemistry projects got ruined. Some papers got wet. But, by and large, the labs survived the messy downpour just fine. Not too surprising, I guess, for *chemistry* labs.

As it became clear that no permanent damage had been done, the tension eased, and Tom and I and the others began to loosen up. I'm afraid Tom had to put up with quite a ribbing that night.

But he was good-natured about it. I told him I wouldn't say anything to the rest of the group. Of course, that was after he reminded me that I had been responsible for a few mishaps myself.

We did learn later that the reason for the disaster was a water pressure surge during the night that popped one of the clamps on the radiator inlet hose.

How could Tom have foreseen *that*? Perhaps no more than I could have foreseen what would happen when we re-designed the flash photolysis apparatus.

I should have known better.

# CHAPTER 21

## The Big Bang

While walking back to my office after a lecture, I noticed a small crowd outside of Jim Birk's lab. They parted when they saw me, revealing Tom Oyster standing just inside the door. I could see Jim in the middle of the lab reaching for something on the floor.

"What happened?" I asked.

Tom made a mock-serious face. "J.R.'s gone one up on me."

"What?" I cried, slipping past Tom.

There on his knees, picking up debris from the floor, Jim looked up and gave me a silly grin. "You missed the fireworks, S.P." He rose to his feet as I approached.

"Are you OK?" I asked, pulling closer to the mess.

"Yeah, but it was pretty exciting for a while."

Staring into Jim's grin prompted a recollection of how we had gotten here....

I had rushed into print with a quick communication—Jim Birk's paper announcing that we could monitor transient photolytic free radicals electrochemically. But a Czech group had beaten us to press with a more primitive experimental approach.

I was determined to establish ours as the premier research group in this exciting new area. It was a key part of my campaign for promotion. My publications' list was growing, but it didn't cry out "no-brainer." With the clock ticking closer to that tenure decision date, I was desperate to dazzle the promotions committee.

But it would not be easy. There were a number of problems with the flash photolysis studies, the biggest of which was a lack of sensitivity. That is, it was difficult to get enough light energy around the microelectrode to produce detectable intermediates.

Then Jim had a bright idea. Rather than producing the light externally and reflecting it into the cell, we would put the lamp *inside* the cell and capture *all* of the light.

Sounded good to me.

Jim translated the idea into a cell design. It was tricky. The flash lamp—charged to a couple thousand volts—had to be insulated electrically from the cell, solution, monitoring electronics, etc. Accordingly, we designed a cell pierced by an insulating quartz tube, through which was mounted the linear flash lamp.

We put it together, and it worked fine. But there was no improvement.

So we went back to the drawing board to design a better reflecting system.

But Jim hadn't given up.

"What happened?" I asked Jim.

"Not sure. Big bang, and then flames shot out. But the Faraday box around the cell contained most of it."

I looked inside the box—not a difficult task, as the door had been blown off its hinges. Fortunately, the heavy glass of the mercury reservoir and the stout mercury tubing had been shielded from the blast.

I examined the remnants of the cell and the dangling flash lamp that had cracked in two.

"What voltage were you using?" I asked.

"Two thousand volts."

I wagged my head. "I don't understand. The insulation must have broken down."

"Uh ... not exactly."

I grew a frown. "What are you saying?"

"I mean, the insulation was OK, but—." Jim peered at me over his black-rimmed glasses. "But the flash lamp cracked."

My head snapped back toward the flash box, and I scanned the debris more carefully. "What happened to the quartz tube?"

"Well … umm … I was thinking, you know, it was cutting out too much light." He grew a guilty grin.

"Don't tell me you put the flash lamp directly through the solution!" I cried.

Jim snickered mischievously. "You can't do any better than that, S.P."

"What … how … you … I don't believe it," I sputtered. "*Alcohol* solutions. What did you think was going to happen?"

He shrugged, still grinning. "Aw, c'mon, S.P. Wait till you see the data I got before it popped."

Jim came clean on the whole thing.

He had reasoned that, if we needed more intensity, the obvious ploy was to eliminate anything between the flash lamp and the monitoring electrode. Therefore, he concluded, the original design (see [1] in illustration) with a quartz tube surrounding the flash lamp had to go.

In his new design (see [2]) the flash lamp was mounted directly through the cell body and sealed to the cell walls with Tygon tubing and wax. The sample solution surrounded the lamp, with the monitoring electrode positioned in the cell directly above it.

I'm sorry to say that

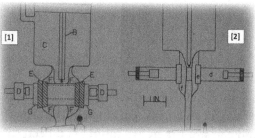

*Jim Birk's Flash Photolysis Cell Designs. [1] Original (Flash lamp, D, encased by quartz tube, G.) [2] "Big Bang" Design. (Flash lamp, d, in direct contact with test solution.) [Copyright, S. P. Perone]*

this approach did work, and Jim got improvements in measured photocurrents. In fact he collected lots of data for our publication. The risk paid off; at least until it went up in smoke.

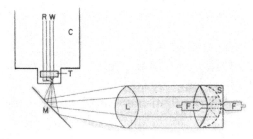

*External flash lamp design. [Copyright, S. P. Perone]*

Thankfully, no one was hurt, and the "big bang" event was the source of countless ribbings for many years to come.

We did re-work the design for an exterior flash lamp—using a focusing reflector to increase the light flux around the monitoring electrode.

The new design worked great but wasn't nearly as exciting. Excitement, however, can come from many unexpected directions.

# CHAPTER 22

## 'Searching

Karen knocked on the door and poked her head into my office. The short sandy hair was characteristically tousled. "You have a minute, Doc?" she asked.

An undergraduate research student, Karen had a tomboyish personality that fit well with my male grad students. They quickly learned that she excelled at both partying and sports. She was one of a number of undergraduates that chose to work with me in the mid-1960s, while I was still an untenured, uncommonly young professor.

I beckoned her to come in and have a seat by my desk.

"Doc, my sorority has a dinner-thing," she began after sitting and crossing her legs. "I'm supposed to invite you." She leaned against the back of the hard chair and gave me a crooked grin. "Yeah, grub at the house. Girls doing any 'searching invite their professors. You OK with that?"

"I thought you lived at home?"

"I'm a *Lambda Phi* 'townie.' They let me crash there for a hundred bucks a month."

"What's this 'dinner' about?"

Karen uncrossed her long, tan legs and slumped down in the chair, sliding her feet forward and slipping her hands into the side pockets of her straight khaki skirt.

"It's a tradition," she replied. "Once a year, research advisors get invited to dinner." She shrugged. "It'll be short. No speeches or anything."

I dragged more information from her and agreed to attend the dinner. I learned that a number of her sorority sisters would be inviting their research professors also. She added that she would never be *'searching*—as she and her friends referred to independent *research*—for any of those "old farts."

Surprisingly, the dinner was scheduled for six o'clock on a Friday evening. Karen's description of the other professors, to be kind, had been fairly accurate. Her prediction that it would be over by seven had not.

By eight o'clock I had thanked the housemother and was preparing to leave. Karen ushered me to the door, where we were joined by one of the other women from our table. Her name was Jane—a petite brunette who amply bolstered those rumors that Biology got the best looking female science majors.

Karen leaned over to hear Jane's whispered message. Her face lit up with a mischievous smile. Raising a hand to hide her mouth, Karen whispered to me, "We're goin' for a beer. Wanta come?"

I glanced from Karen to Jane. Their eager faces told me that replying "no thanks" was unacceptable.

We left in my car.

I had anticipated a quick trip to Harry's Chocolate Shop for a beer and then home. Not this night. Karen directed me to the home of another "townie" sorority sister across the river in Lafayette. The house was located just off Ninth Street, south of the Lafayette Country Club, in one of the upscale wooded developments.

A tall, willowy blonde in a dark blue straight skirt and powder blue cashmere sweater opened the door. I met "Wanda," and we were led down a half-flight of stairs to a large, carpeted lower-level family room. All the lighting came from a number of candles spread about the room. Seated on the floor, arranged in a circle about a candlelit central cocktail table, were several young women engaged in animated conversation. Each was attired in a skirt and sweater. The din of chatter subsided, with a bit of squirming and re-arranging of assets, as the only man in the house descended the stairs.

Wanda introduced me to her friends, told us where to get our drinks—hard, soft, or beer—and we joined the circle. The chatter had risen again to a soothing cacophony that allowed one to converse almost privately with the adjacent person. *Norwegian Wood,* from the Beatles' *Rubber Soul* album, could be heard just below the ambient decibels of prattle.

I leaned to my left and asked Karen, "Are you sure it's OK for me to be here?"

"Sure, Doc. Relax. We unwind like this every Friday."

"But—"

"It's OK. The girls wanted me to bring you."

"Why?"

Karen gave me a coy smile and shrugged.

I glanced around the room. What were these young women expecting? I decided to take Karen's advice—*relax and enjoy.* The soothing scotch-rocks helped.

I turned to Jane on my right. "Did you invite your major professor here?" I asked.

She giggled and covered her mouth. "Are you kidding? I'd be blackballed for life."

I chuckled to myself, recalling the brief, stuffy chat that I had had with her professor at the dinner. He was fiftyish and projected that all-to-typical bloated perception of his academic and social status. I nodded. "Yeah, I understand."

"Do you?" she asked, tilting her head. An impish smile flashed briefly.

I hesitated and then decided to open up. "I guess he's like a lot of faculty—thinking they're the center of the universe."

"Yeah, most of 'em don't realize they're just arrogant pricks."

I blinked. Jane wasn't inaccurate, just colorful. "Couldn't have put it better myself," I declared, suddenly feeling more at ease.

We chatted for a while longer, and I learned that she hailed from a small southern Indiana town near the Ohio border. She was dating a biology grad student. And she hoped to go to graduate school after getting her B.S.

A tap on my shoulder prompted me to turn around. Karen had disappeared, and there, getting comfortable on the carpet next to me, was Wanda. She leaned forward, lightly touching my back, and said to Jane, "Sorry. Didn't mean to interrupt, but I wanted a chance to talk to Dr. Perone. Do you mind?" It was more a command than a request.

Jane shrugged and started to rise. "Good time to get a refill," she explained.

She sauntered away in the direction of the wet bar located one step up from the carpeted area where we sat. She passed the bar and continued down a dark hallway. I assumed she was heading for a bathroom. She seemed a little unsteady.

Wanda quickly distracted me with conversation while another young woman—a lithesome redhead—slid into the spot vacated by Jane. I didn't know her name, but soon learned that she and Wanda were taking introductory chemistry courses taught by my colleagues. That didn't surprise me. In the 1960s nearly all Purdue students took chemistry. That's why we had freshman chemistry courses with thousands of students enrolled. That's why we taught introductory chemistry at a dozen different levels. And that's why we needed to recruit a hundred new grad students each year to maintain this remarkable machine. (Conversely, this unusual policy funded a large annual influx of graduate students to the chemistry department, fueling professors' research programs.)

"My chem. instructor is Dr. Hansen," Wanda was saying. "Do you know him?"

"Not very well, but I've seen him in action. I sneaked into the balcony of the big lecture hall during one of his Ag. Chem. classes."

She chuckled. "Did he throw anything at anybody?"

"No. Not that day. But he gave a tongue lashing to two strapping farm boys. Kicked them out of the room."

Her head bobbed. "Students are scared of him. That's one class I don't walk into unless I'm prepared."

"How are you doing?"

"Getting a 'B'. But I hate chemistry. Don't understand why I have to take it. I'm an Econ. major."

I did my best to explain the university's antiquated policy.

Wanda waved off my explanation. "I bet I'd enjoy chemistry ... with a different instructor." She bounced a sly glance off me.

"You have the best teacher right now," I responded quickly.

"What? I can't stand Hansen."

"Doesn't matter. When it's over, you'll know you've learned something."

"What about those Ag. students he picks on? I'll bet they're not happy."

"You'd lose that bet. In my senior course, I had a guy that started out in the Ag. program. A football player. He claimed all the guys 'loved' Hansen."

"Hard to believe."

"There was an incident a couple years ago. A student challenged Hansen in class. That's when half-a-dozen other students—big guys—stood up and carted him off."

Wanda shook her head absently. "Who was the football player in your class?"

I chuckled. "I can see you're really into this teaching philosophy thing. He was a backup kicker. You wouldn't know him.'

Wanda persisted. "Did you ever get any pressure from the coaches?"

"Why would you ask that?"

"I've heard stories."

"I've had athletes in different classes. Never had any pressure." I thought for a moment and then added, "But they do want progress reports. I get phone calls. They throw tutors around like candy."

"Bet they'd be upset if you didn't warn them, and a student flunked."

I shrugged. "Don't know. That never happened."

Wanda seemed to lose interest and became absorbed with her drink. So I turned to chat with the redhead on my right. She was another biology major and, surprisingly, asked about my research. Fearing that I would bore her to death, I mentioned the only work that was remotely related to biology—the flash photolysis studies for which I had gotten a NIH grant. The redhead's eyes lighted up. Would I consider her for a senior research project, she blurted excitedly. After finishing a double scotch, I nearly said yes. But instead I politely suggested that she should work with a biology professor.

Once again I felt a tap on my shoulder. I turned to discover that Jane had returned and taken Wanda's place. She greeted me by extending a smoking, crudely wrapped cigarette, grasped lightly between her delicate thumb and forefinger.

"Want a hit?" she asked, exhaling smoke.

I hadn't been prepared for a 'hit' that night. In fact, I didn't smoke, period. The closest I had ever come to marijuana was to enjoy the sweet smell of its smoke drifting over a rock concert.

I glanced briefly around the room. Karen had taken a spot in the circle far across from me. Her eyes caught mine just as she took a hit from a second joint making the rounds. She took a deep drag and then gestured toward me, as if offering the smoking cannabis in her hand. Her eyes remained locked with mine while she passed the joint to her right. She exhaled and smiled as I accepted Jane's offering and brought the smoking stub to my lips.

The drag was short. I didn't want to embarrass myself by choking and coughing. I passed the joint to the redhead, as I slowly inhaled the smoke into my lungs. I liked the taste and smell.

With a few more hits I grew braver, inhaling more of the sweet smoke. I still didn't feel anything unusual. I noticed that the room had become quiet. People were whispering and giggling.

Like the others around the circle, Jane and I hadn't talked much. Then she leaned closer and whispered in my ear, "What were you and Wanda talking about? Looked serious."

I turned and grinned. "Football," I replied.

She arched her eyebrows. "Really? Looked more personal."

"Some people think football is *real* personal," I quipped.

She patted my thigh, smiled coyly, and murmured, "Could be." Her hand remained for a moment, and I searched her eyes. They were brown, like mine, and sending messages that set off alarm bells in my foggy brain.

I suddenly discovered I needed to pee and decided to head for the dark hallway that several of the ladies had visited previously. The first indication that I was slightly incapacitated was when I went to stand up. Jane reached out a hand as I rose. I grabbed it to steady myself.

"You OK?" she asked.

I nodded. "My foot went to sleep. I'll be right back."

Concentrating on putting one foot steadily in front of the other, and taking the single step up to the wood flooring with careful deliberation, I managed to navigate down the hallway about ten feet to the bathroom. It was illuminated with a night-light. I went in, locked the door, and did my business.

Before leaving the bathroom, I examined myself in the mirror by the dim light. I leaned closer and looked into the eyes. *Perone*, I said to myself, *you'd better get out of here.*

I opened the door and stepped out into the dark hallway. I was startled to discover Jane standing just to the right of the doorway. She reached out to touch my arm.

"Are you all right?" she asked for the second time.

"Of course," I replied, grinning like a goat. I noticed that she hadn't let go of my arm.

"That's good," she sighed. Then she drew herself to me, wrapped her free hand behind my head and pulled me down so that her lips could reach mine.

I was stunned, but I didn't resist. She wrapped her arms around and pressed her body to mine—an act that quickly squelched for me the rumors about pot's stifling effects.

Then—as suddenly as it had all begun—Jane pulled away, threw me a coy smile, and slid into the bathroom.

I stared blankly at the closed door for a while.

*Yes*, I thought, *it's time to go.*


I never saw Jane again. Nor did I ever see Wanda or any of her friends, except for my student, Karen. I don't know if Karen ever learned about the brief, strange encounter between Jane and me. I hope not. It surely meant nothing to Jane. And it would not lead to anything as far as I was concerned.

Sometimes I wonder if Karen had set me up. She had that kind of sense of humor.

But it had been a memorable evening; and it would not be the last time that I would find myself on the brink of potential disaster.

Not always would I be able to extricate myself so readily.

# CHAPTER 23

## Reflections

It was the summer of 1966. Harry Pardue had just been promoted. I knew this next year would be the one where I would either be promoted or not.

Was I concerned? *Concerned* doesn't begin to describe it.

Many times I wondered why I hadn't taken one of those plush industrial jobs. My friends from Wisconsin that had done so were making good money and were seemingly unconcerned about anything resembling a tenure decision.

As a graduate student, I had interviewed both Kodak Research, in Rochester, N.Y., and Esso (later Exxon) Research & Engineering, in Linden, New Jersey. Both had offered me good-paying jobs as a research chemist.

It was time to reflect on why I had instead chosen an academic career.

I was a college sophomore—in 1956— when it happened.

I hadn't yet committed to a major field but was leaning strongly toward history. Yes, that's right, *history*. Rockford was a liberal arts college, and my early courses were selected accordingly. I took chemistry, physics and math but also got a healthy dose of history, political science, philosophy, literature and art.

I was totally captivated by the field of history. I saw myself pursuing a lifetime of scholarly activity—delving into the past to dissect events in the manner of the noted historians whose works I'd been reading.

Of course, to pursue such a career would require getting an academic job—becoming a history professor.

That's what I announced to my family.

And that's when I got a visit from Uncle Nick.

My mother's brother, Nick Parrinello, was thirty-six at the time, and he was the first ever college graduate in our family's history. He had gotten an engineering degree at Armour Tech (now Illinois Institute of Technology) in Chicago. His high school advisor had gotten him into a co-op program where he worked at a Rockford tool and die company six months and went to school six months.

Nick was my godfather, mentor, advisor, donor of coats, ties and loaner cars for important high school dances, and the person my parents expected me to emulate. With a tall, athletic frame, dark wavy hair, movie-star handsome features, and a college degree, Nick had found his way into a good job with Western Electric in Chicago after serving in the Navy during World War II.

But he soon found that the corporate world of the 1940s had not yet fully embraced Italian-Americans, and his options for advancement were limited. Nick solved that problem by abandoning his engineering career and becoming an independent insurance agent back in Rockford. His engaging personality and ability to speak fluent Italian, particularly the locally predominant Sicilian dialect, contributed to his quickly building a very successful agency.

My fondness and admiration for Uncle Nick prompted my parents to call on him to "talk" to me about any important decisions.

Not surprisingly, I found myself sitting on the front porch of our family home one Sunday afternoon "discussing" with Uncle Nick my decision to become a history professor.

"Won't you have to get a doctorate," he asked, "to become a professor?"

I nodded.

"What would that take? Three, four, five years of graduate school?"

I shrugged. "Something like that."

"Can you afford it?"

"My professors tell me I can get a teaching assistantship, and the school will waive tuition."

My uncle's eyebrows raised slightly. "Sounds like a good deal." He stroked his chin for a moment and then asked, "Do you know what you'll make as a history professor?"

I wagged my head.

"Well, I looked it up," he declared.

It was my turn to arch eyebrows. "Where? How——?"

Big toothy grin. "It's my job—digging up information like that."

I matched his grin, remembering that he was an insurance underwriter. I guess he could get that kind of information if he wanted.

"Five thousand a year for an assistant professor," he declared. "Not much money."

"I know. I know. But they're doing what they want to do."

"What's that?"

"Teaching. Research. Writing."

He shook his head. "That's a tough price to pay," he remarked. Then he asked, "Aren't you interested in anything else? I remember that you got the science award in high school. Your mom tells me you're doing well in chemistry."

I chuckled. "That science award was Father Glynn's mistake. He had to give out four graduation awards and played eeny-meeny-miney-mo. He taught me Latin, not science."

"That's too bad. Chemistry's a good field. Right out of college you'd make more than a history professor. With a master's or doctor's degree, the sky's the limit."

Well, that conversation gave me pause. I loved history. But I had had enough of financial stress. I had shined shoes to get through high school; I was working thirty hours a week repairing shoes to get through college; and I was eagerly looking forward to the "rich rewards of education" that my parents had extolled since I was a toddler.

I took a fresh look at chemistry. My grades in the freshman course had been good, and the professor had urged me to take the sophomore course. It was analytical chemistry, and the concept of detecting and identifying the components of materials inherently appealed to me.

I decided to select chemistry as my major, but kept history as my minor field of study. At a liberal arts college you could do things like that.

It was a pragmatic choice. I had chosen to study something I was good at, but less enthused about, over the less practical but more appealing career path—not the first nor the last of my pragmatic life choices.

Choosing chemistry also meant that I wouldn't be compelled to pursue an advanced degree to get a job in my field.

But choosing chemistry made pursuing a graduate degree much more likely. The Soviet launching in 1957 of *Sputnik*, the first orbiting satellite, jolted the United States into realizing that a serious science gap existed between our two countries. Not unexpectedly, the U.S. Congress reacted swiftly and dramatically by establishing NASA and numerous programs to encourage and facilitate the training of many more scientists and engineers. Financial support for science graduate students became plentiful.

Rockford College joined this scientific surge by hiring two freshly minted Ph.D.s on the chemistry faculty. Justine Walhout, with a degree in organic chemistry from Northwestern, and Cal Huber, with a degree in analytical chemistry from Wisconsin, jolted my chemistry aptitude into high gear. They both encouraged me to go on to graduate school. Naturally, I considered graduate programs at Northwestern and Wisconsin. Ultimately, of course, I chose Wisconsin and the same major professor, Irv Shain, for whom Huber had worked.

Largely because of their efforts, I was fortunate to compete successfully for a fellowship from the Woodrow Wilson Foundation to subsidize my first year of graduate study. Recipients of this award were expected to pursue a career in college teaching.

My subsequent years of graduate school were funded by suddenly-plentiful National Science Foundation fellowships. Likewise, a federal student loan program for graduate students in science, math and engineering became available, where half the loan principal would be forgiven for graduates who went into college teaching.

*Sputnik* had put money into my pockets.

With all of these financial inducements to choose a teaching career, I began considering that possible choice early during my graduate tenure at Wisconsin. But the clincher was the influence of my major professor, Irv Shain. Not that he overtly pushed me in that direction. I simply observed what he did—picking his research studies; guiding fresh, young, talented graduate students; teaching courses that excited him;

traveling to distant places to give talks; and engaging in daily intellectual and social interactions with colorful students and colleagues.

In other words, Shain was having fun and getting paid for it.

That's what I wanted to do.

Hence, I found myself at Purdue in 1966 in the academic job I had wanted. I had sacrificed only money and security—that which had been offered as an industrial job. I was living the life of a professor just as rewarding and satisfying as I had observed for Shain at Wisconsin.

But it could all go away in an instant.

That is, I hadn't yet made tenure at Purdue. Without achieving tenure, everything else would be meaningless, because it would abruptly end.

Not that the experience hadn't been totally without its own reward.

I had had the opportunity to interact with a group of intelligent, highly motivated young people and to see them blossom before my eyes. I had also learned that the sharing of knowledge went both ways.

I had benefited, unexpectedly, from relationships with those same students—contributing a crucial missing segment to my previously neglected social maturity.

I had been given the freedom and resources to develop a personal research program. No one could say I hadn't taken advantage of that—for better or worse.

I had discovered that attaining the Ph.D. did not mean the end of an education. Indeed, for me, it had only opened the door to learning. But that learning no longer came from traditional sources. Now that learning came from research, reading publications, attending conferences, and interacting with colleagues.

I had grown scientifically and professionally. By the fall of 1966, when the promotions committee would gather for its annual meeting, I expected to have sixteen papers published and two more accepted for publication. Other universities were beginning to take notice of my work and invite me to give talks. I had landed two major research grants, one from NIH—the National Institutes of Health—and one from NSF—the National Science Foundation.

But none of this would mean a thing if I didn't get promoted to associate professor. And that would be in the hands of the full professors. They would throw up every legitimate impediment.

Because that was their job.

# CHAPTER 24

## Storm Warnings

Years later—when I would be a member of the promotions committee at Purdue—I would hear the renowned Nobel Laureate, Professor H. C. Brown of our department, say: "A candidate should not be promoted unless doing so will elevate the median talent level of the tenured faculty."

I'm glad I hadn't heard that in 1966. I believed I had done all the right science things. The numbers were good.

But what about the *quality?*

The promotions committee would not simply accept my work based on the numbers. Nor would it accept the endorsements of Buck and the other full professors in the analytical division. They would want to see supporting letters from established scientists at other universities— people who were qualified to evaluate my work.

What would outside experts have to say? I had a hint of that from people that had reviewed my papers or from comments during my outside talks.

And that gave me pause.

My former major professor, Irv Shain, had simply chuckled when he first heard my report about studying "ultra-fast" reactions electrochemically.

It was the Great Lakes Regional Meeting of the American Chemical Society (A.C.S.) in Chicago, summer 1964. I had only been at Purdue a couple years. I had gotten two papers accepted for presentations at the meeting. Jim Birk would talk about his flash photolysis work; and I would talk about what I had done, working alone, to study ultra-fast electrochemical reactions.

I was very excited about both pieces of work. Jim's work was breaking new ground scientifically; and my work was pushing the high-speed electronics envelope for electrochemical measurements. I was pretty pleased. Sure, this was just the tip of the iceberg. There was so much more to be done. But I believed we were establishing ourselves firmly at the forefront of these two areas of study

I was thinking about that—and feeling pretty good about it, actually—as I walked down the broad hotel hallway to the meeting room where I would present my talk.

That was when I saw Irv Shain. Walking with him were Dick Nicholson and Bill Schwarz—my contemporaries from Shain's research group at Wisconsin, now gainfully employed elsewhere. With them was Willie Reinmuth—the young Columbia University electrochemist cranking out theoretical papers even faster than Shain. There couldn't have been four others whose work I admired more.

Nicholson, Shain and Schwarz had done the groundbreaking theoretical and experimental work that was the basis of my Purdue studies. Reinmuth, who I had met at a previous meeting, had become Shain's best buddy. Along with Nicholson, they huddled together at meetings, talking LaPlace transforms and integral equations, chuckling and sneering at those of us who didn't speak their language.

Their dream, as well as mine, was to apply the new theory to studies of ultra-fast chemical reactions. So they were more than casually interested in the work I was presenting, and I had given them an advance look.

Shain was the first to greet me. "There he is," he declared as they approached, "the fifty thousand volts per second guy."

Shain and Reinmuth smirked while Nicholson and Schwarz snickered. I *cringed*. Shain's remark was delivered good-naturedly—a friendly poke at a former student that might have been meant to sharpen me up—but the underlying skepticism hurt.

I stuck out a hand to greet them. Shain took it first, while Nicholson asked with tongue firmly planted in cheek, "Hey, Sam, are you going to show us one million volts per second today?"

Already shaken by their barbs, I extended my hand to Nicholson. My heart was sinking, but I did a little self-deprecating laugh and responded, "Well, we can dream, can't we?"

Schwarz and Reinmuth each shook my hand and spared me any further insults. "I'm looking forward to hearing your talk," said Schwarz.

I went on to give my talk that day. But my confidence had been shaken. If my friends didn't believe my work, what would my detractors do?

My talk was well-received. Although, the formidable four were there, only Reinmuth asked a question. He challenged the electronics, and I was able to toss back the manufacturer's specs as a rebuttal. That quieted him but couldn't alter the collective cynical body language of the quartet.

Bill Schwarz stopped me afterward and asked if I wanted to have a drink. I did, badly.

"I'm really interested in your work," Schwarz began. "We've seen behavior just like you're reporting—the large oscillations when the voltage is reversed. Aren't you concerned about that?"

"Yes, we can eliminate oscillations by nudging the reference probe a hair away from the working electrode, but that hurts response time. Ultra-micro electrodes minimize the oscillations even with minimal gaps and preserve large bandwidth."

"Do you understand what's going on?" He swirled the ice cubes in his drink for a moment. "Do you think you're getting valid data at the fastest times?"

"The data that we get for cadmium at the highest scan rates are consistent with what we get at the lowest rates."

"That's true." He made a face. "But your amplifiers are teetering on the edge of instability at the highest scan rates. That's what those oscillations mean."

"But the oscillations are over by the time we make measurements."

"Yes, but can you be sure that the amplifier is controlling the voltage properly? Do you know what the Bode Plot looks like?"

We were now getting into an area of electronics that Schwarz understood quite well and I did not. But I did know the answer to his question. "Sure," I replied, "the amplifier has a band pass of four megacycles."

Schwarz threw me a "gotcha" kind of look. "That's for a linear impedance, but not for an electrochemical cell."

"I don't understand."

"That's the problem, Sam. You need to understand that. The overall transfer function depends on the transfer functions of *both* the amplifier and the cell. And you *know* the cell isn't linear."

The light went off. "I see what you're getting at." I got a hollow feeling in the pit of my stomach—wondering if this was the missing linchpin that might bring everything tumbling down.

Schwarz leaned back from the bar. There was the hint of a knowing smile. "I think your data are OK, Sam," he said slowly. "You're on the right track. But you need to look closer at the cell transfer function. Don't be in such a hurry to publish."

I left that meeting with mixed feelings. Thankfully, Schwarz had expressed confidence in my data. But he had also pinpointed my own inadequate appreciation of instrumental limitations. Clearly, the people I was trying to impress were not impressed.

I vowed then and there to make it right. Eventually, I assigned one of my grad students, Jim Mumby, the task of re-doing the project I had reported, but doing it right.

After a long, intensive study, that's exactly what he did. In 1971— in a Ph.D. thesis and landmark 38-page publication in *Chemical Instrumentation*—we reported a thorough characterization of the combined amplifier-cell transfer functions with solid scientific and engineering principles. This work would impact a generation of electrochemists interested in pushing the limits of ultra-fast electrode reactions.

Mumby's 1971 paper also confirmed my 1964 studies, and that was very gratifying.

But in the summer of 1966, things didn't look that way. I was facing the immediate problem of getting promoted, and my thoughts wandered back to that Great Lakes meeting two years earlier. Surely, Shain, Nicholson, Reinmuth or Schwarz would be asked to write an evaluation letter for the promotions committee. What would they say?

Did they question my competence? Did they think I had published too quickly?

But what if I hadn't rushed publication of a couple papers? What if that made the difference between promotion and dismissal?

Then again, had I risked being labeled "superficial" or, even worse, publishing bogus results?

Doubt and anxiety nearly consumed me. I needed to talk to someone.

# CHAPTER 25

## Mike

During the 1960s, Buck Rogers brought in a series of postdoctoral associates to Purdue to work with him. As I mentioned earlier, the proximity of Buck's labs to me and my labs catalyzed friendships between his students and mine. My wife and I enjoyed warm social interactions with each of Buck's postdocs and their spouses.

I've already mentioned the close friendship I had with Jerry Fitzgerald who arrived at Purdue shortly after my arrival. After a couple years, Jerry and his wife, Laura, moved to New Jersey where Jerry became assistant professor of chemistry at Seton Hall University. We continued to see each other professionally and socially.

Buck's next postdoc was Mike Burke who had just finished his Ph.D. at Virginia Tech. It turned out that Mike's appointment at Purdue in 1965 would correspond to the final two years of my quest for tenure—and also embrace his search for a professorial position. For that reason—and many, many others—we formed a very strong bond.

One of the first things that brought us together was that Mike, his wife Jini, and their two daughters rented a home in Lafayette, not far from our home. Their two daughters, Patti and Colleen, were close to the ages of our two daughters, Vita and Amy, and we made a special effort to welcome the family.

There was an instantaneous rapport. Like us, Mike and Jini were Catholic and had married young. Like me, they had gone through Catholic schools, even attending a Catholic college. They were struggling with their beliefs just as we were. Although we were feeling slightly more comfortable financially, we were still stressed and very sympathetic to their tight economic situation.

Although we were all close in age, Mike was the youngest of our group of four. But he was probably the wisest. A wonderful listener, with keen insight, his advice was sought by many. Very astute about academia and academic politics, Mike soon became my closest confidant. Our relationship blossomed into a lifelong friendship.

In one way or another, Mike Burke played a role in most of the critical junctures in my professional and personal life that followed. Nothing epitomized that relationship more than our conversations in 1966....

# CHAPTER 26

## Tenure or Not?

"I hear you ran into your old boss," said Mike Burke as he fake-knocked on my open office door. "Want to talk about it?"

I made a sour face but waved him in. "I guess J.R.'s been blabbing again," I remarked. I had made the mistake of sharing with Jim Birk my concern about that meeting with Shain and his comrades two years earlier at the 1964 Great Lakes Meeting.

Mike showed me his other hand. A cigarette burned between two fingers. The others grasped a small glass beaker. "Do you mind?" he asked before walking in.

"No. Come on." I motioned him in again. "Looks like you're carrying an ashtray with you."

First setting the beaker and cigarette on the lab bench next to my desk, he then pulled up a chair and turned it around. Mounting it backwards, he leaned over the back and asked, "What's the story?"

"Didn't J.R. fill you in?"

"He suggested you might be having nightmares."

I shook my head. "It happened a couple years ago. I still can't get it out of my mind."

"It can't be that bad."

I gave him a sharp look. "Shain kinda punched a hole in my parade."

Mike laughed. "Do you do that on purpose—mixing metaphors?"

"I like 'em that way," I snapped.

He wagged his head. "My, you're in a good mood."

"How would you feel if your former major professor told you the work you're doing isn't worth a crap?"

Mike's eyebrows raised. "Did he say that?"

"Not in so many words."

He looked me over for a moment. "Tell me about it."

I described the deflating brief exchange I had had with Shain and the others at the 1964 Great Lakes meeting. And I gave him the drift of the more detailed conversation I had had with Bill Schwarz. I mentioned my concern that any one of them might have been asked to write an evaluation letter about me to the promotions committee.

When I finished, he took a drag on his cigarette and flicked the ashes in the beaker. Then he squinted and looked at me sideways a moment. It was a look that always preceded some insightful question or comment. "Sounds like they thought you published too quickly, S.P.," he remarked.

*Mike Burke, 1966 [Copyright, Mike Burke, Jr., Used with permission.]*

"That's the kindest interpretation."

"What do you think?"

"I think they were right."

Mike wagged his head. "I think if people waited until they completely understood *all* the science in their work, they'd never publish anything."

"You're patronizing me, Dr. Burke."

A twisted smile. "You know I'd never do *that*, S.P." Then he put on a sober face. "Seriously, you should've asked Shain if he didn't hurry up publications when *he* was working on tenure."

"Yeah, you're right. I'll probably look at things a lot differently when *I'm* tenured—*if* and when, I mean."

"Oh, Christ, S.P., don't worry. You're going to get promoted. You've come a long way since that Great Lakes meeting. What have you got now? A dozen publications?"

"I should have sixteen by the end of this year—when the full professors meet."

"Jeezuz! That's probably twice what you need."

"If you'll recall, we were talking about *quality* not quantity."

Mike offered a sly grin. "Hey, if you had chosen to work in chromatography—I mean doing something *worthwhile*—you wouldn't have to worry."

I chuckled. "You chromatographers don't worry about much of anything."

He took a final drag on the cigarette and crushed it in the beaker. "Frankly, S.P.—now don't quote me because I'll deny it—when I get an academic job, I can't imagine getting off to a better start, quality *and* quantity, than you have."

I believed him. "Thanks, Mike. I hope you get to a place like Purdue. I mean, look at what I've got—a *dozen* top-notch research students."

"You know what Buck always says: 'Great professors are made by great graduate students'."

"True. I'm totally dependent."

Mike winked. "Kretlow tells me they do their best to educate you."

I laughed. "He ought to know. He was in the first course I taught." I shook my head. "Did I ever tell you about those guys? They were *all* smarter than me; and they knew it. I never sweated so much in my life."

Mike shook his head. "Bill wasn't talking about *technical* stuff."

"Oh...." I grinned. "Yeah, did he ever tell you about that party—before you got here? Kretlow brought his brand new GTO—that red convertible. Everybody gave him a hard time because he sprang for *air conditioning*, old tight-fisted Bill."

"I haven't heard this one."

"Party went till two in the morning. Oyster furnished lab gin for our bottomless punch bowl. You know, like we partied after the group put my patio in."

"That was a disaster. Didn't your neighbors call the cops?"

"No, they called *us*. That's why we moved the party inside. But that was a hot summer night, like Kretlow's party."

"Kretlow's?"

"Well, he topped it off. You see, it broke up after I played the Beach Boys' *409* four or five times in a row. I lost track."

"Hey, *your* stereo...."

"That's what I figured. Anyway, Kretlow was the first to bail. But then he came back, saying he'd lost a contact lens and could we help him look for it."

"Where'd he lose it?"

"That was the problem. He lost it crossing the front lawn."

"On the lawn?"

"Yup. There we were, two in the morning. Bill's GTO pulled up onto the lawn—headlights over the grass—and a dozen half-blind drunks on hands and knees scouring the ground."

I thought Mike was about to go into convulsions. Finally, he asked, "Did you find the contact?"

I nodded. "Incredible as it seems."

"What did the neighbors think?"

"I can only hope there were no witnesses."

Mike wagged his head and began to get up from the chair. "I'm sorry I missed that one, S.P." He moved the chair back in place and grew a crooked grin. "Gotta go. Hope I'm leaving you in a better mood."

I threw him my own crooked grin.

As he sauntered toward the door, a thought struck me. I cried out, "Hey, Mike."

He looked back over his shoulder.

"My group's goin' over to the Wabash Hotel tonight for beer. After the seminar. Like to join us?"

He turned and asked, "What kind of place is it?"

I shrugged. "I hear they have country music. It's my first time."

He wagged his head. "They want *two* virgins for sacrifice?"

I laughed. "How bad can it be?"

He threw me a sloppy salute and turned to open the door. "All right. See you tonight."

I called his name once more. "Mike?"

He paused halfway through the door and looked back.

"Thanks. Thanks for the pep talk."

He winked. "Anytime, S.P." Then he slipped away.

# CHAPTER 27

## Country Time

Above the din of the rowdy crowd, and above the strains of a first-rate imitation of Johnny Cash's *Walk the Line* by Chet and his Country Cats, a low rumble began to swell. Everyone in the lounge of the Wabash Hotel sensed it. The rumble grew until the booze in the glasses began to ripple and the glasses began to rattle.

An excited buzz swept through the lounge. Chet stopped picking and halted his song in mid-verse. Holding up a hand to the rest of the band, he didn't say a word. With a silent count of "One, two, three, four—" they launched into a rousing rendition of *Wabash Cannonball.*

*Listen to the jingle the rumble and the roar ...*

The crowd cheered. And the walls began to rock—as the *real* Wabash Cannonball thundered down the tracks just behind the hotel. Everyone joined in to sing the chorus.

*... he's riding through the jungle on the Wabash Cannonball.*

Chet timed it perfectly, driving home the final line of the final chorus with a crescendo just as the roar of the train began to fade away.

"God, I could listen to that every night!" exclaimed Vic Evins.

I caught his eyes glazing over and wondered if he did, every night.

Vic had lured some of my group to the Wabash Hotel after a visiting speaker's lecture. The hotel was an old two-story wooden structure in one of the oldest Lafayette neighborhoods. At one time there had been a train stop nearby, and the hotel had thrived among vibrant surroundings.

Now the Wabash Hotel was a local hangout in a rundown neighborhood dissected by aging railroad tracks. The hotel still thrived, but in a different way. The kitchen provided good food, and the bar provided great country entertainment. It attracted crowds from all over town.

"Sounds like you've been here before," I said to Vic.

"At least once a week. These guys are great."

"They play here all the time?"

Jim Birk spoke up. "No. There's a gal that does Patsy Cline on the weekends."

I looked around at the group—Vic, Jim, and Bill Kretlow were there. Some of my students hadn't come. But Al Moreland and Mike Burke from Buck's group had joined us.

Mike asked the question that was on my mind. "Was that train *really* the Wabash Cannonball?"

Vic replied. "You bet. Comes by every night."

Jim was the railroad junkie, so we turned to him for confirmation.

"Yup, it's the real thing. Wabash Railroad named the train after the song. Makes the run between Detroit and St. Louis every night."

"You mean the song came first?"

Jim grinned. "Carter family made it popular in the thirties. Wabash Railroad named the train in the fifties."

Six of us crowded around an aluminum table with a dark red plastic top that must have been part of a 1950s renovation. We were close to the stage. With the band on a break, I looked around the room. Smoke and boisterous chatter filled the air. Our table of university dudes stood out like ants in a beehive—we enjoyed the offerings but didn't really belong. The local guys were older, hard-working types. The ladies were middle-aged, heavily-painted, and loud.

But it was a friendly crowd. The lanky blonde waitress called Doree, in tight jeans and barely-buttoned checkered blouse, hovered impatiently at our table, offering refilled pitchers. Nobody objected.

I nudged Vic. "I'm gonna have to get going."

"Oh, no, Doc. You gotta stay for the next set."

I looked at my watch. "It better be worth it."

"Trust me, you don't want to miss it."

I shook my head and held out my mug for a refill.

Mike, sitting at my side, asked, "Hey, S.P., I hear you and Pardue are teaching the electronics short course this summer?"

"That's right,"

"That's the same as the Malmstadt course at Illinois? A whole semester in three weeks?"

I nodded. "We'll run the labs 8 a.m. to midnight."

"Sounds pretty intense for paying customers."

"Talk to Vic about it." I leaned back and pointed to Vic. "He volunteered to be a lab instructor."

Vic snorted. "*Volunteered?*"

Mike grinned at Vic. "Sounds like you're in for a real grind."

"Hell!" Vic shrugged. "I think you can do *anything* for three weeks." He cracked a grin. "Anyway the pay is good."

"We'll see what you think when the course is over," said Mike.


I sensed something different when Chet took the stage alone and sat on a chair. Vic leaned over to say, "Get ready."

Picking up his guitar and adjusting the microphone to his seated position, Chet proceeded to strum a few chords. Then he began to play the recognizable lead-in chords to *Ring of Fire*, following with the opening verse,

*Love is a burning thing. And makes a fiery ring . . .*

He followed with the first chorus, ending with,

*And it burns, burns, burns. The ring of fire. The ring of fire.*

But then, instead of singing the next verse, the clear, sweet sound of a trumpet playing the melody filled the air. The crowded bar erupted with cheers and hoots.

I looked around. Chet was still alone on the stage. I turned to Vic. "That's him," he whispered in my ear. "That's Chet. Take a look."

My eyes found Chet once again. I noticed that he had leaned closer to the microphone. His cheeks puffed out and pulsated in harmony with the trumpet melody.

There was no trumpet. The sound came from *Chet.*

Looking back at Vic, I wagged my head and mouthed, "What the hell?"

Vic was beaming like he had discovered gold in his back yard. I didn't know what to say. Had this suddenly turned into a freak show?

Chet finished the entire song with a "trumpet" solo, accompanied by guitar chords—while all the regulars in the bar stood and cheered.

I quietly joined in the applause while Chet took a couple bows. The rest of the band slipped back onto the stage, picked up their instruments, and began to play upbeat background chords for the next song.

Vic nudged me. "What'd you think?"

"I don't know. Never seen anything like it. Is that talent? Or indigestion?"

"Man, that's *talent,*" Vic insisted. "I've heard the real thing that doesn't sound that good."

I shrugged. "Could be. You couldn't tell the difference with your eyes closed."

"Listen, Doc. Stick around. He's gonna play one I know you like."

Vic called Doree over and whispered something in her ear. She walked toward the back of the bar and through a door that took her up on the stage. She shouted in Chet's ear above the sounds of the band, and he nodded.

"What did you request?" I asked Vic.

"It's one you always play at your parties."

I heard the music stop and then heard Chet's words in the microphone. "Here's a request for Doc," he announced.

The rest of the band had obviously gotten the signal as they began to play the opening notes, and then Chet broke into one of the most soulful renditions of Jim Reeves that I had ever heard.

*Out where the bright lights are glowing, you're drawn like a moth to a flame ...*

*Four walls to hear you. Four walls to see. Four walls too near me. Closing in on me ...*

This time I joined the rest of the crowd in rising to my feet and cheering.

No, it wasn't Jim Reeves. It wasn't Johnny Cash. And it wasn't Harry James on the trumpet. But for a broken down bar in a broken down neighborhood of Lafayette, Indiana, it was one hell of a show.

# CHAPTER 28

## Choices

"Hey, Doc," cried Bill Kretlow, sticking his head inside my partly-open office door. "Can we talk?"

It was a polite request, but I was apprehensive. I waved him in, and he took a seat next to my desk, setting his research notebook on the desktop edge.

"Did you get a chance to read my first draft?" he asked.

Bill had written up the work on electro-oxidation of ascorbic acid (vitamin C). This work would constitute his Ph.D. thesis, but I had asked him to write it up first for publication in *Analytical Chemistry*. I pulled a marked-up draft from my briefcase and said, "I've read it. Got some comments."

I flipped through the pages of the draft, showing him the high density of red pencil marks. "You can look at the details later," I suggested. "Let's talk about the overview."

He sat back in the chair and gazed at me warily.

"Don't worry," I began, "I like your writing."

His gaze relaxed a bit. "What's all the red pencilling about?"

I chuckled. "It's not the writing. You've just included too much detail."

He grew a frown. "Like what?"

I took a breath. "Let me back up. I'd like to get this paper published as a *correspondence* to *Analytical Chemistry*, rather than a full article."

"Why should we do that?"

S. P. Perone

"For the same reason we're publishing J.R.'s flash photolysis paper as a *correspondence*. It gets into print much faster."

"Should I care about that?"

"Well, yes. A *correspondence* allows workers to establish priority."

"You think someone could publish this work before us?"

I shrugged. "Maybe not the same work, with ascorbic acid. But other groups are studying electrode-coupled chemical reactions—Shain, Nicholson, Schwarz, Reinmuth."

"But no one's reported studying fast reactions like us."

"That's right. That's exactly why we need to get this out quickly; before someone else does."

Bill scratched his chin and thought for a moment. "What's the difference for *me*, Doc? I mean, what's better on my resumé—*article* or *correspondence*?"

"They both count the same on a list of publications."

"Are you thinking of stretching this work into *two* publications?"

I shook my head. "No. I'm not playing that game. We'll do *one* publication—reporting everything we can get into three or four journal pages."

"What do we leave out?"

"The details of the literature study and transfer function theory. We can put the full discussion in your thesis."

Bill looked away for a moment. Then he turned to me with a pained look on his face. "Doc, I talked to J.R. about his publication."

I had a bad feeling about where this was going. "And?" I responded.

The painful look deepened. "J.R. said you wanted to get his work into print quickly because you're up for promotion this year."

I took a breath. "That's true. It's not the *only* reason, though. We needed to establish ourselves in that research area. Too many others are knocking on the same door—just like in your research."

"But he said you're planning to publish a full article later."

I nodded. "That's because J.R.'s doing work beyond what we put into the *correspondence*."

Bill blinked and moved back in his seat. "I'm not asking to do more research, Doc. I was just concerned about short-changing my publication."

"I understand. But a correspondence is *not* a second-class publication. It's a brief, quick paper to tell the world you've done something that lots of other people are trying to do."

He threw a wry smile back at me. "And if that help's you get promoted?"

"So much the better."

# CHAPTER 29

## A Conversation

After a brief vacation, I was back on campus getting ready for the 1966 fall semester. For me, that first day back was depressing.

Don't get me wrong. I loved my job. I just didn't enjoy leaving summer behind.

I loved the freedom and productivity of summers. My graduate students and I worked our tails off. But the lack of constraints on how and when and in what order we might attack things made that time exquisitely enjoyable.

But summers devoted to research inevitably flowed into fall semesters—with classes, meetings, and other demands that decimated scientific productivity.

My anxiety level began to elevate immediately after the Fourth of July and peaked just as fall semester preparatory meetings got underway.

Dragging myself up the stairs to my new third-floor corner office—the one recently abandoned by Buck when he moved to the more spacious second-floor suite—I regretted getting a late start that morning. It was nearly nine o'clock. My first meeting was at ten. I expected to find a number of phone messages. And I was certain that one or more of my research students would be waiting for me.

I arrived on the third floor landing to a surprisingly quiet hallway. Only one of the research lab doors was open—that next to my office. That lab was occupied by one of Buck's students, Al Moreland. Al enjoyed his isolation from Buck's new research complex on the second floor and was connected socially to my research group.

So, before entering my office, I poked my head into his lab.

Surprisingly, I saw Mike Burke seated on a lab stool, smoking a cigarette and chatting with Al. Mike returned my greeting, explaining that he'd been waiting for me.

I motioned him into my office.


"This is your big year, S.P.," declared Mike after we occupied my office. He ditched his cigarette and took a seat on the surplus wooden church pew I had added.

"What do you mean?" I asked, knowing full well.

"Come on," he shot back, "promotion, tenure, all that stuff."

I smirked. "Any late-breaking news?"

He grinned back at me. "You're not worried, are you?"

"I'd be lying if I said I wasn't."

"Have you turned in your up-dated Curriculum Vitae to Buck yet?"

I shook my head. "He wants the C.V. by October 1."

"They should be impressed with the numbers of publications."

"You don't think other stuff counts? Teaching? Grants? Not important?"

"Well, maybe that crazy teaching assignment you had last semester will get you a point or two?"

"1500 freshmen?" I grunted. "Not fun."

"What was it? Four professors taking four weeks each?"

"Yeah. We gave the same lecture four times a day, nearly 400 students at a time. I was totally wasted by the end of the week."

"I hear some professors like it. Gets their semester's teaching over in four weeks."

I shook my head. "It's a nightmare. By the third lecture of the day you can't remember if you already said it or not. Fourth lecture you finish in thirty minutes, and your voice is gone. By week's end you just want to go home and die."

"That big lecture hall's got to be a challenge."

"Well, at least you have a microphone and someone to set up demos. But it's like a theater—balcony and all. 400 pairs of eyes watching every move. You're a performer, not a teacher."

Mike chuckled. "Didn't know there was a difference."

I glared at him. "You'll find out some day."

Mike ignored my look. "So much for your teaching credentials. How about research money? The promotions committee should like your NSF and NIH grants."

I nodded slowly. "I hope it's enough."

"Look, S.P. This is a *tenure* decision. They aren't giving a Nobel Prize. Hell, they know you've got exciting stuff coming—like that departmental talk you gave last semester."

I recalled the departmental talk. I had described J.R.'s work—studying the electrochemistry of transients in flash photolysis. "You liked that?" I asked.

"Your *colleagues* liked it. I thought Margerum was going to swoon."

I chuckled. "Yeah, he gets that way whenever we talk about microsecond time scales. But I'm not sure he can help me with the promotions committee. I mean, he's an analytical colleague."

Mike eyed me askance. "What's your take on Dale? Is he really an *analytical* chemist?"

"He teaches analytical. He's in the analytical division," I responded unconvincingly.

"Come on, S.P., Dale's in the analytical division because that's where all the grad students are. He publishes in *Inorganic Chemistry* and *J. Phys. Chem.*"

"I don't care where he publishes," I insisted. 'Dale *thinks* like an analytical chemist, and—"

"Whoa! Back up. He *thinks* like an analytical chemist? What's that?"

"I mean, he realizes that scientific progress requires measurements research."

"So that makes him an *analytical* chemist, not an inorganic or physical chemist?"

"Absolutely."

Mike pursed his lips and thought about it. "It's got to be more than that. I mean, any physical chemist knows he needs sound measurement technology. But they *use* it. They don't get their kicks out of *developing* it, like *we* do."

"But physical chemists *do* develop measurement technology."

"Sure, but that's not what they hang their hats on. And they don't respect those that do."

"Then how did I sell NIH my proposal about electrochemical monitoring of photolytic reactions? *That's* analytical chemistry."

"Don't tell NIH. They think you're studying reactions that cause skin cancer."

"That's true. We are … soon as we develop the techniques."

Mike shook his head. "I guarantee they won't be happy if the only thing you do is develop measurement techniques."

I glared at him.

"Look, S.P., I don't mean to diminish your NIH grant. It's a real accomplishment."

"But you think I got it under false pretenses?"

"No, no, that's not what I mean." He pushed out a palm to calm me down. "I mean that you should put *analytical chemistry* in perspective. Purdue is an exception. Buck says it all the time. Most chemistry departments don't believe analytical chemistry is a legitimate discipline."

"Yeah, I know that," I admitted. "When I was looking for an academic job, I didn't see analytical openings outside the Midwest." I wagged my head. "I just don't understand it."

"It's historical. Most academic chemists think *analytical chemists* are *analysts*—lab technicians."

"That's ridiculous. My job is training *technicians?*"

He smirked. "You begin to see what I'm getting at."

I regained my speech. "Surely people realize that developing measurement principles—*measurement science*—is just as fundamental as bonding theory or chemical synthesis."

Shaking his head, Mike declared, "That's just the point. They don't. Schools like Purdue, Illinois, Wisconsin, and others mostly in the Midwest, are exceptions. Some good analytical chemists got an early foothold—like M. G. Mellon here, Kolthoff at Minnesota, and Meloche at Wisconsin."

"I guess that's why Dale or Harry or I can succeed at Purdue."

"Dale would do well anywhere," Mike corrected. "Other schools think he's an inorganic chemist. But you or Harry or me, we'd better find the right school. You and Harry did. I hope I will."

We sat silent for a few moments, pondering the dilemma we had just detailed. Mike lit up a fresh cigarette.

Finally, he spoke. "You know what, S.P., there was something you said."

I contemplated silently on which words of mine he might pounce.

"Maybe the big mistake we've been making," he continued, "is that we *call* ourselves *analytical chemists*. It suggests that we're *analyzers* or *analysts.*"

"What do you suggest?"

"You said it yourself, just a minute ago," he said. Then, after a slow drag on his cigarette, blowing the smoke away, he gave me that squinting askance gaze and declared, "We're *measurement scientists,* S.P."

The light bulb finally went off. "You're right!" I exclaimed. We should call ourselves *measurement scientists* not *analytical chemists.*"

"It's not just the *name,* S.P." Gesturing for emphasis with the smoldering cigarette, he added. "We need to change the way we *think* about ourselves."

I offered him a blank stare.

"I mean, physical chemists think that all chemistry springs from them. Physicists believe that physics explains *everything.* So, where does that leave analytical chemists?"

"How do we change that?" I asked.

"Isn't *measurement science* the foundation of everything real? After all, theories aren't credible until measurements confirm them. Einstein learned that."

I grinned and gave Mike a nod of approval. "I think you've got something, Burke—a mission to take up when I'm *tenured.* You think?"

He winked. "All right, put it on the calendar for next summer—*after* you get promoted."

Mike's optimism reflected no inkling of what I could yet do to screw things up during that academic year.

# CHAPTER 30

## An Exam for the Ages

Although it hadn't started that way, by the fall of 1966, Vic Evins had become my most productive graduate student.

Vic hailed from Frankfort, Kentucky. But he had earned his B.S. in chemistry from M.I.T. in Boston. He had been an average student there—with grades that wouldn't ordinarily impress our graduate admissions committee. He had gotten strong letters of recommendation from M.I.T. faculty, however. Buck—having recently taught at M.I.T.—had urged the committee to accept Vic into our chemistry graduate program. Buck had claimed something like, "I'd rather have a C-student from M.I.T. than an A-student from other schools."

Now that might have been a bit too strong, and the admissions committee probably relished the thought of possibly making Buck eat his words. In any event, Vic was accepted at Purdue.

I don't know if Vic hadn't expected to get into Purdue, but he arrived with a bit of an attitude. Perhaps he felt obligated to prove his supporters right or detractors wrong. It made him determined to succeed—not a bad thing. But it sometimes made him a little defensive—something that didn't really cause a problem until his final Ph.D. oral exam.

And that was really *my* fault.


"It's in the departmental guidelines," Vic declared. "Every Ph.D. thesis in the chemistry library is formatted that way."

I shifted my gaze from the tall, crew-cut student standing beside my desk to the printed sheet of thesis guidelines he had thrown down. There it was in black-and-white:

> *Every Ph.D. thesis shall include an extended abstract of the body of the thesis, suitable for publication in an appropriate chemical journal.*

I was familiar with the requirement. I had already served on a number of Ph.D. final oral exams and had read each candidate's thesis. Vic was right. The theses had all adhered to the letter of the law.

I thought the law was stupid, at least in Vic's case.

"I understand the requirement," I declared finally, raising my gaze back to Vic. He shifted nervously from one foot to the other. "But do you know why it's there?"

Vic shrugged off the question. "I just want to know what'll happen if I don't follow it."

"I'm confused. I thought you didn't want to do your thesis in this format."

Vic huffed and sat down in the chair next to my desk. "I don't. It makes no sense for my thesis." Pointing at the guidelines, he explained, "That rule prevents people from leaving without writing up their work for publication, but that doesn't apply to me."

I nodded. Vic had already published two of the three papers that comprised his thesis work. The third was submitted for publication. We had already agreed that his thesis should consist only of those three papers, verbatim, in their publication form—with appendices to document the extensive programming.

"Yeah," I said, staring off into space, "it doesn't make sense to simply duplicate the body of your thesis and call that the extended abstract."

"So you agree with me?" Vic asked. "We won't do it?"

Our eyes met, and I nodded slowly.

"What if the committee objects?" he asked.

"I'll explain. It's my call."

Vic gave me a skeptical look. "You're sure?"

"Yup." I pointed to my office door. "Now go get it finished."

Despite my assurances to Vic, he remained nervous about distributing his thesis to the four committee members, three from chemistry and one from another department. He had chosen Bob Squires from chemical engineering—a young professor with research interests much like our own—as the outside member.

He had good reason to be nervous. Although Vic had entered graduate school a year after my first students, he had been able to complete requirements for the Ph.D. in just over three years. Bill Kretlow and Vic would finish up at virtually the same time. Their oral exams would take place in the fall semester of 1966.

Vic and Bill Kretlow would be my *first* students to complete a Ph.D.—which meant I would be learning on the job.

No wonder Vic was nervous.


I knew the ritual. The committee gathers in the reserved conference room at the appointed hour. I ask the candidate to step outside briefly while the committee has a quick meeting. The candidate is then called back in to begin his or her presentation; answer questions; ultimately leave the room again while the committee deliberates; and then is recalled to hear the verdict.

Rarely does a candidate fail the Ph.D. oral exam. It is understood that the Ph.D. candidate has arrived at this stage with the major professor's stamp of approval and that the candidate has independently completed the work. The candidate will have demonstrated no further need for guidance from the major professor. It is a given that the work is a novel contribution to some narrow scientific discipline. In addition, the candidate would necessarily have satisfied all of the lower prerequisites—courses, preliminary exams, residency, etc.

In other words, the candidate *is* a Ph.D. in everything but name. It is the committee's duty to confirm that and sign off on the thesis so that the candidate can acquire the Ph.D. title as well.

That's the way it works nearly every time. Oh yes, the committee has some fun at the candidate's expense—asking probing questions about the work or the procedures or the relevance to the real world. They might even ask the candidate about chemistry *fundamentals* if they are in a particularly devious mood. But ultimately, they take the candidate off the hook, shake his or her hand, and congratulate them on their new Ph.D. status.

That's the way it's supposed to work.

But not this time. Not with Vic's exam. Not a chance.


Just as Vic closed the door, sliding out into the hallway, I spoke to his committee. "Thank you, gentlemen, for being here," I began. "You've all met Vic. I hope you all got your copy of the thesis in time."

I looked around the table at the three other members of the committee. Bob Squires—crew-cut, mid-thirties, looking a bit uncomfortable, as though his shirt collar was too tight—sat across from me. Buck, in his usual drab gray suit, sat quietly at my side. At one end of the table sat Donald Millen—beefy, fiftyish, thinning hair slicked back— representing physical chemistry. Only Millen had foregone coat and tie. Everyone nodded, so I moved on. "I've asked Vic to—"

"Hold on!" demanded Millen.

Surprised by the interruption, I snapped my gaze to the end of the table. "Yes?" I responded.

"I've got a question about the thesis format," he explained, peering at me over his rimless glasses.

"What's the problem?" I asked, feeling my pulse quicken.

Millen opened his copy of Vic's thesis, flipping through the initial pages. "The extended abstract is missing," he declared. "Does he intend to add that later?"

The armpits of my shirt were beginning to soak, and my collar was tightening. I wanted to loosen my tie. "Well...." I croaked. "We ... that is ... *I* asked Vic to leave out the extended abstract."

With a puzzled frown, Buck asked, "Why would you do that?"

"It ... it just seemed ... redundant," I replied. "You see, each section of Vic's thesis is already published or in press."

"That doesn't matter," countered Millen. "It's a format requirement. The thesis isn't complete."

I cleared my throat. "I believe we satisfied the intent of the requirement—that is, the entire thesis is in publishable form. In fact, the thesis is a collection of three papers exactly as written for *Analytical Chemistry*. With the appendix, it's a complete thesis."

There it was. The *rationale*. I had thrown it out on the table. I held my breath.

After a moment's reflection, Millen said, "I get your point. But this...." He slapped a hand on the thesis. "This isn't a chemistry department thesis. Not in this format."

There was a tone of finality to his statement. I wasn't sure how to respond. This was a full professor and I was an assistant professor—*untenured*. This man was part of the promotions committee. How far did I want to push this?

I looked to the other committee members. My eyes must have been pleading, as Buck stepped up to the plate. God bless him.

He directed his attention to me. "Is this the accepted protocol at Wisconsin?"

I saw where he was going. He was trying to get me off the hook. Allow me to claim ignorance.

Tempting as that was, I couldn't go there. "Yes," I responded, "but that wasn't the reason we did it. I thought we satisfied the *spirit* of our departmental guidelines."

I stopped there. I could see Millen getting agitated.

That was when Squires spoke up.

"Well, I can see Dr. Perone's point," he offered. "We don't have the extended abstract—or publication preprint—requirement for theses in our department. Obviously, it's not a university requirement."

Buck nodded and then added, while flipping through the thesis, "You know, it's actually pretty impressive that Vic has gotten all this work accepted for publication already." He threw a questioning glance at me. "He's been here only *three* years?"

"Yeah," I replied, throwing a mental *thank you* to Buck, who knew very well how long Vic had been here. "He's been very productive."

"Is he thinking about an academic job?" he asked.

"No. He wants to go into industry. He's got a job waiting for him at Celanese."

Just as I began to breathe a bit easier, Millen brought us back. "Regardless of Mr. Evins' achievements—and a job waiting—can we agree that his thesis is incomplete?"

"Not really, it's—" I began. But Buck interrupted.

"Dr. Millen is perfectly correct," he declared. "On the other hand...." He paused. "Dr. Perone makes a valid point about satisfying the *spirit* of the guidelines. So, if we agree that Vic has been remarkably productive, perhaps we should—"

"Make an exception?" suggested Millen.

"Well, yes," responded Buck, looking at me, "assuming Mr. Evins lives up to expectations in defending his thesis." He turned back to Millen. "Would that meet with your approval?"

I realized that Buck was treading dangerous ground here. I had put him in the difficult position of defending me against another full professor. He had to be at his diplomatic best. I would *owe* him, big time.

Despite the sour expression on Millen's face, he gave a grudging nod to Buck's idea. Squires quickly agreed.

"All right," said Buck, turning back to me. "Maybe we ought to bring Mr. Evins in before he has a heart attack out there."

Vic had walked halfway down the hall, probably to avoid hearing any of the committee's discussion. I motioned him back to the conference room, and he shuffled toward me.

As soon as I saw Vic's flushed face, I knew there would be trouble.

"Nothing to be concerned about," I lied. "We just lost track of time."

"It's been twenty minutes," he said, looking at his wristwatch.

"Don't worry, we weren't talking about you," I lied again. "Department gossip."


It was no surprise to me that Vic's presentation was clear and concise. It was also obvious to me that he was struggling to mask an inner anxiety.

In helping to prepare for this oral exam, I had cautioned Vic that committee members would interrupt him with questions. I assured him that this was not adversarial, but rather genuine scientific curiosity. At least, that's what I had observed at other Ph.D. orals. Committee members perceive the candidate as an expert and asked questions out of curiosity, not because they wanted to trip up the candidate.

Apparently, Vic had forgotten our conversation. Or his elevated anxiety took over. I don't know. But the periodic interruptions seemed to put him on edge. Soon his replies became terse, clipped phrases.

That was when Millen asked about something Vic hadn't anticipated.

"I'm looking at the theoretical equations on pages 79 and following," Millen began. "I'm curious about this *gamma* term."

Vic picked up his copy of the thesis and flipped the pages. "Yeah. That's the square root of the ratio of diffusion coefficients," he declared tersely.

"Yes. I know. But it doesn't seem to appear in any of your theoretical computations."

"Oh, that's because you assume the ratio is one."

Millen's eyebrows raised. "Is that legitimate? I can think of cases where they might be very different."

"Well, that's what all the theoretical electrochemists assume," Vic shot back.

I could sense the tension rising.

"Is that necessary?" asked Millen.

"Of course," replied Vic quickly. "Otherwise you couldn't solve the equations."

"But what if it's not valid? What does that do to theoretical predictions?"

Vic's arms flailed in a wild aggravated gesture. "I don't know. They probably wouldn't work."

I tried to intervene. "Vic, perhaps you could answer Dr. Millen's question by pointing out where the *gamma* term appears in each equation."

It was too late. Everything had come to a head. My attempt at calming the waters had the opposite effect.

"It doesn't matter," he snapped. "Go ask Shain or Reinmuth or other theoretical electrochemists. I'm just doing what everyone does. Hell! I won't be doing any of this stuff anymore *anyways*."

Then, realizing what he had just said, he followed up with a nervous laugh.

No one had anything else to say.


I watched Vic leave the conference room so that the committee could deliberate. Vic didn't seem upset, just detached, as if he were in shock. I wanted to join him. I really didn't want to face the committee.

I turned to them. "Well?" I asked.

Buck responded quickly. "I guess we pushed too many buttons."

Squires added, "Up to the end, his presentation was very good. It's darn good work."

I looked at Millen.

"I agree with Bob," he admitted. "It's very nice work. But I am concerned about the attitude."

"Well, I can tell you this," I responded. "Vic doesn't talk much. But when he does, he tends to say exactly what he thinks. It's one of the things I admire most about him. I think that's what we saw today."

"Do you agree with what he said?"

I thought for a moment. "He's probably correct that he will never again have to deal with the specific issue we questioned. In fact, he has a job where he'll probably never do any more electrochemistry."

"But you can't condone the cavalier way that he dismissed it," declared Millen.

"No, I don't. I plan to discuss it with him."

When no one spoke further, I scanned the table and, with some trepidation, asked, "What's your pleasure, Gentlemen?"

Squires didn't hesitate. "*Pass*. He's a little rough on the edges, but he'll do well."

Buck murmured agreement but looked over at Millen.

Then Millen declared, "I've never failed anyone on a Ph.D. oral. But I have my reservations this time. The thesis format. The attitude." He shook his head.

There was an awkward silence for a few moments. Then Squires spoke up. "Look, I'm the outsider here. But maybe that will help. I don't see the thesis format as an issue. I like the way it was done. It makes sense."

Then he turned to Millen. "Dr. Millen, you're concerned about 'attitude.' I actually found it refreshing to hear a Ph.D. candidate speak his mind frankly. Perhaps it was misguided. But I'll let Dr. Perone deal with that."

An uncomfortable pause was followed by Buck declaring, "I say we go get Vic and tell him he's a Ph.D. What do you say?" He looked directly at Millen.

Millen did a slight bob and weave with his head as if searching for a better way to say what was on his mind. But finally he nodded his assent.

I breathed a sigh of relief.

Millen wasn't a happy camper, but at least he didn't hold the formatting fiasco against Vic. I had fallen on the sword, and Buck had come to the rescue. Only time would tell if any permanent damage had been done.

Vic and I had a long talk in my office before leaving to join his wife, Ellen, and my wife for a celebration dinner. I explained about the long delay before beginning the exam, and I apologized for nearly sinking him with the thesis formatting.

He admitted to being set on edge by the start delay—and to some anxiety about the thesis formatting issue—culminating in his outburst at the end.

But he refused to back away from what he had said.

I didn't expect that he would. I admired his determination to speak truth to power. But I wondered how that would work with his future industrial colleagues.

*Vic Evins. early '60s. [Copyright, C. V. Evins, used with permission.]*

Vic would leave Purdue and perhaps never again think of those turbulent moments during his Ph.D. oral exam. He would go on to a very successful industrial career, served well it turns out, by his penchant for "straight talk." In fact, years later he would return to Purdue to lecture to graduate students that "communications skills" were the most important attributes for success in the industrial world.

But in 1966, remembering Millen's sour disposition after Vic's thesis exam, I wasn't sure that it wasn't my own aspirations—for tenure—that had suffered a blow.

# CHAPTER 31

## The Day Arrives

Buck was true to his word. He didn't utter a peep about my promotion before the big announcement.

I got the word first by looking at the official list published in the morning newspaper. Each year during the first week of March, the *Lafayette Journal and Courier* reported all the academic promotions across all of the university's departments.

In early March, 1967, of course, I was eagerly awaiting the delivery of each morning newspaper. I was cautiously optimistic. After all, if the promotions committee meeting the previous November hadn't gone my way, wouldn't Buck have let me know? Wouldn't he have said something like, "Sam, you need to be looking for a new job?"

Buck's silence notwithstanding—none of the full professors had given me so much as a smile, a wink or a nod either. Well, not completely true. The department head, E. T. McBee, had, surprisingly, called me by name at a departmental social function.

So, on an early March morning, I was ecstatic to read my name listed as promoted to *associate professor* in Purdue's chemistry department.

Anita and the girls were delighted to see me running up from the foyer, all grins and whoops. Of all the people in the world, my wife had to be the most relieved—after living with my constant paranoia and all those nights and weekends writing papers or proposals.

Surely, she must have believed that the future looked much more stress-free—perhaps even *normal*.

She would have been correct—at least for a while.

I soon began thinking about the academic consequences of tenure. Did I feel less pressure to publish? Not really. Instead, I feared I would soon be consumed by the quest to make *full professor*. More precisely, I knew that I must make a name for myself if I wanted to reach that next plateau.

Sure, I was making a small splash with publications. And I was being seen at national meetings, delivering papers.

But where would that get me? Would it get me to full professor? Would it get me to the elite corps of distinguished professors? Would it make any improvement in my economic status?

One thing I firmly believed was that it did little good to simply impress the folks at Purdue. My future good fortune would be determined by what people thought of me *outside* of Purdue. Impress the scientists at Illinois, Wisconsin, M.I.T., and dozens of other institutions around the world, and that would assure a golden future at *Purdue.*

A corollary of that belief is that you must attach a high priority to professional activities that take you away from the university. Another corollary is that you shouldn't be too devoted to tasks that are only appreciated within your university—like committees and teaching.

Sounds wrong, doesn't it? But that's reality.

At a university like Purdue, the rewards of full professorships, distinguished professorships, large salaries, attractive research space and other perks are usually reserved for faculty that have outstanding national or international research reputations. Rarely is a professor rewarded bountifully for outstanding *teaching* or other activities that are mostly appreciated within the local university community.

Where did that leave me in the spring of 1967? I had a long, long way to go. The next few years would probably be filled with dizzying activities that would make my first few years look like child's play.

But I did take a moment to enjoy the warm, fuzzy feeling that went along with just being awarded tenure in the job of my dreams. My wife and I attended the spring Victory Varieties convocation in the Hall of Music.

The Victory Varieties series of the 1960s featured established entertainers. For example, Jack Benny appeared in both 1967 and 1968. Fall shows were scheduled on home football weekends. Ray Charles might perform one weekend and Bill Cosby the next. Others included: Steve Lawrence; Eydie Gorme; Nat King Cole; the Smothers Brothers; Johnny Cash; Sonny and Cher; Louis Armstrong; Earl Grant; the Kingston Trio; Peter, Paul and Mary; Trini Lopez; and so on. Hardly any feature performer of that era escaped Victory Varieties. It was New York's *Ed Sullivan Show* transported to West Lafayette, Indiana.

The venue for these performances was the 6000-seat Hall of Music on campus. It was a remarkable structure, comparable to Radio City Music Hall. The cost of seats was nominal—less than ten dollars in the mid-1960s—because the university subsidized these convocations out of student fees.

*Hall of Music, Purdue University. [From wikimediacommons, "Purdue University" by Amerique, used under CC BY 3.0, cropped.]*

If the acts listed above don't sound like preferences of eighteen- to twenty-two-year old students, you would be right. Bookings for Victory Varieties obviously catered to an older demographic. With time, students would demand change, but not in the 1960s.

I remember the feeling that came over me when we first took our main floor seats for the spring Victory Varieties. I sat down and took in the spectacle of this grand theater as the main floor and upper balcony gradually filled up.

*Hall of Music interior. [#PPBUC00317, Courtesy of Purdue University Libraries, Karnes Archives & Special Collections, cropped.]*

Finally, the seats were filled, and the lights dimmed. The

single spotlight narrowed to a life-size circle at the foot and center of high plush curtains spread across the spacious stage. As the M.C. appeared from behind the center flap—dwarfed by comparison to the cavernous venue—the Hall of Music erupted in applause.

That was when I felt it—that palpable sense of *belonging*. Finally—after nearly five years—I felt like I really was a part of this great university.

# PART 4
# California Calling

# CHAPTER 32

## Opportunity Knocks

The female voice on the phone was pleasant, almost casual. But the message was all business.

"Dr. Perone, this is Evelyn at the Lawrence Radiation Lab in Livermore, California. I'm calling for Jack Frazer. I believe you and Jack have met?"

I had met him six months earlier. A friend of Buck's, Frazer headed analytical chemistry at the Livermore Lab. He was doing pioneering work linking digital computers to laboratory instruments. In 1967, that required dedicating a mainframe computer the size of a small lab. Only a national laboratory like LRL had the skills and resources needed.

But I could think of no reason for Frazer to be calling *me*.

I replied to Evelyn. "Yes, we met in New York last fall, at the Eastern Analytical Symposium."

"Well, Jack would like to speak with you. Do you have some time right now?"

It was spring, 1967, and I was in the midst of a grueling four-week total immersion lecture series for the freshman course. I glanced at the incomplete set of lecture notes on my desk and sighed. "Yes. Of course."

Within seconds I heard Frazer's loud voice.

"Sam!" he shouted. "Hope I didn't drag you out of the lab." He followed with a boisterous laugh.

"I traded lab time to teach freshmen this semester," I replied dryly, wondering what he found so funny.

We exchanged pleasantries. He asked about Buck, and he congratulated me on my recent promotion. Then he told me what he wanted.

"Sam, you know that we like to bring professors out here during the summer?"

"Yeah. Dale Margerum told me he was there one summer. In fact, my major professor, Irv Shain, spent some time out there."

"That's right. Irv worked with Jack Harrar. I recall that he *really* enjoyed San Francisco." He punctuated the last sentence with another sharp burst of chuckling. I would soon recognize his loud chortling as part of the vocabulary that defined this incredible bundle of energy.

He continued. "The reason I'm calling is to invite *you* out for the summer. Do you think you might be interested?"

I was stunned. Spending a summer away from Purdue and my research program was the last thing on my mind. And that's what I told him.

"Hah!" he shouted. "What can I do to persuade you?"

"I don't know. What would you expect of me?"

Frazer quickly described the program. There would be no specific duties. I could define my own project. I would get a salary plus travel and per diem expenses.

"It sounds like a good deal," I remarked. "But I really need to think about it. When would you need a decision?"

"Yesterday," he quipped. Then he laughed. "Not my choice. You will need a security clearance, and that takes time."

"Security clearance?" I asked.

He chuckled loudly. "Don't you know what we do out here?"

I did, sort of. Like its sister lab in Los Alamos, Livermore Lab designed and developed nuclear weapons, and they tested and maintained the nuclear stockpile. Much of the cutting-edge science done there helped sustain a weapons program that defined U.S. security in a Cold War era.

"I know about the weapons work," I answered. "Would I be involved in that?"

"Not unless you want to. But everything we do supports the weapons program. That means you will need a Q-clearance to work here."

The only thing I knew about "clearances" had been learned from spy movies. So I queried Frazer about a "Q-clearance."

"The FBI has to make sure you can be trusted with classified information. They'll talk to your relatives, neighbors, friends and so on." He cackled loudly and added, "Hope you don't have anybody mad at you."

The whole idea of prying agents made me a little queasy. I didn't tell him that, but I asked, "Is the Q-clearance really necessary?"

Frazer's tone took a serious turn. "We bring in people without a 'Q,' but frankly, those people aren't very useful to us."

I decided not to make an issue of it. I probably wouldn't accept the offer anyway. So I changed the subject. "You know, I'm really impressed with what you've been doing with computers in the laboratory."

"You can't see me right now, but there's a big grin on my face," he replied. "I was hoping you might be interested in that project. Our engineers have created a cutting-edge solution in search of a *problem*. What we need is a chemist—like you—to show us how to solve some real laboratory problems."

Mixed emotions hit me. I was flattered. But buried in his statement were expectations that I wasn't prepared to deliver. "Hell," I said to him, "I know practically nothing about computers."

Once again he laughed raucously. "Doesn't matter."

Out of curiosity, I asked if I could set up to conduct flash photolysis studies at the Lab, and he assured me it was not only OK, but they would provide equipment, space and technician help. That was impressive, but I remained skeptical. I tried to end the conversation by asking him to send me some information.

"Do you know Jim Oberholtzer?" he asked. "Buck's grad student? He spent last summer out here."

"Sure, I know Jim. He works in the lab next to my office."

"He does?" Frazer chortled. "Good ol' Buck. Hanging on to his lab space, huh?" His words teased. It was a good-natured allusion to the perennial problem of tight lab space. I wondered if Frazer *knew* that I had ten research students squeezed into three two-man labs. No matter. He had touched a nerve.

I shook it off and said, "I actually enjoy having Buck's students nearby." That was true. I had good relationships with his students. But I chafed at the fact that two of the five labs surrounding my office still belonged to Buck. I was cramped, while he had ample lab space and a large office on the floor directly below me.

Frazer chuckled. "Well, you'd better go next door and talk to Jim. He can tell you what life is like at LRL and the Bay Area."

I told him I'd talk to Jim and get back to him. But I was far from enthusiastic.

"Livermore's a strange place," Jim Olberholtzer began. He wiped his hands on the white lab coat and turned away from the gas chromatograph in his lab. He continued with an answer to my first question. "It's a small town surrounded by cattle ranches and vineyards. But it also has LRL and Sandia Labs, with thousands of the sharpest scientists and engineers in the world. Lab people commute from all over the Bay Area—even San Francisco."

"San Francisco?"

"Yeah. Forty-five miles west. Beautiful city. Great food. Lots to do. Summers— when Livermore's a hundred degrees—San Francisco might be sixty or seventy."

I shrugged my shoulders.

"You've never been there?" he asked.

"Sure. 1950. I was eleven. My dad drove us out from Illinois in a two-door '46 Dodge. I remember Fisherman's Wharf and *DiMaggio's* restaurant—the only thing my dad wanted to see."

"They're still there. But there are better places to eat."

"Wouldn't know. We never ate there. Just drove by. I think my dad was expecting to see 'Joltin' Joe'."

"Well, San Francisco's changed a lot since 1950."

I gave him a puzzled look.

"Do you remember North Beach?" he asked.

I wagged my head. "That's just a name. I read that hippies have taken over."

"It's not that simple. North Beach is the Italian district. But it also attracts artists and intellectuals—free spirits, hippies. It includes Broadway. That's where all the topless night spots are."

"Yeah, I heard about that."

"Would you believe, even topless shoe shine girls?"

The visual image was just too much for *me*—an old shoe shine boy who knew all the moves. I chuckled. "Was that part of your report to Buck?"

Jim grinned. "I learned a *lot* at LRL, Doc. You will too. I brought back a whole new *digital* approach to my research instrumentation. It's going to blow the competition away."

"What would I learn?" I smiled. "At LRL, I mean."

"I don't know. Things change so quickly out there. I hear that Frazer is getting a new D.E.C. PDP-8/S. It's the first 'desktop' computer. Can you imagine having one of those in your lab?"

"Hmmm, Frazer *said* they were looking to attack chemistry problems with their lab computer."

Jim nodded. "It's a whole new world, Doc. Even instrument companies don't have a handle. Engineers aren't going to learn chemistry. Chemists will have to learn digital electronics and machine language."

"Machine language?"

"Ones and zeroes. Binary-coded instructions. To get a computer to operate an instrument, you have to talk to it in machine language."

"Sounds challenging."

"It is. But just think about it. With just a small instruction set, you can compose thousands of sophisticated control programs."

I stared at him for a few moments. I was beginning to understand the excitement that showed in his voice. I had a tiny glimpse of the vast potential of this whole new field.

And that tiny glimpse—as pitifully inadequate as it would turn out to be—began to ignite my scientific curiosity. But could I convince myself to abandon my research group for the entire summer?

I had to talk to Mike Burke.


"S.P., you're looking at this all wrong," Mike protested. He twisted the stub of his smoldering cigarette into the Petri dish sitting on my desk. Then he sat back and suggested, "Your students will get along just fine without you."

"Thanks for the compliment," I shot back.

"Trust me. You'll be doing them a favor," Mike said.

"Thanks again. Who do they turn to while I'm gone?"

Mike chuckled. "Not *me*. I'd tell 'em to forget electrochemistry and get into something worthwhile."

I threw him a scornful glance. Because his field of chromatography solved perhaps ninety percent of the world's analytical chemistry problems at that time, he took pleasure in belittling my less practical specialty.

"Don't worry, they won't be seeking advice from a glorified plumber," I shot back. We electrochemists *were* elitists, after all.

"You're funny, S.P. But that's my point. If you're not here, they'll figure things out for themselves."

"That's what I'm afraid of," I protested.

"You've got a couple of advanced students. They'll guide the younger ones. How do you think Buck runs *his* research group?"

"My most advanced student is the one I'm most concerned about."

"You mean Heinz?"

"I want him to take charge of his thesis research. But he won't go on to the next experiment without talking to me first"

Mike chuckled. "That's his way of showing respect, S.P.—an old German tradition. The head chemist gets all the credit—deserving or not. You're not around, Heinz becomes the independent researcher you want to see. Believe me, he'll thrive in your absence."

*Heinz Stapelfeldt, with flash photolysis set-up, 1965. [Copyright, Heinz Stapelfeldt, used with permission]*

I grew a pained expression. "Thanks a lot."

"You know what I mean. How do you know you can ride until the training wheels come off?"

I stuck out a palm. "All right. I get it. But all that aside, look at the other issues. What do we do about our house for three months?"

Mike wagged his head. "We'll watch your house. Hell, we'll probably be living in your basement during tornado season."

He gave me that knowing gaze while digging into his shirt pocket for another smoke. He lit up and slouched in the chair, blowing smoke toward the office door. His eyes never left mine. "There's something else bothering you, isn't there?" he asked.

"All right," I replied, after a few seconds, "I'll level with you. I ... I think I'll be in over my head. Those Livermore guys are really into computers. I'm a total zero."

"What do they expect you to do?"

I looked away. "I think I could do flash photolysis if I wanted." My gaze returned slowly to Mike.

He took a drag on the cigarette and parked it on the rim of the Petri dish. Leaning forward, he said, "Sounds like you're covered, S.P. What's your problem?"

I shrugged. "Don't know. I guess I worry about fitting in."

Mike laughed. "Are you kidding? They *invited* you. Just be yourself."

"Wouldn't I be able to do that better right here?"

Mike picked up his cigarette again. But just as the tip reached his lips, he pushed it away. "Look, S.P., Livermore's got top notch people and buckets of money," he declared. "And any equipment you want. Just show up and soak it in."

"Then what?"

"Then bring it back to Purdue and make a name for yourself."

Mike's arguments eventually won me over. I didn't believe any of that crap about making a name for myself. But I did learn later that he was right about one thing. My grad students, particularly Heinz, would thrive in my absence.

Would he be right about anything else?

I didn't know. But I took the Livermore offer and hoped for the best.

# CHAPTER 33

## Summer of Love

*If you're going to San Francisco*
*Be sure to wear some flowers in your hair …*

The Scott McKenzie siren song that called flower children from every corner of the world during the summer of 1967 seemed to guide our Chevy wagon from Indiana to California.

It couldn't have been more fitting than to hear McKenzie's lyrics once more as we sped west over the thousand-foot Altamont Pass, beholding for the first time the sprawling Livermore Valley. Framed by golden brown rolling hills, vast ranch lands and verdant vineyards, it stretched north to Mount Diablo, south to Mount Hamilton, and west to the green coastal hills surrounding San Francisco Bay.

Anita, the girls, and I were eager to see San Francisco, the Golden Gate Bridge, and the flower children we had been hearing about. But that would have to wait until we first unloaded the wagon into the furnished Livermore apartment we had secured for the summer. We had driven all the way from Salt Lake City that day, and an excursion into the City—a 45-mile drive from Livermore—wouldn't happen until the following day.

Unburdened by the tons of luggage, books, portable TV, and stereo receiver we had toted from Indiana, the Chevy wagon took us around the Oakland hills and onto the approach to the Oakland-Bay Bridge. It was an early Sunday morning. The fog still hovered over the City. But, as we passed through the Treasure Island tunnel and emerged onto the suspension span of the bridge, the full San Francisco panorama burst into view. Sailboats peppered the bay. The skyline—from the Transamerica Building to Coit Tower—took our breaths away. Then we were stunned to behold far off in the distance the unmistakable reddish-orange expanse of the Golden Gate Bridge.

As we would do many more times that summer, we toured the City by car before choosing one of the many local attractions—Fisherman's Wharf, Ghirardelli Square, Chinatown, North Beach, Haight-Ashbury,

*Vita(left) and Amy(right), cleaning wagon for San Francisco trip, summer 1967. [Copyright, S. P. Perone]*

Golden Gate Park, and many, many others—to enjoy on foot.

Flower children were everywhere. Young, long-haired, barefoot, in colorful flowing garb, and always with flowers in their hair—they walked, laughed, danced and sang. It was a scene that even Scott McKenzie's lyrics had not captured. It was a scene we would enjoy over and over that summer in many different ways—the rise of a young generation that questioned everything that had gone before. They embraced love and rejected war. There was a spirit of innocence and fellowship that summer in San Francisco that hadn't happened before and, sadly, would not ever be the same again.

*Flower Children in San Francisco. [Copyright, Don Ebert. Used with permission.]*

No one who was there that summer will ever forget it. You couldn't help but get caught up in it, even if it was only to observe spontaneous musical performances in the park, or to adopt some of the colorful garb, or simply to wear flowers in your hair—as our girls did.

But one thing I didn't see happening that day was that *my* "summer of love" would unfold in a most unexpected way.

# CHAPTER 34

## A Love Affair

After seemingly endless orientation meetings, I was issued my "green badge"—a Lab photo I.D. signifying I had been granted a Q-clearance. I was now cleared to enter any classified area of the Lab where I needed to work.

I enjoyed the feeling of power. But the somber tone of the orientation had left me anxious about "spies and leaks and moles" and, most of all, about accidentally revealing something classified.

Little did I know that all this anxiety was unwarranted. It wouldn't be until years later that I would get deeply involved in classified work. This first summer at Livermore would be more like postdoctoral study at a university.

But, oh, what a trip it would be!

Jack Frazer guided me through the guard gates, and I got my first close look at Livermore Lab—about a one-mile square campus. It didn't take long to note the striking dichotomy between the remnants of the old military base and the newer high-tech structures. It wasn't the most appealing facility. Flat. Arid. Lots of concrete and asphalt. Laid out in squares with paved streets and sidewalks, buildings were spread out, and only Lab vehicles were allowed. But the Lab provided hundreds of bicycles for employee transport around campus.

Frazer and I took two bikes from a nearby rack and pedaled to our first destination. Building 222—the one-story chemistry facility divided into three flat, rectangular wings—had to be a military base remnant.

There I met other Lab chemists, often in tee shirts and jeans, in striking contrast to shirts and ties typical of other contemporary labs. After a quick tour, Frazer brought me to the area that would be my home for the summer. He left me there in the capable hands of Jack Harrar—the chemist whose lab and office I would be sharing.

Having gotten his Ph.D. in analytical chemistry at the University of Washington in the late fifties, Jack Harrar had worked there with Professor Crittenden—who had also been Irv Shain's major professor. Moreover, Jack was from Indiana and had gotten his bachelor's degree at Purdue. Irv Shain—while I was working for him at Wisconsin—had visited Livermore to work with Jack.

It was amazing to discover that, in so many ways, Jack and I were already connected. But that day we began a new connection—an enduring relationship as scientific colleagues and close friends.

"Here are the materials you ordered," said Jack, as he opened the cabinet.

I stared at the shelf filled with xenon flash lamps, electrolysis cells, and electrodes. On a separate shelf was the three thousand-volt power supply and capacitor bank to drive the flash lamps. The accompanying electrochemical monitoring hardware had been built to my specifications and was sitting on the lab bench.

Everything was ready to go. And Jack had introduced me to another chemist, Fred Stephens, who had been assigned to help me set up and run experiments in the lab across the hall from our offices.

I was ecstatic. I hadn't yet been able to put together this kind of state-of-the-art system at Purdue. Now here it was, sitting and waiting for me to use. All I had done was put in a requisition. I was super-impressed.

"Wow!" I exclaimed. "When can I get started?"

"Fred will help you set everything up. He's ready when you are."

I shook my head. "Where have you been all my life?"

Jack chuckled. "We like to do things right." Then he pointed toward the door. "Should we take a look at what's going on in the other lab?"

We walked out of Fred's lab and into the lab adjacent to our shared office. That's when I met Roger Anderson for the second time. I had attended his talk a few months earlier at the Eastern Analytical

Symposium. That was when I had first learned of the exciting new stuff the Lab was doing with computers in the laboratory.

Roger was a physical chemist, but his passion at that time was exploring how digital computers could be programmed to do laboratory tasks.

In this lab with him was something I had never seen before—a brand new Digital Equipment Corporation PDP-8/S *minicomputer.*

The only computers I had seen before had been in movies—the electronic brains that filled enormous rooms and required a small army of technicians to operate. But here was a full-fledged computer, specifically designed to fit on a lab bench. It was the size of a large suitcase. The front panel had an array of tiny lights. Sticking out from the front panel was a long row of flat plastic two-position switches. Parked next to the lab bench was a Teletype with a keyboard and punched paper tape module. Next to it was a tall, portable, instrument rack with a number of

*D.E.C. PDP-8/S. [From everystockphoto. com, computer-history-pdp8-189478-o by ajmexico, used under CC BY 2.5, resized.]*

different electronic panels. Long connector leads stretched between the back of the computer and selected panels in the instrument rack.

"Ever seen anything like this before?" asked Roger.

I shook my head. "What are you doing with it?"

"Putting it through its paces. It's *really* slow compared to the PDP-7 down the hall."

"What's a PDP-7?"

"That's an earlier D.E.C. lab computer. It takes up about half the lab. We hooked it up to the mass spec."

I screwed up my face. "Why would they make a *slower* computer?"

Roger laughed. "It's a slower version of their PDP-8, the upgrade to the PDP-7. It's still a hell of a lot faster than you. It's got an eight microsecond cycle time."

I had nothing but a puzzled look for him.

"That means it can do several thousand math operations in a second." He grinned. "Beats the hell out of a slide rule."

"I meant, why produce a *new* computer that's *slower?*"

"They weren't going for speed. They were looking for something cheap and compact; and *voila!*" He waved a hand at the PDP-8/S.

"What did you lose in speed?" I asked, trying to act intelligent.

"About a factor of ten—3.5 millisecond multiplication compared to 300 microseconds for the PDP-8—but still that's 300 multiplications per second. Fast enough for government work." Roger chuckled.

"What kind of applications are you working on?"

He smirked. "We're hoping you might tell *us*."

My mouth opened. "What? Me? The only thing I've ever done is write simple FORTRAN programs, through the computer center at Purdue."

"FORTRAN isn't going to help you much with *this* computer. You'll have to learn machine language."

"I hope it speaks English."

He laughed. "Ones and zeroes. Twelve-bit data. Twelve-bit instructions."

I shook my head.

Roger twisted toward the lab bench, opened up his briefcase, and pulled out a book. About the size of a paperback novel, the book's cover had a picture of the PDP-8/S. It was the "User's Manual."

"Take this home with you, Sam. Read it through. Then we'll talk."


I was so curious that I postponed for a few days setting up the flash photolysis experiments.

I read the D.E.C. User's Manual. And Roger showed me how to generate machine language code by typing simple three-letter mnemonic instructions on a Teletype that punched out corresponding binary-coded characters on paper tape. The coded tape could then be read directly by the minicomputer's "assembler" program to produce twelve-bit machine code for execution by the computer.

I began to explore this intriguing world of ones and zeroes that could program a minicomputer to perform an infinite variety of tasks—from evaluating complex math expressions to collecting enormous amounts of data—all within the blink of an eye.

This was a world that had previously been accessible to only a privileged few that worked with large mainframe computers. But with the arrival of affordable laboratory-scale minicomputers, this world had suddenly opened up to other scientists—like me.

Now here I was at one of the labs at the cutting edge of this new technology.

I dived further into the machine language of the PDP-8/S. Within a few days I was writing math and data handling codes. I learned to use the punched paper tape media. Then Roger introduced me to the coding that would communicate with the digital data acquisition hardware that sat in a D.E.C. Logic Lab module—connected to the minicomputer's input/output terminals with simple patchcords.

That's when I knew I was hooked—totally and completely addicted.

I forgot all about the flash photolysis studies. I had found something infinitely more exciting.

The affair had begun.

While the flower children enjoyed the passions of a *Summer of Love* in San Francisco—just over the coastal hills in the Livermore Valley I had become hopelessly enchanted by an inanimate, pint-sized computer.

I had no inkling then of the extraordinary consequences of the choice I had made.

# CHAPTER 35

## All's Fair....

For all I know the flash photolysis equipment rounded up for my summer of '67 may still be on the shelf gathering dust at Livermore Lab.

But I never used it. And I never looked back.

I was completely and totally enthralled with the world of minicomputers. I learned machine language programming; digital interfacing; and programming the computer to talk to laboratory experiments.

It was a mind-blowing experience—my psychedelic event of 1967. But it didn't come without a little pushing and shoving.

The PDP-8/S was a hot, new commodity. It was "affordable" but not cheap—about twenty-five to fifty thousand dollars, depending on bells and whistles. That was a lot of money in 1967. Livermore Lab was one of a handful of places where chemists had one to play with at that time.

There were a number of people that wanted to play with the minicomputer in my lab. Roger Anderson was one. But he had gladly deferred to me. He was happy to be my mentor. There was a bigger plan.

But I had to fight off a passel of folks that were as eager as I to get their hands on the PDP-8/S. Lab employees were quickly handled by Jack Frazer. He told them to let the summer visitors work with it.

But I wasn't the *only* summer visitor.

After my first week of work with the computer, I had settled into a routine. Our East Avenue apartment was only minutes from the Lab. I would rise and get to my office each morning by about eight or eight-thirty. I would work until about five—faithfully taking a daily lunch break with Jack Harrar at the west cafeteria. Jack and I had a seemingly endless number of topics to discuss—Purdue football, Oakland Raiders football, mutual friends and acquaintances; and, always, the best places for food and entertainment in the Bay Area. On this latter subject, Jack and I and our spouses took a number of field trips. More on that later.

But my second week on the job brought a big surprise.

I walked into the lab on Monday morning, eager to get to work on the next phase of machine language programming, and discovered a strange, new occupant of the lab.

There, seated in front of the computer, was a tall, heavy-set, balding gentleman in his forties. Dressed in a short-sleeved green shirt and khaki pants, he was busily preparing a punched tape program at the Teletype.

"Hello," I called out, and he looked up.

Without standing, he stuck out a hand and said, "Hi. I'm Don Hill. I'm here for the summer."

I looked at his green badge. It looked just like mine. "I'm Sam Perone," I responded. "I'm a summer visitor, too."

"Is this your lab?" he inquired.

"Yeah. I've been working with the PDP-8/S."

"Oh, I see. Are you running an experiment?"

"Uh … no, not yet. I'm learning the language."

He nodded. "Me, too." He looked down at the Teletype printout. "I'm in the middle of something. Do you mind if I finish?"

"Umm … sure. Go ahead. Do you know when you'll be done?"

He shrugged. "Shouldn't be too long."

Then he turned back to the Teletype and began typing.

I had been dismissed.


I sought out Roger Anderson in the PDP-7 lab.

"Hey, Roger," I called out. "Got a second?"

"Sure." He looked up from the keyboard and grinned. "You stuck?"

"No. Not exactly," I replied. "Do you know this guy—Don Hill—another summer visitor like me?"

Roger's grin faded to a half-smile. "Oh, you've met?"

"Yeah. He's working on the 8/S."

He threw me a knowing glance. "Looks like you've got some competition."

I gave him my desperate look. "What can I do?"

He shrugged. "Share. Work out a schedule."

I shook my head and began to walk away.

"Oh, by the way," Roger called out as I reached the door. "I hear that Hill has a rental house in Dublin."

I turned back to him with a puzzled look. But Roger just grinned and turned back to his work.


Don Hill's stint on the computer that day took the entire day. And the next. He didn't even look up when I walked into the lab.

When Hill didn't show up the following day, I got back on the system. But he was there the next day when I arrived.

That did it for me. If it would be first come, first serve, I would damn well be first.

That's when Roger's words hit me. Of course! Hill's rental was in Dublin—about 15 miles from Livermore. His longer morning commute would give me an advantage.

We would see who was more determined.


I began getting into the lab by six in the morning, sometimes earlier.

After three or four days of finding me on the computer no matter how early he pushed his arrival time, Hill gave up. I had won.

The 8/S was *mine* for the summer.

Did I feel guilty? Maybe a little. But Frazer had undoubtedly brought me to the Lab that summer to get involved in the computer automation projects. That was why Roger's time was my time for the entire summer. Hill was at the Lab for another project. He had simply been curious about the 8/S. I can't blame him. But if he had really been dedicated, he would have found a way to work with it. Then, frankly, I would have begun to work nights and evenings.

I was sooooo hooked on computers.

# CHAPTER 36

## Play Time

My summer visit to Livermore Lab lasted only about ten weeks. Barely enough time to accomplish what I wanted, scientifically.

Yet there was so much more than science to do during the summer of '67.

For two Midwesterners who hadn't seen much outside the cornfields of Illinois and Indiana, my wife and I were of course very eager to sample the North Beach scene—*Italian cuisine and topless bars.*

Jack and Rosemary Harrar were glad to accommodate. They lived in Castro Valley—positioned in the hills halfway between Livermore and San Francisco—and were eager to introduce us to the many tastes of the City.

On one of these outings, we had dinner at a restaurant off Columbus and then took a short walk to Broadway. We did the tourist thing, strolling up and down, listening to the spiels of the sidewalk barkers and checking out the enticing billboards.

*"North Beach Scene" [everystockphoto.com, by atl10trader, used under CC BY 2.5, resized.]*

The barkers assured us that the real showgirls were even better than the leggy beauties on the signs and would show us a "real good time." We had decided beforehand that the establishment we would visit would be *The Condor*—the most notorious of the day. Located at the corner of Columbus and Broadway, *The Condor* had become famous because of its featured performer, Carol Doda. Her name had become synonymous with "breast enhancement," as she was a somewhat extreme example, and, as we were to learn, she sure did put on a show.

Of course, topless bars are nothing new today. But it was a relatively new phenomenon in 1967. San Francisco had led the way. There were topless bars; topless restaurants; and a remarkable range of topless entertainment in the City.

Fortunately, all of these attractions were off-limits to minors. But we often cruised around the City in our '67 wagon touring all the sights with our two daughters. And, yes, they loved cruising through North Beach at night. My wife and I provided a sanitized narrative.

One of their favorite sights was the go-go-girl that danced in a cage above the entrance to one of the nightspots on Columbus. Well, I guess we all enjoyed that.

I'm sure their grandparents were shocked to hear about these North Beach excursions. But, for the girls, it was all part of the San Francisco experience—no more or less exciting than touring Chinatown; cruising over the Golden Gate Bridge; riding a cable car down the Hyde Street hill; or walking among the flower children in Haight-Ashbury or Golden Gate Park.

Of course, the summer would not have been complete without an excursion to southern California and Disneyland.

We made the trip on a long weekend, taking time also to spend an afternoon with my former student, Jim Birk, his wife Cathy, and their baby girl, Linda. Jim had taken a job at Atomics International in Canoga Park.

Jim and I left our families at their home one afternoon so he could take me to his lab. Well, that's what he said when we left.

He took me instead to a topless bar that he frequented for lunches near his workplace.

That's where I met Tiffany.

She was a dancer on the day shift, and Jim had made her acquaintance. (Don't read anything into this. Jim was a long way from the cornfields of Iowa—a stranger in a strange land. He was just a curious, friendly, outgoing guy.)

*Jim "J.R." Birk, post grad. school era. [Copyright, S. P. Perone]*

Our experience that day might be a testament to how the world around us was changing. Jim Birk and I grew up in the conservative, restrained world of the 1940s and 1950s. We weren't rebels. Except for our mutual enjoyment of the popular music of the sixties—Beatles, folk rock, psychedelic, and others—we contributed nothing to the emerging liberated counter-culture. Neither of us could have conceived—even a few years earlier—of holding a conversation with a topless dancer.

But here we were.

The place was sparsely filled at this hour. Jim and I ordered drinks at the bar. A half-dozen other customers—all male—were spread around the horseshoe.

Music started, and Tiffany took the stage at the center of the horseshoe. She appeared to be in her mid-twenties, creamy complexion, with shoulder-length auburn hair and a leggy, well-toned body. She had on only a white sequined string bikini bottom, and she swayed seductively to the music. After directing her smile to every guy at the bar, she offered a wink to Jim.

After a while, she broke into a more energetic dance and then followed a walkway to the bar top. She dance-stepped toward us on spike-heeled silver pumps and shimmied for a while directly above Jim.

Jim tucked a bill under one string of the bikini and spoke toward her ear. "Hey, Tiffany, this is my old boss from Indiana." He pointed to me. "He wants to meet you."

I hadn't said that, but it seemed like an interesting idea. So I just shot a silly grin at her and got a wink in return.

She mouthed the words, "I'll stop by," and then danced on down the bar.

After a while Tiffany danced off the center stage and disappeared. No other dancer took her place, but the music continued, somewhat muted, in the background. Within minutes she re-entered the bar at floor level through a backstage door.

Still in high heels, but wearing a long, men's dress shirt over her outfit, she glided over to us. I moved over to the next barstool so she could sit between us. Twirling around so that her back was to the bar, she leaned back and crossed one long leg over the other. She couldn't have had time for a shower, but she appeared cool, dry and pleasantly fragrant. The chilled air from the overhead air conditioner caused long wisps of her hair to flutter; and left no doubt that she remained bra-less under her shirt.

Smiling at Jim, she asked, "Aren't you going to introduce me to your boss?"

"Sure," he replied, "S.P., this is Tiffany. Tiffany, this is my major professor, from Purdue, Sam Perone."

She offered me a coy smile. "You're from Purdue? What're you doing *here?*"

"I came to see *you.*"

She laughed. "All that way?"

I chuckled. "Well, I came to Canoga Park to see J.R., but he brought me here to see *you.*"

"Hope you weren't disappointed."

"Not a bit."

She smiled and turned to Jim. "So, you're *J.R.?*"

Jim smiled back. "Friends call me that."

"How about me?" she teased.

"Are you my friend?" he asked, peering slyly over his glasses, with that devious half-grin of his.

"I hope so," she replied, winking.

"Hey," I interrupted, "could we buy you a drink?"

"Thanks, I'll have a Coke."

I got the bartender's attention and ordered drinks while Jim and Tiffany had a little private joke.

When I turned back to them, Jim said to Tiffany, "Why don't you tell S.P. about yourself."

She frowned at him. "There's nothing to tell."

"Oh, I don't know," I offered. "I'd like to hear how you got into this business."

She threw me a scathing glance.

"I ... I'm sorry," I said quickly. "You must get questions like that all the time."

She rolled her eyes.

"Look. Let's start over," I suggested. "Tell me where you're from."

She thawed and flashed a toothy grin. "I'm from Ohio. Moved to California when I was ten."

"Oh, so you're from back east like us." I looked over at Jim. "Did you know that?"

He nodded. "You're asking the questions, S.P."

I turned back to Tiffany. "Did you go to college?"

"Sure. Got a B.A. in psychology from U.C.L.A."

I felt my eyebrows elevate. "What ... why—?"

"Because," she interrupted, "because I got lousy job offers and—*here*—I make good money." She looked away, quietly regarding the silver pump dangling from the toe of her extended foot.

Jim used the pause to slip in a question. "Hey, you never told me you had a degree in psychology."

She turned to him with a smirk. "What did you think? I came in off the street?"

He shrugged. "You're always talking about *religion.*"

"Religion?" I asked. Now I was really curious.

"Scientology," she replied. "I'm really into it."

"Scientology?" I asked. "I don't know anything about it."

"I bet you've heard of L. Ron Hubbard."

"Sure. Science fiction writer."

"Well, he's more than that. Did you read his book on *Dianetics?*"

"You know, I remember it—a big deal in the early fifties. But I never read it."

She laughed. "I guess you might say it was a 'big deal.' It only led to the Church of Scientology."

"What kind of religion is it?"

She shook her head. "You're Catholic, right?"

I nodded.

She looked at Jim. "Your wife, too?"

Jim nodded but didn't reply. I was pretty sure they had covered this ground before.

Turning back to me, she explained, "Scientology isn't a Christian religion. It's not a *religion* in the traditional sense. It's a set of *beliefs*; beliefs about the human soul; the human spirit."

"*Christians* believe in a soul."

"Yeah, sure, because someone *tells* you to believe. You have faith. Scientologists actually *experience* the human soul."

"What's *that* like?" I asked.

"I'm not there yet. It takes years."

"Do you believe in God?"

"Of course. We believe in a Supreme Being. But that's it. No fairy tales."

"Fairy tales?"

"You know—about God hearing prayers or passing judgment."

"Sounds like some kind of 'do-it-yourself' religion," I remarked.

"That's exactly right. We practice self-improvement—reaching for the ultimate experience, the Eighth Dynamic."

"What's that?"

"Hard to explain. I'm a long way—"

Jim interrupted. "Tell him about the *Second* Dynamic."

She poked him with an elbow, and he gave her that devious half-grin again. Then she turned back to me and said, "Jim doesn't take any of this seriously."

"What's the Second Dynamic?" I asked.

"There are eight Dynamics. They really define different levels of the basic urges of human beings. The Second—as *J.R.* will tell you—is the urge toward *sexual activity*."

"Yeah," added Jim, "that's the one Tiffany's working on." He chuckled and warded off a second shot to the ribs.

She threw me a stern look. "Are you *really* interested? Or do you want to poke fun like Jim?"

"No, really, I'm fascinated," I insisted, confirming my sincerity by averting my eyes from her barely concealed bosom.

She threw a long, pensive look at me. Then she asked, "Are you satisfied with *your* religion? Are you a good Catholic?"

Caught off-guard, I didn't answer for a few seconds. Through my mind flashed snippets of the many spirited conversations about religion I had had over the past two years with Mike Burke back in Lafayette. Finally, I replied, "You know, like many Catholics today, I'm disillusioned with the Church. But we still go to church on Sundays and raise our kids Catholic."

"But you don't follow the rules, do you?"

I shook my head. "I guess I'm one of those 'Cafeteria Catholics.' I pick and choose."

"Birth control?" she asked.

"That's where the Church has gone off the tracks; or maybe stayed on the track and gone over the ravine. I don't agree with them."

She laughed. "You sound like a lot of my Catholic friends. One reason I prefer Scientology."

Jim snickered. "Yeah," he said, "Scientologists *enjoy* the sex urge, while Catholics *stifle* it."

We laughed with him for a moment. Then Tiffany wagged her head at him and said, "You can't be serious about anything, can you?"

He chuckled. "Not about religion."

She shook her head and slipped off the barstool. Turning to face us, she put a hand on each of our knees. "It's been fun, boys. But I've got to get back to work."

Then she whirled around and dashed back to the stage door.

Jim and I settled the tab and left the bar. I never saw Tiffany again. I don't know whether she was really into Scientology or just pulling our legs. But Jim and I often recalled that intriguing conversation with a fascinating young lady who just happened to be a topless dancer in the summer of '67.

# CHAPTER 37

# What Have We Wrought?

The summer wound down quickly. Too quickly.

With only a week left before packing up and returning to Indiana, it seemed inconceivable that I could complete the ambitious project undertaken at the Lab.

Yes, I had mastered machine language programming of the PDP-8/S. And Roger Anderson had schooled me in digital electronics for interfacing lab instruments to the computer. But I wanted more than that.

I wanted to complete a publishable piece of work.

That's where Jack Harrar and Fred Stephens became indispensable. Together, we defined a cutting-edge electrochemical study that required computer control. We proposed to extend the detection limits of rapid-sweep voltammetry by signal-averaging currents from multiple repetitive voltage sweeps.

At least, that was the hypothesis.

Jack pulled together the instrumentation, and Fred Stephens did all the chemistry—preparing samples and electrodes. Fred, Roger and I conjured up a computerized data system that collected voltammetric data from repeatedly refreshed mercury drop electrodes. By synchronizing each voltammetric experiment with the last second of the life of each droplet, repetitive experiments could be run at the rate of one every few seconds.

It's impossible to overstate the significance of this kind of study. Prior to the availability of a laboratory digital computer, scientists had very

185

limited ability to control or modify conditions during an experiment. They would have to capture data, at best, by using strip-chart recorders or photographs of oscilloscope traces. At worst they would have to use visual observations with manual written records. To analyze data with a computer required manually converting the data to digital form on punched cards or paper tape and then manually transporting these media—including a Fortran data analysis program—to an institutional computer center. With luck, the results would be received back the next day.

With our laboratory computer system, I had written the machine language program to run the experiment, automatically collect data, ensemble average the data, and analyze the averaged signal to compute analyte concentrations—all within the several seconds time frame of the experiment. This represented an extraordinary leap forward in experimental capability.

For the final week of my stay at Livermore Lab, that instrument was humming a tune. We collected reams of data that plainly demonstrated the advantages of the computer-automated technique. I collected all the printouts, photos, circuit diagrams, and data summaries into a big cardboard box and headed back to Purdue to write up a paper for publication.

Fred and Jack, with Roger's help, were able to conduct a number of studies after my exit that managed to complete the story we wanted to tell. I had the paper written—with lots of inputs from the folks at the Lab—by the end of the year; and it was published in *Analytical Chemistry*, May, 1968.

By that time, a few other analytical chemists—notably Don Smith at Northwestern, Fred Anson at Cal Tech and Lauer and Osteryoung at North American Rockwell—had begun publishing articles describing computer automated electrochemical instrumentation. Many of these early workers were on the program at the American Chemical Society meeting in San Francisco in April, 1968, when I presented our Livermore work for the first time. The room was jammed, and there was an air of excitement about the dawn of a new era in laboratory instrumentation.

The competition was heating up in this field that was about to explode. It was clear that soon everyone working in the laboratory would have to understand and use computer instrumentation.

I had gotten in on the ground floor, and I was planning to make the most of it.

# PART 5
## 1968

# Chapter 38

## What Was It about 1968?

Looking back at an eventful career, most people can point to a time when everything came together. For me, it was 1968.

Coincidentally, 1968 was perhaps the signature year of the decade in many other ways. Political and cultural conflict reached unprecedented heights. An unpopular war forced out an incumbent president; his likely successor was assassinated; and the revered face of the civil rights movement was silenced. Deep fissures spawned by Vietnam were never more dramatically demonstrated than at the Democratic presidential convention, as Chicago police mauled student protestors before a national television audience.

*Chicago police confronting anti-war protests at Democratic Convention, 1968. [Copyright AP//Corbis, used with permission.]*

These world-shaking events impacted everyone, and the effects on my life will be described later. But so many other things affected me personally that year that I need to put things in perspective.

A recurring theme in this memoir is that many fortuitous events have impacted my life. Everything that came together for me in 1968 exemplified that notion and provided a quantum leap forward in my professional life.

Nothing quantifies this more than the astounding change in the role of computers. Prior to the mid-1960s, scientists accessed computers by writing programs and providing data for analysis to centralized large computer centers that housed expensive institutional computer systems. Interaction with the computer was severely limited; turnaround times could be hours to days. Direct access was limited to a privileged few.

About this time, as space-age technology produced solid state microelectronic devices, more compact, powerful and comparatively "inexpensive" computers became available. A leader of this development was the Digital Equipment Corporation of Maynard, Mass. They produced their revolutionary compact PDP-1 model in 1960 for a cost of about $120,000 (or nearly one million dollars today). It featured an eighteen-bit word size, came with 4096 words

*D.E.C. PDP-1, circa 1960. [From everystockphoto.com, "PDP-1" by Marcin Wichary, used under CC BY 2.5, cropped.]*

of core memory, and could execute 100,000 operations per second. By today's standards it was slow as molasses and practically moronic. However, it was comparable in power to an IBM 1800 business computer—capable of performing very sophisticated data processing with efficient high-level programming—and it was compact enough to fit in a laboratory.

Scientists were very excited about the possibility of capturing their own computer and connecting it to their laboratory experiments.

However, only a handful of academic chemists were capable of investigating computers connected to laboratory experiments. Until about 1967, this line of research was limited severely by the cost. Before the bench-top size Digital Equipment Corporation PDP-8/S came out that year, researchers attempted to bring into the laboratory bulky, expensive business computers like the IBM 1800 or the more compact but still quite expensive PDP-1.

The PDP-8/S excited researchers all over the country with its small size and "affordable" price. There was a burst of energy moving through the scientific community in 1968 regarding the imminent incorporation of computer technology into everybody's laboratory.

The problem was that there were only a handful of chemistry labs in the country that had the needed expertise. Even the instrument companies were behind the curve. They desperately needed chemists who understood laboratory computer technology. But that talent pool simply didn't exist.

Enter here the young Dr. Perone, freshly minted laboratory computer "expert." Upon returning from Livermore Lab in the fall of 1967, I made the case to Buck and the rest of my Purdue analytical colleagues that we should institute a special three-week summer course to teach laboratory computer principles to university and college professors and other practicing chemists.

We had an excellent model to emulate. In the 1950s, Howard Malmstadt at the University of Illinois had instituted a highly successful summer short course to teach electronics principles and applications to chemists. That course had been running successfully for several years. Harry Pardue—one of Malmstadt's former students—had taught that same summer course at Purdue with good attendance.

Cognizant of Malmstadt's landmark success at Illinois with electronics training for chemists, my colleagues embraced the Purdue computer course idea enthusiastically.

But there was one very big problem. This would have to be a "hands-on" kind of course. Yet we had absolutely *no* laboratory computer equipment. We would need to raise at least a hundred thousand dollars—and that would be like raising a million dollars in capital funds today. It just wasn't going to happen.

But it *did* happen, just not the way one might expect.


What made everything possible was a series of fortunate events.

First of all, I wouldn't have suddenly become the "lab computer expert" if I hadn't spent the previous summer at Livermore. That wouldn't have happened if I hadn't been at Purdue—with Buck's connections to Livermore Lab and Jack Frazer.

Another fortuitous event was the presence at Purdue of a premier chemistry instrumentation group led by Jon Amy.

Jon was—in his quiet, unassuming way—one of the most powerful figures in the chemistry department. Increasingly, chemistry faculty depended on sophisticated instruments. Jon's counsel and support were essential. He was in demand. Faculty vied for his attention.

Jon's popularity did not stop at department boundaries. He moved easily within instrument company circles. He was a personal friend of the Hewletts and the Packards of Palo Alto. He served as consultant to numerous other instrument companies. He was on a first-name basis with presidents and CEO's and privy to innovations on the drawing boards. In many cases, he was their inspiration.

When Jon became aware of my passion for laboratory computers and desire to develop a course, he offered his help. It was Jon who then persuaded Hewlett-Packard to provide a long-term loan of an early production example of their first integrated-circuit minicomputer in the spring of 1968. (In fact we got the *third* unit produced.)

The H.P. 2116A we received was the size of a small refrigerator. It had 8192 bytes of memory. (That's right, *eight thousand*—not even enough to store one digital photograph today.) For input/ output there was a Teletype with ten characters/sec. punched paper

*H.P. 2116 computer. [Copyright HPMuseum.net, used with permission]*

tape input/output. Later, we would have "high-speed" punched paper tape input/output (150 to 300 char./sec.). The loaner system was probably worth about a quarter million in today's dollars.

As primitive as it might seem, that early H.P. system was far ahead of the D.E.C. PDP-8 machines. (Although D.E.C. would quickly announce an integrated circuit version.)

The availability of the 2116A was a godsend. I was able to introduce a number of graduate students to machine language programming. The chemistry department was motivated to contribute a few thousand dollars for D.E.C. Logic Lab stations—with which students learned digital electronics and interfacing to the computer. I was then able to begin preparing a number of students for one of the biggest adventures of their lives—teaching the nation's first lab computer course for science professionals.

Hewlett-Packard would later loan us additional minicomputers to use during the summer course so that we could have several students or student-pairs working simultaneously.

Another benefit, sometimes lost in the push to develop the computer course, was that the long-term loan of laboratory computer equipment allowed analytical faculty to incorporate it into their research. Suddenly we were all working at the cutting edge of laboratory technology.

We owed all that to the efforts of Jon Amy and the generosity and foresight of Hewlett-Packard.

This brings me to another fortuitous circumstance—the presence of David O. Jones in my research group.

Dave had joined my group during the 1966-67 academic year. He was from the state of Washington and had done his undergraduate work there. He had been a chemistry major, but had developed expertise in both electronics and business. He had been forthright in declaring that he wanted to work with me because he wanted the freedom in conducting his thesis research that he couldn't get with other professors.

It was instantly apparent that Dave would be quite different than my earlier

*Dave Jones, 1966.*
*[Copyright, S. P. Perone]*

students. His decision to work for me was more like a negotiation. He had extraordinary self-confidence; he knew that he had something special to offer me—electronics expertise and other skills I would learn about later—and he wanted a level of freedom and operational latitude rarely bestowed on graduate students.

I agreed, not really knowing what I was in for. But I would learn that I had made an invaluable investment and would be rewarded many fold, despite what would become a very unconventional student-advisor relationship.

Dave rolled into West Lafayette and immediately purchased a home for his family (wife and two young daughters). That alone was quite unusual. Most graduate students rented.

When Dave first joined my research group, I offered to find him a desk in one of my research labs. He thanked me but claimed he had a better deal. Puzzled, I soon discovered that Dave had struck up a relationship with Jon Amy and his technicians, who had a fair portion of the department's basement digs for their operation. They had found a nice spot for Dave to hang out—his own basement getaway. This isolated office space might have been the envy of a postdoc or young professor, and was certainly much better than any chemistry graduate student might hope for.

Should I have objected to this arrangement? Perhaps. But I recognized that Dave's cozy relationship with Jon and the electronics techs was not something to discourage. Why should I turn down space that was, in fact, very precious to come by in the department?

And so it began.

When Dave began to conduct his thesis research program, we agreed on a project that was as much his idea as mine—developing a hardware-based digital instrument that emulated the computer-controlled experiment-optimization innovations we had been implementing with laboratory computers. Today, that is what instrument companies do routinely. But in 1968, it would involve cutting-edge concepts and electronics. Dave would be the first to demonstrate this approach.

There was just one catch—Dave didn't want to do the work in my research labs.

He had outfitted the garage of his home as a first-class electronics lab. He had also demonstrated to me that he had the necessities to conduct his studies there—including the minor amount of chemistry required.

So, once again, I agreed to an unconventional arrangement—with the proviso that I would periodically visit his garage to confirm and observe his studies.

The list goes on and on. We attended a two-week course together—at Hewlett-Packard in Palo Alto, February, 1968—to learn machine language programming of the H.P. 2116A. I gave Dave responsibility for developing the digital electronics part of the laboratory computer course, and I made him the supervisor of the lab. In 1969, after our pioneering summer course had garnered world-wide recognition, we developed a travelling one-day to one-week hands-on course for various companies.

From the outset, Dave and I had planned to write the first book on the subject, and McGraw-Hill published the very successful graduate textbook in 1973, *Digital Computers in Scientific Instrumentation.* The first of its kind, the book was adopted by a number of schools and is referenced even to this day, although it is decidedly out of date.

Dave didn't hang out with the rest of my research students. But to say that he was a "loner" would be inaccurate. He simply didn't believe in wasting time. If he were going to spend time chatting with someone, it was because he needed something from that person. And that included me.

From Dave I learned to recognize where the real "power" resides in any organization—*the support staff.* Dave formed relationships with Jon Amy, the electronics and mech. techs, secretaries, and administrative staff. He knew how to get things done; he knew where things were hidden; and he understood the inner workings of the department perhaps better than any other single individual.

Dave's "aloofness" and his special relationship with me were not lost on the rest of my students. Those that had been around a while let me know about it. To their credit, they recognized that Dave's connections and expertise benefited our group. They both envied and respected him.

195

But they needled me about his "private office" and wondered aloud about the propriety of conducting thesis research in one's home lab.

Did I handle things in the best possible way? I don't know. But it was clear to everyone that Dave was uniquely talented, and I'd like to think that our unconventional working relationship allowed him to make the unprecedented contributions that he did.

Another fortuitous circumstance at Purdue in 1967-68 was the presence of Harry Pardue. I mentioned earlier that his hiring as an analytical professor one year earlier than I was a benefit to my career. I could gauge my own progress by comparison to his. It's like a long-distance runner with a partner that establishes the pace early in the race.

In developing the first laboratory computer course, I benefited from my prior work with Harry. He had set up the Malmstadt-type electronics course for chemistry graduate students, and then he organized a summer short course like that of Malmstadt's at Illinois. He asked me to help him teach the course.

*Harry Pardue, lecturing, late 60s. [Copyright, S. P. Perone]*

In 1965, Harry prepared a proposal for the summer instrumentation course, and I contributed parts of the proposal. The proposal wasn't funded, but I benefited by learning about the NSF program, from which I later sought funding successfully for the computer instrumentation course.

Finally, but not least important, there were a number of first- and second-year graduate students at Purdue that were eager to get engaged in developing this first short course on lab computer instrumentation. So eager were they that they devoted their own time to the intensive training that would be required over the spring semester of 1968.

The students were: Dave Jones, John Patterson, Gerry Kirschner, Mike Fleming—who worked for me—and Barry Willis and Gerry James, who worked for Harry Pardue. These young men were taking courses, doing their own research projects, and in most cases, working as teaching assistants in other courses.

On top of what would normally be a full load, these young men immersed themselves in this strange new world of machine language programming, digital electronics, and interfacing computers to instruments. They were not only learning the fundamentals but were also developing the course materials that others would use. In the following summers they would be instructing college and university professors from all over the world.

Based on the notoriety achieved for developing this first-of-its-kind course, the number of people impacted over the years, the publicity garnered for Purdue, not to mention the associated research contributions from my group, the computer course was probably the pivotal event in my career.

The following sections will address the craziness that came along with this and many other dramatic events of 1968.

# CHAPTER 39

# A Meeting in San Francisco

The 155th National Meeting of the American Chemical Society was scheduled for the first week of April, 1968, in San Francisco.

I was presenting a paper, and I was excited to return to San Francisco. I was planning a reunion with my former student, Jim Birk, now working at Atomics International in Southern California, and with my good friend, Mike Burke, who had left his postdoctoral position at Purdue for a faculty appointment at the University of Arizona.

I was eager to impress them with my newfound knowledge of this exciting city.

But I never anticipated the singular memorable experience the city would offer.

The small saloon in North Beach was just around the corner from the brightly-lit topless joints of Broadway. It could hold perhaps sixty patrons, packed tightly around tiny cocktail tables. One side of the room was a long bar with a dozen stools. At the far end of the bar was a tiny raised stage. Normally a steady procession of topless lovelies would occupy the stage to bump and grind for the patrons.

Mike, Jim, and I knew about the topless lovelies. We had checked the bar out earlier in the week.

But tonight the saloon had been reserved for a private party. A group of young analytical electrochemists—with a taste for science discussions mingled with surfing excursions—had organized this North

Beach outing. Word of the gathering had spread among all the analytical electrochemists attending the A.C.S. meeting. Spouses were welcome.

We arrived early and selected seats at the end of the bar closest to the street exit. As more patrons arrived—nearly all of them recognizable names in the field—we couldn't help but notice a number of ladies in the audience.

"Jesus, do they have any idea what their husbands have dragged them to?" Jim remarked.

"Hey," I replied, "you have to know what's happenin' when you're in *North Beach.*"

"Yeah, but *look* at these ladies," Mike Burke observed. He made a show of surveying the room with his eyes. "Some of them are from the 1930s."

I gazed across the room at one stylishly dressed middle-aged lady, hair dyed and lacquered. "I see one that's gonna drag her husband outside when the bare boobs come out."

"If that's the worst that happens…." Jim speculated.

We had no idea what was in store. Did anybody?

After the joint had been packed full—doors closed and drinks consumed—the loud recorded rock music faded, and one of the party organizers hopped on the stage to grab a microphone. In the glare of the spotlight, our master of ceremonies was forced to endure a number of catcalls and pleas for more comely entertainment.

That was when we first realized we were part of a well juiced rowdy crowd. We joined in with the lusty clamors.

Silencing the crowd by hurling mock insults at the instigators, the M.C. welcomed everyone and thanked the small group of organizers. Then he told us to get ready for a great treat.

That catalyzed a round of cheers and whistles.

"Without further adieu," the M.C. shouted above the noise, "let me introduce *Stephanie!*" He reached behind for the heavy curtain at the back of the stage. He jerked it aside, and Stephanie appeared on stage—with a thundering cheer from the audience.

Stephanie deserved the loud reception. She was a tall, shapely, young lady, with long wavy dark brown hair and creamy white skin, wearing only a pair of polka dot bikini briefs. Responding to the cheers, she raised her arms and struck a provocative pose, wiggling her hips and nudging one knee across the other. The cheers got louder.

Then the M.C. took one of her hands raised high and guided her in a circular tour of the stage. The hips wiggled and the green eyes gazed saucily over her shoulder at several young males in turn. The noise was deafening. The whole scene was all the more incongruous because our M.C. was the same young electrochemist who, earlier that day, had presented a formal scientific paper at the A.C.S. conference.

The M.C. parked Stephanie beside him and attempted to regain the attention of the crowd. "All right. Here's the deal," he shouted into the microphone. The noise subsided.

"Here's what we're going to do: Stephanie here...." He nodded at the smiling young lady, "Stephanie has agreed to let us auction off all the visible parts of her body, from the neck down."

The whistles and cheers started up again, and he raised his hand for quiet. "Once you purchase your section, you get to do this...." He beckoned to an accomplice at the foot of the stage who held up into the spotlight a large metal box about the size of a briefcase. With the box held high over his head so all could see, and with the crowd eerily silent, he popped the lid.

There was an audible gasp, followed a split second later by scattered hoots and cheers. Shortly everyone understood.

The box contained a battery of tiny jars, each with a different colored lid. It was a paint set.

Some of this chipper crowd of electrochemists would become artists this night, practicing their handiwork on the lovely female body occupying center stage.

Calling for quiet once again, the M.C. added, "Now, we know many of you artists out there may be too shy to show off your talent. Therefore, we will entertain bids from anyone on behalf of anyone else."

It took a moment for this statement to settle in. Some of the crowd hooted. A large part became curiously quiet.

"Oh yes," the M.C. continued, "I forgot to mention, we won't be using *paintbrushes.*" That met with a round of lusty howls.

Mike Burke leaned forward on the bar and called to me across Jim Birk. "Gotta hand it to you, S.P. You electrochemists really know how to *party.*"

"Yeah," I responded, gazing back at Mike, "but I hear chromatographers are better with their hands."

Mike's eyes narrowed and he shot back, "Don't even *think* about it."

"Better be careful, S.P.," Jim warned. "More people around here know *you*."

I glanced back at the stage where the bidding was getting underway, then turned to my companions. "Maybe we *all* better lay low."

Mike, Jim, and I looked at one another and silently acknowledged that we would *not* offer bids on the other's behalf. We inched our barstools closer to the exit door and hunkered down.

But there was no way we were leaving.


The auction proceeded in a boisterous yet orderly fashion. The less "choice" body sections were auctioned first. We were entertained by the sight of a number of uninhibited young men first vying for spots and then gingerly smearing colorful designs on parts of thighs, calves, tummy, arms, and back.

Stephanie had obviously done this before. She smiled and bantered with the painters. I was keeping track of the bids. If she kept all the money—and why not—her nightly income would easily top my monthly salary.

But then again she had something more appealing to sell.

Surprisingly, the entire affair took on a matter-of-fact tone—business as usual in North Beach, possibly due to the welcoming, affable behavior of the young lady at the focus. Sounds improbable, I know. You had to be there.

As the more desirable "canvases" came up for auction, there was an interesting lull in the bidding. That was when the "bidding for others" began in earnest. And the beneficiaries were not too happy about it.

It soon became clear that the devious organizers of this debauchery had planned to rope some of the more senior, reserved, and well-known electrochemists into the body-painting orgy—people who wouldn't bid on their own in a million years.

Those that got snagged were good sports—as were, amazingly, the wives who watched warily.

I won't go into the gory details, except for one.

The most memorable artistic effort of the night was rendered by one senior electrochemist, known and respected by everyone there. This man demonstrated to our everlasting delight why he was revered for his shrewdness and wit.

This was the very last painter of the evening. He followed behind a long line of hacks that had done nothing better than smear paint in meaningless designs on charming body parts.

When faced with being "selected" to finger paint the only remaining space—the left boob—this man stoically ascended the stage and stood towering over the smiling Stephanie.

Jim Birk poked me in the ribs. "Hey, S.P., isn't that—?"

"Yeah, that's him. This should be interesting," I replied.

The man put a fist to his chin, leaned back, and gazed for a few moments at the remaining virginal surface. Then a sly grin spread across his face. He picked up the pallet, dipped an index finger into the black jar, and began to paint.

Within seconds it was clear that, contrary to his predecessors, this painter had created a *technically meaningful* sketch. It was a current-voltage plot—a *cyclic voltammogram*. Not only did the diagram frame the perky bosom perfectly, but it was also recognizable to every electrochemist there—and tied historically to the man who *drew* it.

Stephanie had no idea why the crowd went crazy as the sketch emerged.

But, for a room full of electrochemists, there could have been no more perfect symbolism. It was a fitting and memorable exclamation point to a bizarre evening.

# CHAPTER 40

## Flying Home

The United flight out of SFO seemed to climb forever. The *no smoking* and *fasten seat belt* signs remained lit on the Boeing 707. I wanted to get up and stretch. Four hours to Chicago O'Hare and a couple more to fly "Leaky Central" (Lake Central Airline's ancient DC-3) into the Purdue Airport, added to the time spent at the conference, would make this a very long Thursday.

I never could understand why the flight attendants were free to roam the aisles while passengers remained confined. At the moment, however, the view from my aisle seat of the mini-skirted petite blonde stewardess climbing up to retrieve a blanket from the overhead bin ahead was pleasant compensation.

Her eventual departure to deliver the blanket evoked sighs from a number of males in the immediate vicinity.

The disappearance of the distraction allowed time for reflection on the highlights of the A.C.S. meeting I had just attended. My talk about the lab computer work done at Livermore had attracted a big crowd. As Mike Burke had predicted a year earlier, this was *the* hot area of analytical chemistry. Everybody wanted to get computers in their labs. But very few had.

It had been exciting to talk shop with that small group of peers at the meeting who were breaking new ground with lab computers. One of those was Bob Osteryoung from North American Rockwell. I chuckled to myself recalling Bob's astute observation about my data slides. I had used the simpler binary-to-octal printouts. He called me on that. Couldn't blame him. Who could make sense of *octal* numbers?

Don Smith of Northwestern was using a PDP-8/S like Livermore's, and we bemoaned its lack of speed, anticipating the faster generation of integrated circuit lab computers. Hewlett-Packard had already produced one. (Don was envious to learn that we had gotten one for our lab.) Varian and D.E.C. each claimed to have upgraded products. We chuckled at that, considering the vendors' proclivity for promising more than they could deliver.

A satisfied grin appeared on my face as I recalled the considerable buzz at the meeting about my recently announced summer short course on lab computer instrumentation. It would be the first course of its kind. When the announcement appeared in trade journals, I had immediately received a number of applications. Several were from analytical professors. Mike Burke from Arizona had applied, along with professors from Nebraska, Oregon, Georgia Tech, and a host of smaller schools.

My grin suddenly turned to a frown as I succumbed to that perverse game played upon returning from business trips—torturing myself with thoughts of all the work left behind. Contemplating the upcoming summer short course prompted me to ponder the enormous preparation effort. I had given a series of lectures in the fall semester, but now I was locked into a summer course providing "hands-on" *laboratory* experience.

What *chutzpah*, I thought to myself, to even dream of offering a "hands-on" short course before any hardware was in sight. Thank God Hewlett-Packard had come through.

Six graduate students had volunteered to work with the borrowed H.P. computer during the spring semester. But that was only part of the preparation. In addition to teaching machine language programming, we would teach digital electronics and interfacing computers to instruments.

I was the only one in the chemistry department at Purdue who had done this previously. And I had been working with an entirely *different* minicomputer.

I had convinced the department to provide funds to purchase digital interfacing breadboards manufactured by Digital Equipment Corporation. Never mind that the D.E.C. hardware couldn't even *talk* to the Hewlett-Packard hardware. Somehow we had to solve the compatibility problem before June. My grad student, Dave Jones, was working the problem. He was confident. I was concerned.

The loud "bong" that extinguished the *no smoking* and *seat belt* lights brought my thoughts back to my surroundings. I unsnapped my seat belt and started to rise, but stopped when I saw the beverage cart bearing down. I needed a drink.

I peered through a window and noticed darker skies ahead. My watch and my appetite told me it was well after six o'clock central time. I wondered if they would be serving filet mignon like they had on the flight out. Sure, it had been a tiny portion. But it *was* a filet.

That prompted me to reminisce about the wonderful meals in San Francisco the past week. On arrival at SFO on Sunday afternoon, I had shuttled to my hotel, checked in, and then hopped on a cable car to Fisherman's Wharf. There I headed directly to Fisherman's Grotto Number 6 and ordered a bowl of white clam chowder, crab Louis with sourdough bread and butter, and a glass of white wine.

One evening was spent at Scoma's on the Wharf—enjoying *Cioppino* and the company of friends from Livermore.

Finally, as the cute blonde stewardess delivered my gin and tonic, my thoughts—for some reason—returned to that crazy evening in the North Beach nightspot. That first week of April, 1968, would be permanently etched in the memories of those who had been there. I sipped my drink and smiled, replaying the highlights.

Suddenly, my reverie was interrupted by the sound of the P.A. system coming to life. I heard the deep, crisp voice of the captain. "Ladies and gentlemen, pardon the interruption. We've picked up some breaking news and been asked to pass it on to our passengers and crew."

I sat up and looked down the long aisle toward the curtain separating our coach section from the first class passengers. The taller brunette flight attendant stood there, dabbing at her eyes with a tissue.

The captain's amplified voice continued, "We've just learned that the Reverend Martin Luther King was *assassinated* in Memphis about half-an-hour ago, at six o'clock local time. We know that a number of our passengers are connecting to flights to Memphis. We will keep you informed as we learn more.

"I'm sorry to bring you this tragic news," he continued. "United Airlines expresses its condolences to Reverend King's family and all those who grieve with them."

The Captain broke off abruptly, and a stunned silence followed. Slowly, a buzz of chatter arose throughout the aircraft. My thoughts turned inward.

I had never forgotten, nor would I ever forget, the moment that I had learned of John Kennedy's assassination. Now another horrible event would be blazed into my memory—all the more grotesque because of its juxtaposition with the recollections of camaraderie, achievement, and entertainment in San Francisco.

I didn't follow the Reverend King's activities daily; but no one of that era was unaware of his pivotal position in the struggle for civil rights. Most of those that weren't directly involved admired him greatly. The emotions of those directly engaged ranged from adoration to bitter hate. Now, with a single cruel stroke, the hope that King had inspired in millions would instantly turn to despair. I feared for the unrest that was sure to follow.

I wasn't disappointed. Race riots erupted in large cities throughout the country over the following several days, most notably in Washington, D.C., where the riot endured for five days, nearly destroying the inner city. Thousands of federal and National Guard troops were needed to restore order.

It was only April, and already 1968 promised to be a turbulent year.

# CHAPTER 41

## Getting Ready

Almost as one, the seven of us gawked as Sherry jiggled her way to our table with a pitcher of beer in each hand. She flicked a knowing smile. No strangers to The Pub or to the voluptuous middle-aged barmaid, we were getting quick service.

And we needed it.

It was ten o'clock on a Tuesday evening in early June, and the very first offering of the three-week lab computer course would begin the following Sunday. I had put the six grad student lab instructors under enormous pressure all semester.

The least I could do was to treat them to a break for pizza and beer at The Pub.

This week—the last week of preparation—had been ridiculous. The good news was that the spring semester was over and we all had free time. The bad news was that, realistically, we needed to squeeze a *month's* work into the following *four days*.

We were literally working around the clock.

*Last minute, late night preparations. June, 1968. Left to right, S.P., Gerry Kirschner, Dave Jones. [Copyright, S. P. Perone]*

Some of the married instructors had taken a cue from me and sent their wives and kids off somewhere for the month of June. My wife and two daughters were staying in Rockford with her parents for the duration. Any other relationships were being seriously neglected.

Sherry delivered the beer; I told her to run a tab and keep an eye on our pitchers. She winked and said the pizzas would be out in about 10 minutes. Before she could turn away, seven mugs had been filled.

I turned to my crew and hoisted a mug. "Cheers! *Five* more days." I heard some groans. But the beer was cold and sweet.

I looked around the table. Harry Pardue hadn't joined us this night, but all six of the graduate instructors were there. Two of Harry's students, Barry Willis and Gerry James, sat at the opposite end of the table. Dave Jones—my designated lab supervisor—sat to my left. John Patterson, Gerry Kirschner and Mike Fleming—my other students— were scattered around the table.

Already these six grad students had forged a lasting bond. They called themselves the "pioneers." Except for Dave, they had started with zero background and pursued a steep learning curve. They were now the resident "experts," preparing to teach a group of twenty-four seasoned scientists about this new world of laboratory computers—if the preparations didn't kill them first.

I took a moment to glance back at the bar. Sherry was busy shuttling drinks to tables. Indiana had this weird law that patrons couldn't carry their own drinks, assuring jobs for all the Sherrys in the state.

The seventeen-inch black-and-white TV above the bar caught my attention for a moment as a graphic flashed that Bobby Kennedy was ahead of Hubert Humphrey in early California presidential primary results.

Dave Jones brought my attention back to the table. "Hey, Doc, what's the latest from the other vendors?"

Digital Equipment Corp. and Varian Instruments, once they learned we had chosen the new Hewlett-Packard computer to teach our course, had rushed to volunteer scarce copies of their new integrated circuit minicomputers—a D.E.C. PDP-8i and a Varian 620i. "They'll be delivered the last week of the course," I replied. Then I chuckled. "They offered to 'help us out' by keeping their techs here for a week."

"What'd you tell 'em, Doc?" John Patterson queried from the other side of the table. "I mean, we don't know *anything* about those systems."

"We can't let any vendors near our students," Dave interjected. "We'll set aside time for students to play with other systems on their own."

I nodded silently in Dave's direction. He was the acknowledged "take charge" guy in the group—a bit more experienced, with electronics know-how and business savvy.

"You used a PDP-8 out at Livermore, didn't you, Doc?" asked Barry Willis.

"Yeah, the 8/S. I thought we'd base the course on it. But D.E.C. couldn't compete with what H.P. did for us."

Dave chimed in. "Have you guys looked at the lab schedule yet? Eight in the morning to midnight, six days a week. There's no time to work in anything extra."

The class would be brutal. "Total immersion" was the descriptor. Three separate three-hour lab sections per day, eight students and two instructors per section. All students would attend ninety-minute lectures each morning and evening. Supervised open lab time would be available every evening until midnight and all day on Saturdays. "Free time" would be used for reading, writing machine language programs, and bugging instructors for help.

"We'll give 'em one break," I remarked. "Thursday, the second week. We'll party out at the cabin that night."

"The cabin" was a rustic two-bedroom weekend getaway spot in the Lafayette countryside belonging to a friend of one of the electronics techs in the department. With a full kitchen and a spacious family room, it made a great place for parties. We could have it anytime, as long as the electronics techs were invited.

Mentioning a "party" stimulated a flurry of excited chatter about kegs of beer, pizzas, and all-night poker. It wasn't long before the fact was tossed up that it would be a "stag" party.

"I'll bet a couple gals from *Lorraine's* would put on a show for our students," suggested Dave, with a sly smile. He knew about the remarkable flexibility of our "continuing education" budget.

His remark was received with a round of hoots and knuckles pounding on the table.

*Lorraine's* was a rugged saloon in downtown Lafayette that entertained its patrons with "go-go girls"—young ladies that might be called "exotic dancers" these days. We sometimes quaffed beers there instead of at The Pub. The girls weren't topless but were quite fetching and practiced the fine art of pole dancing with great gusto. I had a feeling our course participants would discover *Lorraine's* at some point during the three-week course, with or without the help of their lab instructors.

But I had to quickly squelch the idea of providing "entertainment" at the cabin.

"Hold it!" I protested above the hoots. "You want us to be the lead story for the *Kernel and Journal?*" I used the popular mangled name of the local *Journal and Courier* newspaper.

John Patterson chuckled. "Yeah, great headline, Doc. *Purdue Professor Engages Go-Go Girls to Entertain Old Farts.*"

More hoots.

"*Exactly,*" I shouted. "*No* entertainment. OK? But I need volunteers to organize the party."

I volunteered two of the instructors, and our pizzas arrived, along with two more pitchers of beer. Perhaps it was the food or the late hour, but a number of different simultaneous conversations evolved. I turned to one of my first-year students, Mike Fleming, who had been relatively quiet.

"So, Mike, did you think you'd be 'majoring' in minicomputers when you came to Purdue?" I asked.

"Well, I had a lot of electronics at Oregon State. I thought I'd be working for Pardue, actually. When I saw what you were doing with minicomputers, well...." He shrugged his shoulders.

Mike had offered more than I asked, so I decided to probe further. "Were you thinking about Pardue's instrumentation research?"

"Well, yeah, sort of."

I gave him a quizzical look, but remained silent.

Mike took a breath. "To be honest, Doc, I'm just here to stay out of the draft," he explained.

I frowned. "You want to get a Ph.D., right?"

He shrugged once again and took a sip of beer. There was a serious expression on his face.

I persisted. "What *do* you want, Mike?"

He sighed. "I don't know, Doc. It's a screwed up world. Two of my buddies went to Canada."

I shook my head. "I don't understand the Canada thing. They can't come back."

"So....?" He was staring at me now. Dark eyes glaring behind large plain spectacles. "This war is all *wrong*."

A year earlier I would have rebuked him with my staunch recitation of the "domino theory" espoused by President Lyndon Johnson and the other hawks.

But the "Summer of Love" had changed me. Those who stood up to question authority had changed me. The daily tragedy of Vietnam playing out on the nightly news had changed me. Young men serving and dying in deadly jungle crossfire for a murky cause half-a-world away had changed me.

Johnson had felt the groundswell—deciding not to run for re-election.

I listened to Mike and nodded slowly. "Yeah, I know," I murmured.


By two thirty in the morning everyone had bailed from our return trip to the lab—all but me, that is. I continued struggling with a simple machine language program that would tell the computer to electronically initiate a simulated experiment and then monitor the simulated signal. The whole thing would last only a fraction of a second. This was supposed to be an illustration of rapid digital acquisition of transient data.

But, at this hour, it was more an illustration of sheer *frustration.*

I used the Teletype keyboard to interact with a crude "editor" program to modify my machine language program and punch it out on a paper tape punch module—at the astonishing speed of *150* digitized characters per second. Subsequently, the punched tape could be read into the computer by a high-speed photoreader at 300 characters per second. Then, after executing the program to expose other uncorrected errors, the editing, punching, reading and debugging would begin again.

*Tedious* is too kind a word. But that was the state of the art. Really.

I was tired, but returning home wasn't an option. Fortunately, no one waited for me there. I reached over to the nearby workbench where my tiny transistor radio relayed the late night chatter of a Chicago disk jockey occasionally playing the kind of psychedelic rock I had enjoyed in San Francisco. I cranked up the volume.

Then I returned to version seventeen of my transient data acquisition program.

I scanned the mnemonic printout of the sequence of binary-coded instructions, struggling to figure out why my infallible logic simply didn't work. My fingers were poised over the keyboard, ready to enter the edits, as soon as I could figure out what new logic to apply.

But my line of reasoning was interrupted by a sudden change in the tone of the chatter droning from the radio. I half tuned in. It was some kind of announcement.

> "… just received a bulletin from the Associated Press that Senator Robert Kennedy has been *shot* … shortly after midnight … the Senator had just completed a victory speech … Ambassador Hotel in Los Angeles … decisive victory over Hubert Humphrey in the California Presidential Primary … shot twice in the head … Rosie Grier … grave condition … gunman captured … no official identification … eyewitnesses say the assassin was a Middle Eastern.…"

*Oh my God!* I cried to myself. *Not again.*

It had been every thoughtful person's worst fear—another Kennedy assassination.

For what? For being a Kennedy?

The world had gone mad. John Kennedy—*gone.* Martin Luther King—*gone.* Robert Kennedy—*dying.* Lyndon Johnson—*irrelevant.* Richard Nixon—*presidential?*

Robert Kennedy had his detractors. But so many—including me—saw him as a breath of fresh air in a political stink hole. We longed for another "Camelot" in Washington.

But that would never be. A young assassin by the name—belatedly, if unofficially, relayed over the radio—of Sirhan Sirhan had seen to that.

In shock, I turned off the radio and the H.P. minicomputer. I scooped up my frustrating printouts, turned out the lights, and left the lab. I began the slow walk down the stairs, headed eventually to my car parked in front of the chemistry building—a prime but lonely spot at three in the morning.

I wondered what Kennedy's chances were for survival. The voice on the radio said that he was alive. But what had been left unsaid was foreboding.

I knew there would be a vigil—a pathetic wishful thinking. A national soul-searching over yet another arbitrary, violent act directed at a national figure.

I wanted to join with those that would cry out in anguish.

But I knew that I couldn't.

The debut of the short course was now only four days away.

# Chapter 42
## Pressure Cooker

It was nine o'clock, and Dave Jones slid inside the door to the classroom where I had just finished the evening lecture to the twenty-four short course participants. They had scattered, most of them eager to get more time in the lab.

"It's got to be a paperback, Doc," declared Dave, picking up an eraser to begin cleaning the blackboard.

"What?" I asked. "What are you talking about?" I continued stuffing the lecture transparencies into my notebook but threw him a puzzled glance.

"Our book," he replied, continuing the erasing and slowly moving in my direction.

I paused and turned. The longer strands of his fine blond hair fluttered over clear eyeglasses as he swept the eraser in large circles, sending chalk dust flying. "Aren't you getting ahead of yourself?" I asked.

He stopped and turned. That determined gaze of his snared me. "Look, Doc. The outline is done. We need to pick a publisher."

Dave was alluding to the agreement we had made during our training visit to Hewlett Packard-Palo Alto back in February. We had planned the curriculum for the summer short course and worked up a set of lectures on laboratory computer technology and digital logic. Putting these into a textbook would be groundbreaking.

"Why would you want the book to be a *paperback?*" I asked.

"It's for grad students, right? They can't afford twenty, thirty dollar textbooks."

I shrugged. "I never had anything but hardcover texts."

He waved the eraser toward me, using it as a pointer. "We can set an example, Doc. Let people know it's not about the money."

I had no illusions about getting rich by writing an advanced textbook. "Are you kidding?" I responded. "The market's not that big."

"Whatever. The publisher pockets most of the hardcover price difference, even if they double our cut. That's why Malmstadt and Laitenen and all the other advanced texts are hardcover."

"And maybe because they hold up better? You think?"

"High quality paperback will hold up just as well, at *one-third* the cost to students. I'm telling you, Doc—"

"Christ, Dave. All right. Let's talk to a publisher about it."

He broke into a grin and turned back to erasing the blackboard. "I think we ought to go with McGraw-Hill," he declared.

When the news had first broken about our offering the computer short course, I had been deluged with calls from publishers. Dave and I had talked to some. "Why McGraw-Hill?" I asked.

"They publish the best advanced chem. textbooks."

I chuckled. "Maybe that's why they haven't called me yet."

Dave dropped the book discussion—to be continued later many, many times. Its publication was years away. Dave's wishes would eventually prevail. But at that time, right in the middle of the biggest undertaking of our lives, well, as they say, *when you're up to your ass in alligators ...*

Dave finished erasing the board just as I finished stuffing my lecture notebook. He dropped the eraser in the chalk tray and asked, "You ready to go up to the lab?"

I nodded. "Lead the way."

The computer lab was a converted instrumental analysis facility on the third floor, just down the hallway from my office. It was large enough to accommodate eight students, two Hewlett-Packard minicomputer systems, two Digital Equipment Corporation Logic Labs, and two instructors.

Students worked in pairs on each piece of equipment. In the evening, the lab was open to all from nine to midnight. Hardware access was on a sign-up basis. At least two instructors were always available. We had purchased two spare Teletypes for students to use at any time to prepare punched tapes of their test programs.

On this Wednesday evening—halfway through the course—the lab was humming with activity. Of the twenty-four participants, over half of them were there. Most were busy either de-bugging programs or testing digital logic circuits. The rest were busy searching for errors in program scripts or buttonholing lab instructors.

The participants were an impressive bunch. Half were university science professors from all parts of the country, selected from a much larger number that had applied to us for National Science Foundation support. The others were paid for by and represented major chemical or pharmaceutical companies from around the world.

One of the university participants that had applied and been accepted was my good friend, Mike Burke, who was now an assistant professor of analytical chemistry at the University of Arizona. Mike was working in the lab that evening, and, of course, I had to give him a hard time.

I caught Mike sitting in front of the large rolling cart constructed for the H.P. 2116A computer system. The cart allowed us to wheel the computer between the teaching lab and the lecture room. It also allowed research groups to roll it from lab to lab.

Mike was loading a punched paper tape into the high-speed photoreader. It wasn't a very long tape.

"What kind of monster program is that?" I teased.

*Mike Burke, Purdue, summer, 1968.*
*[Copyright, S. P. Perone]*

"Can't you read binary code yet, S.P.?" he quipped, without looking up.

His lab partner, Ed Herlicska, from Varian Aerograph in Walnut Creek, CA, looking over Mike's shoulder, turned to me and grinned. "Dr. Perone, are you here to crack the whip?"

"I just enjoy giving Burke a hard time," I replied, winking.

Ed shook his head. "I haven't worked this hard in a long time."

Mike finished re-spooling his paper tape and looked up at me with a wry smile. "What sadistic lunatic made up this schedule?"

"Yes," Ed added, "a lab and two lectures a day. More lab until midnight. Writing and de-bugging programs in between. When do we sleep?"

"We're planning to put cots in the lab next week."

Eyebrows raised, followed by chuckles.

Dave Jones spoke up. "Seriously, next week you'll be doing both programming *and* digital logic—and wishing for the good old days."

"We're giving you a break tomorrow night," I threw in. "Big party out at the cabin."

"Entertainment?" asked Mike.

"I don't know." I turned to Dave. "Here's the organizer."

Dave shook his head. "Naw, just pizza, beer, music, and a couple of big card tables. A chance for everybody to blow off steam."

Ed nodded and said, "Yeah, we complain about the pace of the work, but, really, we are learning one hell of a lot. What amazes me is the *instructors*."

"Yeah," added Mike, "I see Dave here from eight until midnight every day. The lab instructors do two or three shifts. Then we bug them all day long with questions."

"I hear there's been some after-hours work, too," I remarked, "at The Pub and Lorraine's."

Ed snickered. "We took pity on your guys and treated them a couple nights."

"I thought I saw some bloodshot eyeballs this morning."

Mike chuckled and turned back to the computer. "As much as I enjoy this conversation, I've got work to do," he declared. "Let's see if the tenth de-bugging is the charm."

Dave and I left the pair and moved over to where two others were working on a digital logic lab station. Charlie Wilkins was an assistant professor of organic chemistry from the University of Nebraska, and Chuck Klopfenstein was laboratory director for the chemistry department at the University of Oregon. Long-time friends, they had decided to apply to us for NSF-supported participation in the summer course.

I had learned that they were already well along the way toward implementing minicomputers in their respective labs. They were already conversant with the technology but needed the short course to hone their skills and, also, to learn what they could about our educational approach.

"Hey, Sam," called Wilkins as we approached. "We've got some questions about these logic labs."

"Well, you're in luck," I replied. "The expert is right here." I pointed to Dave Jones at my side.

"What's the problem?" Dave asked.

Klopfenstein replied, "They aren't compatible with Hewlett-Packard computers, are they?"

"If you're talking about the minus-three-volt logic levels, that's right," said Dave. "But

*Chuck Klopfenstein (L) and Charlie Wilkins (R), Purdue, summer 1968. [Copyright, S. P. Perone]*

we'll be using converter cards when we interface to H.P.'s twelve-volt logic."

"Yeah," said Wilkins, "but isn't there also a difference between pulse- and edge-logic?"

"Converter cards take care of that, too."

"Don't timing discrepancies creep in between pulse- and edge-triggered logic?" asked Klopfenstein.

As he often did, Dave tossed his head to one side and showed a clenched-teeth grin for a moment before spewing an authoritative reply. "You're right. But it amounts to less than a microsecond. Not a problem for anything we're doing here."

Wilkins turned to me. "Why did you choose the D.E.C. Logic Labs?"

I turned my gaze to the turquoise blue logic lab at his side. The D.E.C. systems were designed for teaching—seventeen inches wide by twenty-four inches tall, holding up to five plug-in panels. Students could create a large number of digital circuits by using patch cords to connect flip-flops, logic gates, counters, clocks, indicator lights, and switches. All circuit boards were constructed with discrete components—transistors, diodes, resistors, etc.

"It's the only viable logic lab out there," I replied. "We're using it for both teaching and research applications."

"Did you think about using D.E.C. *computers* for this course?" Wilkins asked. "Isn't that what you used at Livermore?"

"Sure," I replied, "but D.E.C. couldn't give us a long-term loaner like H.P. did."

Klopfenstein snickered. "I'll bet D.E.C. would like to re-think that one."

"Yeah," Wilkins added, "H.P.'s getting lots of free publicity. I'll bet a lot of these people...." He swept a hand toward others in the room. "I'll bet they'll end up buying H.P. computers."

I shrugged. "We gave D.E.C. their chance."

Dave added, "Yeah. Now they're begging to bring in their computers. We'll have a PDP-8i or 8/S here for the end of the course."

"What about the Varian computer?" asked Wilkins. "That's what we're getting at Nebraska and Oregon."

"We're going to have one of theirs, too—the 620i."

Klopfenstein whistled. "How did you manage that? We've been trying to get them to loan us a demo. No luck."

"They came to *us,*" Dave declared. "Probably didn't hurt that Jon Amy knows all those guys at Varian. They'll set them up for you guys to *use.*"

"What does H.P. think about their competitors showing up?" asked Wilkins.

"H.P. knows they're in the best spot," Dave replied. "They also know we aren't allowing *any* reps. Not even H.P.'s."

After making the rounds of all the workers in the lab, Dave cut out for home, and I found myself joining Mike Burke for a beer down at The Pub.

Sherry took our orders, and Mike lit up a cigarette. Blowing away that first puff of smoke, he looked at me out of the corner of his eye and asked, "How do you think things are going?"

"You tell me."

Still looking sideways at me, he said, "Don't get a swelled head, S.P., but I'm blown away. Remember, I was here a year ago. I can't believe you put this whole thing together since then."

"Did you forget? You're the one who told me to go to Livermore and bring it back to Purdue."

He chuckled. "Yeah, but I didn't think you'd actually do it."

"Neither did I. But give a lot of credit to the guys—Dave, John Patterson, and the others. Harry jumped in to pick up the digital logic and volunteered two of his best students. They all worked their butts off for the past six months."

"I guarantee the instrument companies will be breaking down the doors to hire your teaching assistants. Ed Herlicska is already doing some recruiting for Varian."

"Jon Amy agrees with you. Without Jon, by the way, none of this would have happened. He got H.P. to come through for us."

Mike wagged his head. "And you got NSF to fund the course. First try. How did that happen?"

"A couple years ago I helped Harry with a NSF short course proposal. So I knew the drill."

Sherry delivered two mugs of beer, and Mike took a moment to flick the ashes off his cigarette before asking, "How are you and Harry getting along?"

I made a face. "What are you getting at?"

"Your course kind of supersedes his electronics short course, doesn't it?"

"Maybe. But Harry's glad to be part of the computer course. He'll probably put together something similar eventually for clinical chemists—maybe with NIH support."

"A summer course?"

I shrugged. "Ask him. He's inviting Phil Hicks—who computerized the Wisconsin University Hospital Lab—to be one of our speakers at the end of the course. I think Harry's leaning that way."

Mike took a sip of beer and set the mug down with a slow, deliberate motion. "S.P., you're avoiding my question. Any hard feelings between you two?"

It was my turn to sample the beer for a moment. "Look, Mike," I replied finally, "Harry and I are fine. When I came to Purdue, I thought his one-year head start would give him the edge. Buck took me aside and explained that I would actually *benefit* from Harry. He was dead right about that. Harry set examples for me to follow.

"Buck also predicted that *Harry* would benefit by needing to stay ahead of *me*. This computer business is making a big splash for me right now. But it will prompt Harry to do something just as exciting. It's a win-win."

Nodding his head slowly, Mike said, "I get it. As usual, Buck is right." Then, after picking up his smoldering cigarette for another drag, he asked, "What would you think if I put together this same course at Arizona?"

"A summer course?"

"No, no, God, no!" He laughed. "I'm thinking of a graduate lab course—like the one you're getting on the books here."

Mike was alluding to the new course proposal I had gotten approved for Chem. 626, a one-semester graduate lab course on computer instrumentation.

"What do the other analytical faculty at Arizona think?" I asked.

He shrugged. "I haven't really talked to them. I'm not sure they'll be as supportive as *your* colleagues."

I shot him a puzzled glance and wagged my head. "Doesn't matter. A year from now, all your faculty will realize that computers are taking over the labs."

Mike made a face. "You don't know these guys." He leaned forward. "How about you come down to Tucson and give a talk next year?"

"You think I might help?"

He nodded. "You know how it is. They'll listen to outsiders. Lab computers are exploding, and you'll be the guru. People will be breaking down your door for advice."

Mike didn't know it then, but he had just forecast the next decade of my life.

# PART 6

# Things We Did Last Summer

# CHAPTER 43

## Computers Anyone?

The Summer Computer Course was offered at Purdue every year from 1968 to 1974. It was supported by the National Science Foundation for all but the last two summers. NSF paid for twelve university faculty participants the first year and for twenty-four each subsequent year. Government and industry scientists, who paid their way, filled the additional slots.

It was a three-week course, but we condensed it to two weeks during the last two summers to accommodate predominately non-academic participants. The equivalent one-semester

graduate-level course was also offered every year. It is still on the books at Purdue—updated, of course, with current technology and content.

From the outset, we were also exploring the introduction of computer technology into undergraduate courses. The National Science Foundation generously supported this effort, too.

The development of the graduate and undergraduate courses was documented in two seminal papers[1] in the *Journal of Chemical Education*. Two subsequent textbooks[2] were written. The graduate textbook (Perone and Jones, 1973) was the first of its kind and was used for many years at a number of universities. Incredibly, some workers still refer to the dated yet often relevant material in the book.

The undergraduate textbook (Wilkins, et al, 1975) was funded by the National Science Foundation, and three of the four other co-authors either worked with me at Purdue or attended our summer short course. Professor Charlie Wilkins (then at the University of Nebraska) was the editor.

Well over 200 professional scientists passed through the summer short course during the seven years it was offered at Purdue. Enduring relationships were formed. Nearly two dozen graduate students served as laboratory instructors over that period. The lecturers, besides me, included Harry Pardue, Dave Jones and Stuart Cram, then from the University of Florida.

Each year we invited outside speakers at the end of the course. One day was devoted to their lectures. They also attended our course "banquet," usually held at a rustic compound called "The Trails" that specialized in grilled steaks and baked potatoes. After three weeks of "total immersion," everyone was ready for a good time; and the lab instructors never failed to put on a great show with hilarious candid slides and gag gifts for "worthy" participants.

We attracted visiting speakers working at the cutting edge of computer instrumentation. Jack Frazer and Roger Anderson from Lawrence Livermore Lab were invited several times. Others included Charlie Reilly from the University of North Carolina and Phil Hicks from the University of Wisconsin Hospital. One year we were joined by Fred Findeis—the NSF program manager for analytical chemistry.

---

[1]  S. P. Perone, "A Laboratory Course on Digital Computers in Chemical Instrumentation," *J. Chem. Educ.*, **47**, 105 (1970); and S. P. Perone and J. F. Eagleston, "Introduction of Digital Computers into the Undergraduate Laboratory," *J. Chem. Educ.*, **48**, 317 (1971).

[2]  Sam P. Perone, David O. Jones, "Digital Computers in Scientific Instrumentation," McGraw-Hill, New York, 1973; Charles L. Wilkins, Sam P. Perone, Charles E. Klopfenstein, Robert C. Williams, and Donald E. Jones, "Digital Laboratory Electronics and Laboratory Computer Experiments," Plenum Press, New York, 1975.

*Trails banquet, 1969 summer course. Inset, Left to right: Dave Jones; Harry*
*Pardue; Roger Anderson (Invited speaker, Livermore Lab); Fred Findeis*
*(Guest, National Science Foundation). [Copyright, S. P. Perone]*

Running the summer courses through the university's conference
center was a huge asset. The guidelines for managing funds from tuition-
paying participants were incredibly flexible compared to NSF funds.
Not surprisingly, we exercised newfound expensive tastes in equipment,
course banquets and visiting speakers.

*Trails banquet, 1969 summer course. Inset, Left to right: Buck Rogers,*
*Harley Griffith (conference coordinator); S.P.; Harry Pardue; Roger*
*Anderson (Invited speaker, Livermore Lab). [Copyright, S. P. Perone]*

*Trails banquet, 1970 summer course. Above inset, Left to right: Fred Lytle (Guest, Purdue Asst. Professor, Jack Frazer, Invited Speaker, Livermore Lab; Gary Hieftje (Indiana U. Asst. Professor, course participant). Below inset: Jon Amy, in a rare photo. [Copyright, S. P. Perone]*

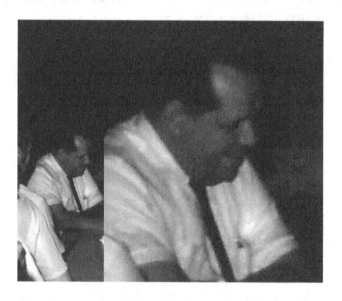

This period at Purdue—when we were at the cutting edge of computer instrumentation for research and education—provided a rich source of legendary events, reflecting the unique scientific and cultural history of the times.

Frankly, many experiences described in the ensuing chapters couldn't have happened anywhere else.

# Chapter 44

## Selected Photos from Summer Computer Course, 1968 – 1974

*Announcement mailer for first summer computer course, 1968.*
*[Source: Perone Archives]*

# SCIENCE LINE

PURDUE UNIVERSITY
VOL. 4, NO. 1   FEBRUARY, 1969

### REPLACES MAN IN THE MIDDLE
## Computer Scheme In Chemistry Speeds Research, Spawns Courses

HOW MANY TIMES have you heard, "He's only human," as an alibi for a costly error? Nowhere can errors be more devastating to productivity than in the research laboratory, where hours -- even years -- of work have often been wiped out by a human error.

This is not to say that machines don't make mistakes, but removing the human element from routine which can be both boring and painfully time-consuming has been found to promote efficiency in the lab.

Although there's nothing new in use of computers to optimize efficiency, a team of Purdue chemists has been exploring the potential of portable, on-line digital computers to the lab with gratifying results.

Their work has not only brought dividends in speed and accuracy in their own experiments, but also introduced a new, integral force in both undergraduate and graduate chemistry education at Purdue.

And produced an incentive short course unlike any other in the United States to provide practicing chemists in Indiana and the rest of the country with know-how vital to performing chemical analyses with unparalleled efficiency.

TWO YEARS AGO Prof. Sam Perone of the Purdue Chemistry Department was on leave of absence at the Lawrence Radiation Laboratory, Livermore, Calif., to work on

the application of digital computers to automated electro-analysis. For this work he was able to incorporate a small, portable digital computer into an on-line system. That is, have the computer in direct communication with the experiment from start to finish, with electronic instrumentation instead of an operator as the link between the computer and experiment.

This would contrast with an off-line approach, which would rely on an operator to be the go-between.

BACK AT PURDUE, Perone talked to associates in analytical chemistry, notably Profs. L. B. Rogers, Dale Margerum and Harry Pardue, about ways of applying the digital computer to their work.

"We could see," says Perone, "that computers would be the heart of chemical instrumentation of the future. Recognizing this, we looked for ways to inject it into our research and work it into our curriculum."

The use of digital computers in the laboratory has been growing fantastically. Perone notes, for several reasons. Modern microtechnology is producing more compact, less expensive, portable computers; automation of routine chemical experiments is faster and more reliable than is human performance in such work; in lab use of the smaller computers is less expensive and provides answers more quickly

rapidly enough to allow modification of experiments for optimized measurements.

STILL MORE EXCITING, believes Perone, is the prospect of "closed loop" operations where the on-line digital computer can instantaneously feed back control information directly to an experiment, bypassing the operator and his relatively small-like pace. Such systems allow making experimental measurements which are impossible when a human is controlling the experiment.

While scientists were becoming increasingly interested in developing capability to use portable digital on-line computers in the labs, Perone and his associates realized that more than interest and funds would be required to put the technique into practice.

"Actually," says Perone, "the task is a forbidding one for most scientists." For one thing, the digital computer and digital instrumentation have a basis unfamiliar to the scientist; while he's accustomed to working with instruments that where information is provided in a continuous, or analog, format, digital computers are basically incompatible with analog information.

All information into and out of the digital computer must be in discrete -- discontinuous -- packets.

Another reason why on-line computer technology is difficult for scientists to grasp initially is that the computer programming must be done, for the most part, in the machine's "language," a group of binary coded instructions which tell the computer to perform the simple, logical and arithmetical functions it can do.

A typical program might include several thousand individual instructions for computer operations; any single incorrect instruction can wipe out the entire operation.

"This type of programming," observes Perone, "appears overwhelming to most scientists," who are accustomed to using what are regarded as the higher-level computer languages. With these languages -- FORTRAN is one of them -- single algebraic statements may generate hundreds or even thousands of machine-language instructions, thus simplifying programming considerably.

(FORTRAN, for formula translation, translates into computer language statements expressed in a format similar to algebraic equations.)

Unfortunately, the Purdue chemist points out, when using computers on-line, there are no higher-level languages yet developed to communicate effectively with experiments. So the scientist must learn to use the machine's language.

Because Perone recognized this formidable stumbling block to scientists he decided to develop a short course designed to provide practicing scientists -- principally chemists -- with a background sufficient to utilize on-line, digital computer technology in their work. He and Professor Pardue then put together such a course.

The inaugural course, "Digital Computers in Chemical Instrumentation," was run last June, a three-week, intensive program which the National Science Foundation financed partially by providing support for academic participants. The NSF also provided funds for a computer and much of the peripheral equipment that will be used in future courses.

Half of the 24 participants were college or university professors; the others were from industrial or government laboratories. They came from 16 states, from Oregon to Georgia, and, for one participant, from Switzerland.

The basic course philosophy was to allow participants to work with computers and associated instrumentation with their own hands in a concentrated program during which progressively more complex computer manipulations would be developed.

The equipment made available for the participants' exclusive use included two Hewlett-Packard 2116 A computers, one Hewlett-Packard 2115 A computer, four Digital Equipment Corporation digital logic laboratories, and a large variety of peripheral equipment such as teletypes, oscilloscopes, analog-to-digital converters and interface electronics.

The course was structured so that at the end of three weeks the participants would be designing and interfacing -- establishing an electronic communications link for -- their own complete on-line computer system.

And it worked out that way.

"INTENSIVE" WASN'T JUST A LABEL. This is how it went: The first day, a Sunday, was devoted to orientation and the first lab lecture. The next 13 weekdays comprised a rigorous schedule of laboratories, formal lectures, lab lectures and open lab time. Lectures were from 8 a.m. and 9 p.m. daily. In addition, the laboratories were open and supervised from 9 p.m. to midnight each evening so those who wished might work ahead, catch up or simply have an informal discussion with some of the staff. Labs also were open and supervised Saturdays from 8 a.m. to 5 p.m.

*Jones, Perone and Pardue (from left) at Hewlett-Packard 2115 computer, typical of the portable, digital computers used in the Purdue chemistry lab studies and courses.*

---

*Purdue's School of Science Publication, Science Line, devoted an issue in February, 1969, featuring the ground-breaking computer instrumentation education and research programs in Purdue's chemistry department. [Source: Perone Archives]*

*Clockwise from upper left: Bill Gutknecht (Perone grad Student) setting up demo with H.P. 2116A system (1969); , Ed Herlicska, (1968 course participant from Varian Aerograph in Walnut Creek, CA.) debugging a program; John Patterson (Perone grad student), 1968 demo with the H.P. 2116A system; Jerry Fitzgerald (1968 participant, assistant professor, Seton Hall University) working with D.E.C. Logic Lab; Dave Jones, (Perone grad student), 1968 demo of logic interface; Gerry Kirschner (Perone grad student), 1969 lab preparation. [Copyright, S. P. Perone]*

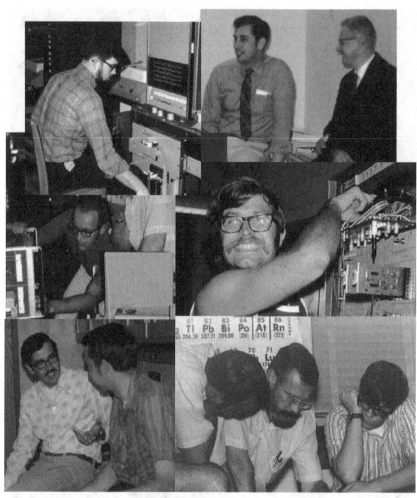

*Clockwise from upper left: Stan Deming (Pardue grad student), 1969 work with H.P. 2116A system; S.P. and Roger Anderson (visiting speaker, Livermore Lab), 1969 summer course; John Zipper (Perone grad student) repairing H.P. 2115A interface logic, 1972; Gordon Woolbert, left, and Keith Dahnke, right, (Perone grad students) working with 1971 summer course participant; Jim "J.R." Birk, talking programming with another 1973 summer course participant; Gary Hieftje (1970 participant, assistant professor, Indiana University) entering a program into the H.P. 2115A system. [Copyright, S. P. Perone]*

1968 Summer Course Participants and Instructors. [Copyright, S. P. Perone]

1973 Summer Course Instructors. Left to Right, Top: Marty Pichler, Quent Thomas, Frank Pater, Terry Berger, Rick Baldwin, Keith Dahnke (all lab instructors and Perone grad students). Bottom: Stu Cram (visiting lecturer, professor of chemistry, Univ. of Florida); S.P., director. [Copyright, S. P. Perone]

# CHAPTER 45

## Computer Games

It was February, 1968. Dave Jones and I were aboard an American Airlines Boeing 707 from Indianapolis to San Francisco. Ahead of us was a two-week course at Hewlett-Packard Palo Alto on programming their new integrated circuit minicomputer, the HP 2116A. An identical long-term loaner system that Jon Amy had arranged for us would show up at Purdue shortly after and would be the foundation of our first summer short course.

As a second year grad student, Dave had already proven himself invaluable in planning for the digital electronics part of the course. He would be my lead lab instructor. However, Dave hadn't done any minicomputer programming, so it was necessary that he accompany me to the Palo Alto course.

As we passed over Lake Tahoe and the surrounding snow-capped Sierras, Dave and I were in the middle of a heated conversation.

"We've only seen the beginning," said Dave. "The 2116A will be replaced by something half its size in a year. In five years it'll be a computer on a chip."

"What are you saying? We're wasting our time?"

"No, the programming and interfacing won't change, but—"

"You're still pushing hardware over software?"

"Naturally. You're designing a course around a programmable minicomputer. But eventually we'll have dedicated cheap, compact *micro*computers—built into each instrument."

"Wait a minute. Yesterday you said you could replace programmable minicomputers with hard-wired instrumentation. Which is it?"

"With today's technology, I'd go hard-wired—combining digital and analog electronics to do whatever the minicomputer does."

"Give me an example."

Dave sighed impatiently and turned to gaze out the window. Looking past him I saw, too, the lush February green of Northern California valleys. "What a difference from my visit last summer," I remarked. "Everything was golden brown."

"Yeah, two or three months of rain fixed that." He turned away from the window and added, "Before we get to San Francisco I want to answer your question."

I nodded.

"Remember what you said about computer instrumentation research you considered worthy of a Ph.D. project?"

"Sure." I nodded. "It can't be simple automation. It has to be something that couldn't be done any other way—a new kind of measurement principle with intelligent computer control."

"You've already begun working on something, right?"

I hunched my shoulders. "As much as I can without a computer."

"Let's go over it. You want to run fast-sweep voltammetry with the computer evaluating data in real time and optimizing the experiment, while it's *running*."

"That's right. The computer adjusts the sweep rate in real time to minimize interferences."

"Right. And it's impossible to know in advance how to optimize the experiment? The computer's real-time computations are crucial?"

"That's the idea."

"What kind of time scale?"

"Collecting data every millisecond means the computer has to complete calculations and decisions in microseconds."

"You mean, once the operator sets evaluation criteria, the computer runs the experiment interactively, on its own?"

"Exactly."

"OK. I'll bet you I can put together a hard-wired system to do the same things, except it'll be compact and inexpensive."

"Why is that important?"

"Christ, Doc. Minicomputers are too expensive to dedicate to *one* instrument."

"Do you think minicomputers will be used mainly to develop techniques that are translated into hardware?"

"Yes. Until we have microcomputers. But I think we can demonstrate hard-wired instrumentation that's just as sophisticated as the programmable minicomputer."

"You're talking about *my* project—interrupted-sweep voltammetry—aren't you?"

He nodded and shot me a sly grin. "*Our* project. You develop the software approach. I'll develop the *hard-wired* system."

I kicked the thought around for a while. "You're thinking—?"

"Ph.D. project." He gave me a questioning glance and waited.

"Hmmm. I don't know. Where's the novelty?"

"No one's done anything like this before—not with software, not with hardware."

"Can't argue with that. But what's novel about the hardware once the programmed solution is done?"

"Are you kidding? State-of-the-art integrated circuit electronics, creating an intelligently interactive instrument? No one's done that yet. We'd be the first—with both software *and* hardware."

I looked past Dave through the window. The sun was low in the west and the lighted skyline of San Francisco appeared in the distance. It was a stunning sight—one appropriate to the research vision he had just described.

Yet neither of us could envision that we would spend the next few years leading a field that was exploding like a supernova. We had hitched a seat on a bolt of lightning, and it would be a wild ride. Dozens of publications would chronicle our investigations—each one fitting the criterion of a novel measurement principle unattainable without computer interaction.

For several years during the late sixties and early seventies, Dave and I and my students would become recognized leaders in the most exciting technology of the day.

We didn't know it then, but within another year, Hewlett-Packard facilities that were teaching us now would then be inviting us to present our computer instrumentation course to *them*.

# CHAPTER 46

## Welcome Additions

One immediate benefit of the summer short courses was funding for several months of a dedicated secretary's time. Each of my research grants also provided for a part-time secretary. So, naturally, I parlayed this into one full-time secretary, year round.

The department sent me Judy—a young lady with a B.A. degree working temporarily as a secretary while her husband finished graduate school. Judy definitely had the experience and smarts to deal with getting our first summer course underway. I gladly welcomed her to the group.

Big problem was finding space.

I certainly didn't want to carve anything out of my precious research space. My office was barely big enough for me. And I didn't like the department's idea of locating my secretary within the departmental pool—where her time would undoubtedly be pilfered away.

This problem would take some creativity.

Back in prehistoric times—when the original Purdue Chemistry building was designed—chemistry professors wanted personal laboratories. Most faculty offices were designed so the occupant could duck in and out of an adjacent lab. My corner space was like that—with lots of doors. Inside my office was a solid door that opened into the corner lab. From the corridor, a door opened into a small entryway that led to two more doors—one left into the corner lab and one straight ahead into my office. Translucent mottled glass panes filled the upper half of each of these three outer doors.

The least amenable of all this space was the tiny entryway, with its three doorways and a wire-caged power distribution panel. Naturally, that's where we found space for a secretary's desk.

I'll never forget the look on Judy's face after our interview when I pointed out her "office space."

Her nose crinkled. "You're kidding me, right?"

I gave her a wagging-head grin. "I'm afraid not."

She turned her head to re-examine the space. The desk and chair hadn't been installed yet. "Can they take out the cage?"

I shook my head again. "You want to change your mind?"

"If they put the desk and chair here...." She gestured toward the L-shaped partition between my office and the corridor door. "Will it fit?"

I nodded. "Already checked it out."

"Are you sure?" She shot me a skeptical glance.

"Everything works, that is, unless you're claustrophobic."

She laughed. "This set up would make a *gopher* claustrophobic."

The corners of my mouth turned down. "I'm not sure what you're telling me."

She sighed. "I'm saying, let's give it a try."

I brightened up. "Great! They'll have it set up for you to start on Monday."

It did work, after a fashion. That is to say, Judy made it work. She got comfortable with the fact that her workspace partially blocked my office doorway. I got comfortable with an attractive young brunette brightening up the pathway.

It wasn't a luxury office, but Judy was the envy of other secretaries in the department. She answered to only *one* boss. The others answered to at least four at a time. They knew only too well the odds of getting at least one jerk out of any four professors.

Between summer course preparations, publications, proposals and correspondence, I kept Judy very busy. And that was just fine with her. She stayed with me for nearly two years, leaving after her husband finished his degree. During that time she was responsible for setting up everything for the summer short courses—from lecture materials to applicant screening procedures—that we would use for years.

Connie came to work for me shortly before I was to leave on my first sabbatical, spring semester, 1970. A pretty, young blonde, she was barely out of high school and recently engaged to a vet school student. Like Judy before her, she planned to work for me until her future husband finished school.

She had no idea what she was getting into.

Judy and Connie barely overlapped, and poor Connie had to rely on me for guidance. Basically, I dropped the short course files in her lap and wished her luck as I flew out the door on my way to a one-semester sabbatical at Lawrence Livermore Lab.

I did arrange to fly back to Lafayette for a few days during the middle of the semester to put finishing touches on acceptance letters and such. Fortunately, Dave Jones had finished his Ph.D. the previous semester and was now working for me as a postdoc. So he virtually managed the short course preparations that year.

Judy was a very serious, hardworking, no-nonsense office manager. She was friendly and worked well with everyone in the group, but she was never "one of the guys." She had a husband and a life.

Connie was just as bright, efficient and friendly as Judy, but not so good at fending off the guys. Where Judy had managed to keep that tiny space we called a "secretary's office" free and clear, Connie frequently found one or more of my students hovering. Don't get me wrong, she didn't seek attention, but the guys clearly made her the social hub of the group.

Despite these distractions, Connie remained amazingly efficient. I never had a complaint—even when she became a co-conspirator in a number of memorable incidents....

# CHAPTER 47

## Pranks, Incorporated

I ran down the hall from the short course computer lab to pick up my lecture notes. Two of the lab instructors were wheeling one of the computer systems down to the lecture room. They would have to use the freight elevator to move it from the third to the first floor.

I found Connie at her desk and pulled out my keys to duck into my office. Surprisingly, she turned and said, "Dr. Perone, here's your lecture notebook."

Sure enough, on her desk was the big black notebook filled with transparencies I would use. She handed it to me and explained, "You've been cutting it close the past two days, so I thought...."

I smiled, thanked her, and then whipped around to sprint down the corner stairway. I *was* running late.

Connie Dowty, Purdue, 1972.
*[Copyright, S. P. Perone]*

After the lecture, I meandered through the computer lab, harassing some of the students. Finally, I left the lab and headed for my office just down the hall.

I could see that the outer door was closed. Not surprising, as Connie was probably away at lunch. She always locked the outer door when neither of us was there.

I got out my key to open the outer door. I pushed the door open, walked in, and found to my surprise that Connie was seated there. With a sack lunch spread out neatly on the desk, she sat with her legs crossed, reading a novel. She looked up and gave me a cheery, "Hi, Dr. Perone."

But I didn't respond. I just stopped and stared at the scene behind her. There, where my office door should have been, was a *brick wall*.

Standing there with my mouth agape, I heard sounds behind me. Turning my head around, I saw half my research group and, further down the hall, a number of the short course students enjoying my reaction to a well-advertised prank.

I put on a silly grin. "Anybody seen my office?"

I was greeted with a chorus of hoots and a smattering of applause, obviously not for me but for the unnamed perpetrators of this elegant trick.

I turned to Connie. "Who did this?"

She shrugged. "Did what?"

"You didn't notice?"

She made a show of turning her head toward the brick wall and brought a hand to her mouth in faux astonishment. "Oh my goodness!"

"So, this wall just appeared out of thin air, right?"

She flashed her most innocent smile. "I guess."

Some professors had joined the crowd in the hall. One of my students, John Zipper, stepped forward from the crowd and observed, "Well, Doc, looks like you're gonna need a different way in."

He was right about that. On closer examination, the "brick wall" was an elegant façade. Yet that veneer of brick certainly looked real. It was solidly in place, neatly trimmed, and stretched along the entire length of wall where my office should have been.

John led me to the back of the corner lab. We moved a cabinet, and I opened the never-before-used-by-me back door to my office. I breathed a sigh of relief at finding everything else intact.

I continued to enter and exit my office that way for a couple days while the entire department had a chance to admire the handiwork. Then the "brick wall" mysteriously disappeared.

No one ever took credit for that prank, at least not to me.

Many other elegant pranks were concocted by my students to let off steam each year during the intensely demanding short course. One year I arrived in the morning to find my office completely filled with balloons.

*Balloon prank, summer, 1972. (Note 4:30 a.m. on wall clock, when students completed job.) [Copyright, S. P. Perone]*

On another occasion, they used their machine programming skills to "booby-trap" the computer system on wheels that I used for lecture demos. After loading a program to acquire and plot data from a transient signal on a large digital display screen, I triggered the signal and turned to explain what was happening.

Amused faces and scattered chuckles greeted me. I turned to look at the display. The signal I saw unfolding slowly was not the familiar pattern of the exponential decay. The class recognized the pattern before I did. What appeared instead of the pulse decay was a design unfolding as though being drawn by hand. In fact, it *was* a hand—or more accurately the back of a clenched fist—with the middle finger *extended*.

I don't know how long it took to develop the "Bird" program. Considering the crude machine language tools we had to use in those days, it must have taken many, many hours. In this case, John Zipper proudly took the blame. The Bird program would mysteriously infiltrate the software of many unsuspecting short course students over the years. You never knew when it might strike.

Except for the Bird program, I never knew for sure who was responsible for any prank. But there was a lot of circumstantial evidence that Connie was a willing accomplice during the three years she worked for me. She knew my schedule, had the keys, etc., etc.

And the first prank was my own fault anyway.

It was the spring semester of 1970. I was on sabbatical at Livermore Lab. Connie and Dave Jones were whipping the short course preparations into shape. Periodically, I sent packages back to Purdue with little samplings from San Francisco—like Ghirardelli chocolate, Chinatown trinkets, and other souvenirs.

One Sunday, during a family excursion to Fisherman's Wharf, we visited Cost Plus Imports—a favorite shopping spot for all of us. On this day I was drawn to one particular item. The more I looked at it the more I thought it would be the perfect decoration for the computer lab.

It was less than twenty dollars, so I bought it. It would be as large as a billboard when installed. In fact it *was* a billboard—a huge poster that came neatly folded into a manageable package.

I sent the package to Connie with a note to have Dave Jones put it up in the computer lab for the summer short course.

I never anticipated what would happen next.


The following week I received my usual mailing containing a set of progress reports. Enclosed in the mailing was an envelope filled with photos. I ripped open the envelope and stared in disbelief at the series of photos. The first was a simple picture of our home—uninhabited for the semester—taken from the front right. It should have captured only the one-and-a-half story high white siding. Instead the image that popped out was as colorful as a billboard!

That's exactly what it had become. I had sent my group a twelve-by-twenty-four foot Cutty Sark scotch whiskey billboard poster, and, of course, they had to put it up on the side of our house.

*John Zipper, inspecting billboard on our Lafayette home.*
*Spring, 1970. [Copyright, S. P. Perone]*

The photos showed the step by step installation of the poster, in all its colorful glory—the iconic Cutty Sark sailing vessel and a twelve foot image of a bottle of Cutty Sark scotch whiskey. For all I knew, the poster was still there and plastered all over the local newspaper as well.

I called Dave Jones and asked what the hell had happened to my poster.

"You got the pictures?" he replied.

"Don't tell me it's still up on the house."

"OK. I won't tell you."

I laughed nervously. "You're having fun with me, aren't you?"

He laughed back. "You bet."

"Please tell me you took the poster down."

"Yeah. Yeah, Doc. We did."

He couldn't have sounded less convincing.

It took a bit of bantering before he finally gave me the truth. They had put up the poster long enough to take the pictures and then taken it down.

I breathed a sigh of relief. Then Dave added, "I think we scared one of your neighbors though."

"What happened?"

"Lady was driving down the street just as we finished hanging the billboard. It kinda shook her up."

"How do you know that?"

"She ran into a garbage can at the curb."

"Oh my god! She get hurt?"

Dave laughed. "No, just spilled some trash."

"Did you talk to her?"

"Yeah, Doc. Don't worry. We explained the whole thing. She thought it was pretty funny."

"Did you get her name?"

"No, but she said you had asked her to keep an eye on the house while you were gone."

"Oh, no! That's Carrie. I wonder why she hasn't said anything to us."

"Hey, she wanted you to get the pictures first."

"Now you've turned our neighbors against us."

"That's what happens when you go to San Francisco and leave your research group back here."

"OK. I get it. Message received."

"And, Doc, did you *really* think you could send us a goddam billboard and it *wouldn't* end up on your house?"

"Honest to God."

"Then you learned a valuable lesson, didn't you?"

# CHAPTER 48
## Other Side of Midnight

The grueling sixteen-hour days of the summer computer course precipitated zany events that could only be explained by fried brain cells. Most of these occurred after the late lab shut down at midnight. Because my students knew that my family took refuge in the grandparents' home in Illinois each year for the duration of the short course, I was often swept into these late night escapades, not altogether unwillingly.

On a warm, late-June evening in 1971, a dozen course participants and instructors—weary and thirsty—fled the chemistry building and packed into cars headed for a new watering hole.

My graduate students had long enjoyed the fabulous student dollar lunch smorgasbord offered by the Morris Bryant Inn north of town on highway 52. A few years earlier, Jim Birk and his roommates had brought me there. After their four trips through the bountiful smorgasbord, I gave up counting. They literally stoked up for the week. Seriously. It was one way of coping with their meager $180/month income.

Our course participants had discovered yet another Morris Bryant offering—a late night lounge that catered to the after midnight crowd. On this evening, they dragged a few of the instructors and me along.

At that time of night, this crowd of young to middle-aged males literally took over the lounge. We filled two booths and some nearby cocktail tables. Two micro-skirted cocktail waitresses were kept very busy. Beer flowed like water. None of the instructors were allowed to pay, and that was a dangerous thing.

I had been coaxed into the middle of one of the booths with two of my grad students, Gordy Woolbert and John Zipper, and a young professor from Tennessee. Dianne, the pretty strawberry-blonde with short hair and shorter skirt had drawn our booth. A lot of good-natured banter ensued, particularly with Gordy. He found that she was a Purdue student from a nearby town. Naturally, she wanted to know about us.

Gordy—attempting possibly to be discreet—impressed me with his instant prevarication.    "We're here with the senator," he offered, nodding at me. "I'm his chief-of-staff." Then he waved his hand at our entire group and added, "We all work for Senator Stone."

As everyone in our crowd bobbed their heads, Dianne gave me a long look and then commented to Gordy, "I thought I knew our senators—Bayh and Hartke?"

Gordy laughed. "We're from Ohio, for a conference at Purdue."

"Oh. That's nice," she remarked. Then she looked over at me. "Well, Senator, what do you think of Purdue?"

Here was my opportunity to bring a halt to the charade. But I didn't. Dianne had obviously swallowed Gordy's line. I didn't want to embarrass her. To be honest, I found this new game enticing. "Actually," I replied, "I've been much too busy to check anything out."

"Yeah," Zipper volunteered, "this is our first night out. The senator's been working us like dogs."

The solid truth behind this little lie brought a round of guffaws from our entire group. The game continued, and I joined in. With several trips to our booth and subsequent friendly jesting with Gordy, Zipper, and the rest, the "senator" story became firmly entrenched and embellished. Everyone was having a good time. Letting off steam. No harm done, I thought.

Finally, Gordy decided to take things a step further. Calling Dianne over to the booth, he declared. "I've been trying to arrange a tour for the senator, and I'm thinking, Dianne, you might be the perfect host."

"Me?" she asked, eyebrows raised.

"Sure. You know Purdue. You know the area."

She eyed me apprehensively. I squirmed a bit. Things were getting out of hand.

Then, unexpectedly, Gordy looked at his wristwatch, turned away from Dianne, and declared, "Hey, look. It's getting pretty late."

As the others grunted agreement and made ready to leave, Gordy slid out of the booth. I slid after him, but he put out a hand. "Hold on, Senator." I paused and gazed blankly. Gordy had taken charge of this bogus event. And he wasn't finished. He turned to Dianne and suggested, "Before we leave, why don't you slide in here and set up a schedule for tomorrow?"

Before I could react, Gordy gently nudged the young lady into the booth. She surprised me by complying. "Is there anything in particular you'd like to see, Senator?" she asked.

"Well, there's … umm.…" I stammered. Dianne was so thoroughly taken in and so darned sweet that I didn't know how to proceed. Play along? Or tell her it was just a joke? Either way seemed wrong.

Playing along did seem the least offensive. Or perhaps it was the easiest path. I didn't know. Regardless, I forged ahead.

"You know," I began again, "perhaps you could recommend some things to see. My … my staff.…" I paused to sweep a hand at our surrounding group, only to realize suddenly that they had disappeared.

I panicked, instantly recognizing the set-up. I turned back to Dianne. "You know what," I said quickly, "my chief-of-staff was dreaming." I began to slide toward the other side of the booth. "I really don't have any time for sightseeing."

I slid out and took a few moments to engage Dianne with an earnest gaze. "I'm so sorry, Dianne. You've been great. I wish I had the time. But I don't, and I have to run."

With that I turned and literally ran for the door. Outside, I raced toward the parking spots.

They were *empty*.

I turned and saw three cars moving toward the exit to the highway. I ran. I waved my hands. I shouted.

The last car stopped.

A back door flew open, and Gordy stuck his head out. "What happened?" he cried.

"Nothing!" I shouted, closing the last few yards to the car. "No thanks to you."

I hopped into the car, slammed the door, and glared at Gordy. But before I could get anything out, the entire car rocked with laughter. The driver—the young Tennessee professor—yelled back at me. "Oh my God, Sam! You should have seen the look on your face."

Gordy elbowed my rib. "We were going to circle back, Doc. We just wanted you to think we left."

"You did a good job of that."

Ignoring my ill humor, Zipper shouted from the front seat, "Do you have a date tomorrow?"

"That wasn't going to happen," I declared.

Grinning at me, Gordy said, "I think she was really into you, Doc."

"You mean she was totally into my chief-of-staff," I countered. "I thought you were setting yourself up."

"Me, Doc? I'm married."

Words failed me. I glared at the grinning face until he burst out laughing.

"I know. I know," he declared, acknowledging the irony.

I shook my head. "That poor kid believed everything you said. She was ready to—"

Gordy shoved out a palm. "Whoa, Doc. It was just a joke." He paused. "You didn't tell her, did you?"

I shook my head. "Hope she doesn't take one of my classes."

He flashed a toothy grin. "It's OK, Doc. We're just trying to make you sweat, like *us*."

"Huh?"

"C'mon, Doc. You work our butts off. We spend a lot of time thinking up ways to get even."

His big grin elicited only a pained grimace in return.

"Yeah," he continued, reading my mind, "you'd better be careful, Doc."

He wasn't kidding.

*Gordy Woolbert, 1971.*
*[Copyright, S. P. Perone]*

In 1973, Bernard Fleet—professor of analytical chemistry at Imperial College, London—spent most of the year as a visiting scientist with me at Purdue. Bernard was eager to learn all about laboratory computers. Along with his wife, Jean, and two young daughters, he settled into a West Lafayette home vacated by a Purdue professor on sabbatical elsewhere.

Tall, slender and somewhat stiff, Bernard appeared the stereotypical British gentleman. In fact, his accent was so thick it brought to mind the old line—*if he were any more British, he couldn't speak at all.*

Bernard's appearance and speech were deceiving, though, until you looked carefully at his devilish eyes. Behind his polite and proper utterances was a bone-dry, razor-sharp sense of humor and a restlessly mischievous soul. He always seemed to be thinking, *what if?* Not only in the sense of scientific research, but more often along the lines of a practical joke.

It didn't take long for Bernard to recruit a number of my graduate students into his schemes. I didn't always know who was involved, but John Zipper, Keith Dahnke, Rick Baldwin, Terry Berger, Frank Pater, and Bill Farrell were the usual suspects. My secretary at the time, Sandra, was pretty convincing as an innocent bystander, but I don't know. Bernard, however, was always suspiciously present in the background snickering when some caper came to fruition.

What happened? Too many things to tell, like the volcano in my office or the vat of beer I found brewing in one of my labs.

And *parties!* Bernard's rented home in West Lafayette became headquarters for some very serious drinking. The home was equipped with an outstanding stereo sound system, a built-in sauna, and a bar that Bernard kept well stocked.

Like Buck Rogers, Bernard didn't believe in pouring short drinks or serving cheap liquor. Parties quickly got loud and crazy. Curiously, Bernard didn't drink much. Like the true practical joker, his pleasure derived from observing the foolish behavior of others. The Perone research group gladly obliged.

Not that Bernard didn't work hard. With his help, my grad students did learn how to play cricket and brew beer.

*Terry Berger (left) with Bernard Fleet at Imperial College, 1975. [Copyright, S. P. Perone]*

Seriously, though, he also inspired our excursion into new scientific areas. In fact, two of my students—Terry Berger and Bill Farrell—subsequently completed their Ph.D.s with Bernard at Imperial College.

Inspired work notwithstanding, this story is about one of Bernard's most memorable schemes.

It unfolded a few days after the conclusion of the summer computer course of 1973. We had condensed the three-week course to two that year, accommodating the increased percentage of industrial participants.

Not that we left anything out of the course. It was more intense than ever, working students even on Saturday and Sunday.

Bernard was given a spot in the course. Like everyone else, he was exhausted at the end. Most participants went home to recover. Bernard and my students were ready to party.

Frank Pater gave us the opportunity. Frank had completed his master's thesis a year earlier but had taken my offer to spend another year as a research associate. He agreed to stay with me through the course. It was over now, and he was ready to leave for a new job.

But not without a party.

And this promised to be a great one.


My family had not yet returned from Illinois. The short course pressure was over for my research group and me. We were all ready for a "roast" down at The Pub, especially because Frank had been the perpetrator of countless pranks on members of the group during his tenure.

We knew this party would be one for the ages, for all of the above reasons, but mostly because the biggest prankster of all time—Bernard Fleet—would be part of the "planning committee."

Unfortunately, I would be at the heart of the caper.

*Frank Pater, M.S. party. The Pub, 1973. [Copyright, S. P. Perone]*

The party itself lived up to expectations. Pitchers of beer were augmented with shots of tequila. Frank got his tee shirt. It was well after midnight before I took my leave. Bernard opted to leave at the same time. That caused the departure of several others that had ridden over to the Pub with him. I had slowed down at the end and felt confident that I could guide my little red '70 Firebird safely home.

I slid into the Firebird, enjoying the coolness of the black leather bucket seat. I twisted the key, and the big V-8 engine turned over—but failed to start. I tried again.

Now Bernard and Terry were at my door peering in. "Hold the accelerator down while you turn it over," Terry advised. "It's probably flooded."

"I smell gas," Bernard added.

I had no success. So Terry offered to look under the hood. He took a minute and then shut it down. "I think it's your fuel pump," he declared.

"Look, Sam," said Bernard, "let me give you a lift home. Tomorrow you can get it towed."

By this time the Firebird

*S.P., '70 Firebird, with Renee (6 yrs). [Copyright, S. P. Perone]*

had drawn a small crowd. John Zipper, Keith Dahnke, Marty Pichler and Rick Baldwin were there, along with a surprisingly sober Frank Pater.

Six of us piled into Bernard's car—an early sixties Buick sedan that had seen too many Indiana winters. I sat in the back between John Zipper and Terry Berger. Keith Dahnke and Rick Baldwin sat in the front with Bernard. Bernard pulled out of the parking lot and crossed over to Union Street, where he made a left turn west toward the bridge.

I thought this strange. My house was south and east from the Pub. Bernard was headed back over the Wabash River to West Lafayette.

Sensing my concern, Bernard turned his head slightly and talked to me. "Hope you don't mind, Sam. These guys all need to get back to campus. It'll only take a few minutes."

"No problem," I declared. Bernard made sense. My home would require a ten-mile detour.

When Bernard turned right on to North River Road after crossing the bridge, I began to smell a rat. "Where're you going?" I asked.

"Williamsburg apartments," Bernard replied over his shoulder.

"Oh," I murmured, somewhat mollified. Many grad students lived there. I shrugged and looked at Zipper. He looked away. I turned to Terry. He was gazing out the side window. When Bernard passed the Williamsburg apartments without stopping, I called out, "You missed the turn."

Nothing.

"Bernard?" I inquired again calmly. "What's going on?"

This time, Rick turned his head to reply. "It's OK, Doc. Nothing to worry about."

"Wait a minute," I protested.

Bernard chuckled. "Come on, Sam. We're just going to have a little fun."

The six passengers in the Buick remained silent as it cruised north along the river road. The Wabash was directly to our right, shimmering in the moonlight. When Bernard pulled into the driveway of the Old Soldiers Home to turn around and proceed back south, I asked, "Are you lost?"

"Just enjoying the ride," Bernard replied. "Aren't you?"

It was a warm, humid night. The windows were open. It might have been a very pleasant excursion, if I weren't so anxious about where the hell we were going. That's roughly what I said to Bernard, except with a bit of gravel in my voice.

Everybody chuckled—which just made me *more* anxious.

When Bernard made a second U-turn just beyond Robinson, proceeding north once again, I began to realize he was probably hunting for something. I scanned the locations on both sides of the road, trying to figure it out. Suddenly, Bernard took a sharp right turn into a poorly marked drive that seemed to lead nowhere. Within seconds, however, we approached an open area that bordered the river. In the moonlight I could see a wooden pier and large sign.

The sign was something that could sometimes be seen from the bridge when the surrounding foliage wasn't too thick. It read, "Purdue Crew."

I didn't see any of the rowing shells that were often observed on the river. The pier was unoccupied. For a moment I wondered if some watercraft might emerge from down river—taking me for a ride.

But that wasn't the plan.

The Buick came to a stop within about twenty yards of the riverfront. That's when I noticed the other car, with the other conspirators from Frank's party. Most of my grad students, including Frank, were there.

Now I understood why Bernard had been driving in circles, waiting for the others to arrive. Who knew what kind of set up awaited us?

Everyone turned to me with Cheshire grins.

"OK," I said, "what's the deal?"

Bernard cleared his throat. "It's come to my attention, Sam, that you're the only one in the group who's not been in the Wabash." His accent made the declaration sound like the introduction to a dramatic stage show—where *I* would be the star.

"What?" I cried, beginning to get the picture. "You're not getting me out there."

"Come on," Bernard persisted. "Even Jesus Christ got baptized in a river."

"I was baptized thirty-four years ago, thank you. And I haven't been in a river since I was old enough to see microbes in a microscope."

Zipper spoke up. "Come on, Doc. Everyone at Purdue has to get dunked in the Wabash."

"Where is that written?"

"In Britain," Bernard interjected, sounding more British than ever, "Oxford Dons punt the Thames."

"I think punting the Wabash is a whole different thing," I countered. "It's muddy enough to walk across."

"I believe Jesus did that, too," Bernard quipped. The conspirators all chuckled.

Terry defined my choices. "Well, Doc, are you going to jump in? Or do we have to throw you in?"

I looked around at five determined, grinning faces. On either side were guys that could overpower me. Clearly, this called for a negotiated solution.

I searched for an out. The only wedge I had was that four of my captors would require my signature on an advanced degree. I wouldn't be shy about using that leverage.

"You guys are willing to forfeit a Ph.D. just for the pleasure of dunking me in the Wabash?"

"You bet!" cried Zipper.

"That's right," added Rick.

Keith and Terry cheerily agreed.

So much for rational negotiations. I had to appeal to something more visceral.

"All right," I began, "what if … umm … I agree to do this … *swim* … another time, and offer an alternative tonight?"

My captors looked at each other with a collective shrug and turned back to me skeptically.

I had to think fast. *Something appealing to everyone? Something tantalizing?*

Then a picture appeared to me. Sitting on a shelf in my office at the university was a very expensive bottle of scotch whiskey that I had brought back from Scotland the previous December when I had traveled to Britain on a lecture tour. There I had first been introduced to Bernard Fleet and the distinctive tastes of single-malt scotch.

That bottle had been the objective of envy and speculation by my entire group. But I had resisted all invitations to crack the seal, until tonight.

I offered. They accepted. An hour later my office was filled with nearly a dozen merry-makers. The 100 watt stereo receiver was cranked up to ear-shattering decibels. A fresh box of fifty-milliliter beakers had provided shot glasses. And we were staring at an empty bottle that had once held the smoothest scotch anyone had ever tasted.

Someone remembered that a number of quart bottles of

*S.P., receiving bottle of "Real-Time '73" from B. Fleet. [Copyright, S. P. Perone]*

beer had been produced from the vat of brew recently conjured by the group. The beer had been dubbed, "Real-Time '73" in a mocking homage to the "real-time" laboratory computer applications the group was researching at the time.

Well, I don't know if this was the moment of truth for "Real-Time '73," but that bottle was the skunkiest brew you would ever want to see, smell, or taste. It was flushed down a lab sink with enough water to sink a battleship.

Several bottles of this brew were saved for posterity. Like prized vintage wines, these would never be opened—but for a very different reason.

The bad beer dampened spirits, but that wasn't the end of it.

The university police took care of that.

Fortunately, they decided to ring my office first. I stabbed the power switch on the old vacuum tube amplifier, shushed the group, and picked up the phone.

"Is this Professor Perone?" the officer asked, after identifying himself.

"Yes, it is," I replied.

"We got a report of a disturbance in your labs? Is everything OK?"

"I'm sorry," I replied. "We … we had a late night … umm … research meeting that's gotten a bit noisy. We … uh … turned up the stereo. Didn't think we'd bother anyone at this … this time of night."

"Yeah, it always amazes us how many of you work the labs all night. You shutting things down now?"

"Yes. We're done. Everyone's leaving." I made a furtive scan of several agreeable faces in the room. "Sorry for the trouble."

"No harm done. But … uh … in the future, I wouldn't plan any noisy late night 'research meetings' in the chemistry building."

We disconnected, and I turned to my group. "Party's over, I guess."

Bernard looked at his watch. "Still time to make the Wabash before sunrise."

I was ready for him this time. "Look, I'm getting hungry, aren't you?"

Their faces told me I had struck the right chord, so I continued. "The Waffle House out on Bypass 52 is open twenty-four hours. How about it? Breakfast on me."

No argument.


Hunger and thirst had trumped the desire to see their major professor soaked in muddy Wabash water. By the time we left the Waffle House, it was daylight. Bernard and the usual suspects drove me to the parking lot outside The Pub where my Firebird sat.

That's when I learned what had really happened. Terry Berger got under the hood and reconnected the distributor cap—about which I had not the least bit of understanding. The engine turned over and roared to life.

I drove home and crawled into bed, dead tired.

But at least I wasn't soaking wet.

# CHAPTER 49

## A Happening

Midway through the summer course of 1971, it was the evening of our traditional party at the cabin on the outskirts of Lafayette. Always a loud, wild event, this one was particularly raucous.

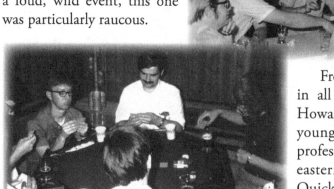

Front and center in all the fun was Howard Bond—a young chemistry professor from an eastern college. Quick-witted and funny, he kept us in stitches as people crowded around the big poker table where he held court.

Howard had struck up a friendship with my grad student, John Patterson, one of the course instructors. Together, they had driven out to the cabin in Howard's dark blue late-model Corvette. Fortunately, John wasn't drinking, and he promised to drive Howard back to the graduate dorm where many participants were staying.

At about one in the morning, I was the last to leave the cabin. My '70 Chevy wagon was the shuttle for a number of participants. After delivering them, I headed for the parking garage across from the student union, with the intention of making a quick trip to my office.

To my surprise, I caught a glimpse of Howard's Corvette entering the garage in front of me. I followed them and parked nearby. We left our cars and headed for the corner stairwell that would bring us down to the underground tunnels leading to both the graduate dorm and the student union. These three facilities formed a triangle, with the dorm about two hundred feet south of the other two.

Howard was feeling no pain—chattering non-stop and changing the subject with each sentence. John and I cracked up as our words were twisted into hilarious quips.

We entered the tunnel that crossed west under the street and would bring us to the lower level of the student union. Just before reaching the union, another long tunnel opened up to the south. That tunnel led to the distant high-rise graduate dorm. The tunnels were well-lighted but deserted.

With Howard still chattering, John leaned toward me and said, "I'll go with Howard."

"Sounds like a good idea," I responded. "I'm heading for my office."

"You gonna be ready for the morning lecture?" he asked.

"You gonna be ready for the morning lab?" I shot back.

John laughed, and I turned to bid Howard good night.

But Howard wasn't there.

Stunned, John and I immediately scanned the tunnels that led to the east and south.

Nothing.

"What the hell?" I cried.

"Where did he go?" John exclaimed.

"He must have gone back to get his car."

Panicking, we began to trot toward the garage.

Suddenly, the tunnels shook with a deafening roar—a sound that literally rattled our bones.

Instinctively, we turned to look back. The noise got louder. It seemed to be coming from where we had just left.

We ran back to the junction. Turning south to explore the long tunnel, we were shocked to see a vehicle the size of a small tank rumbling away from us through the tunnel. In the driver's seat was *Howard.*

"What is that?" I cried as we chased after the vehicle.

"Looks like a street sweeper," shouted John.

Fortunately, the vehicle had a top speed of about three miles per hour, and we quickly caught up with it. We noticed the wide-open set of double doors to the large compartment in the side of the tunnel. In the seconds that we had ignored Howard, he had found the hideaway, climbed into the vehicle, started it, and taken it for a ride.

Waving frantically at Howard had little effect. He was obviously too busy enjoying himself.

Finally, trotting alongside, John reached up to turn off the ignition—bringing the tank-sweeper to a sudden halt. The jarring sounds of the engine echoed on, though, for several seconds.

At that moment I glanced back to see one of the campus police officers tearing around the corner of the junction with the garage tunnel.

The officer caught up with us before we had a chance to extract Howard from the vehicle.

I walked off to the side with the officer while John helped Howard down. I hoped Howard would quiet down, but that didn't happen.

So, with Howard gleefully chattering to John about his brief but adventurous journey, I tried to explain calmly to the officer what had happened.

I'll never know how the officer found us so quickly nor understand why we didn't all end up in the pokey that night. Probably the only thing that saved us was that John and I were cold sober; Howard evidently was not; and we were able to convince the officer that Howard had disappeared from our care in the blink of an eye.

Although he wasn't aware, Howard was doing his best to confirm our assessment of his magical powers of misdirection.

The officer advised us to return Howard safely to his room and he would deal with the hijacked vehicle. We learned that it was some kind of heavy-duty floor waxer.

We held our breath while the police officer berated us with a stern warning—and a barely suppressed grin—as he sent us on our way.

# CHAPTER 50
## Cleaning Solution

In the spring of 1969, we were enjoying a burst of research activity prior to preparing for the summer computer course. It was morning. John Patterson and I were in his lab talking research. We heard a quick rap at the laboratory door and turned to see Barry Willis poking his head inside.

"Hey, Doc, can we talk to you about the 2115?" Barry asked in a subdued voice.

Barry was one of Harry Pardue's students. He was asking about the Hewlett-Packard 2115A minicomputer. We had mounted it and a number of interfacing panels in a tall relay rack on wheels. The system rolled from lab to lab and experiment to experiment.

*H.P. 2115A on wheels, interfaced to an electrochemical cell.*
*[Copyright, S. P. Perone]*

Because we were the only research group in the department with laboratory computer equipment, we allowed the "computer on wheels" to be used by other groups. Harry Pardue's group was the heaviest user.

"Come on in," I shouted at Barry.

He slid inside the doorway, followed quickly by his lab mate, Gerry James.

Barry and Gerry were two of the "pioneer" instructors for me in the computer instrumentation courses, and I had gotten to know them well. They had been using the "computer on wheels" heavily on nighttime shifts.

"What's up?" I asked. They weren't smiling.

Barry looked at Gerry, and Gerry looked at me somewhat sheepishly. "Uh ... Doc ... we had a little problem last night ... with the 2115."

John and I came to full alert. "What's the problem?" I asked.

*Gerry James, tutoring a student, 1968 summer course. [Copyright, S. P. Perone]*

*Barry Willis, giving a demo, 1968 summer course. [Copyright, S. P. Perone]*

While Barry eyed me apprehensively, Gerry explained, "We used the system last night ... and ... well ... we thought maybe you were concerned that ... that we hadn't gotten it back."

"We hadn't talked about it," I lied. In fact, that had been my first question to John that morning.

"Well," Gerry continued, "we wheeled it out of the lab last night."

I nodded. That was the arrangement. John would disconnect the leads before he left in the evening, and Harry's students could come in later to wheel the system out. This had been working smoothly for months. We had mounted an hour-meter on the rack to keep track of usage and joked about adding an odometer to record mileage.

"Well … uh … you know…." He turned toward the doorway. "You see that?"

I followed his gaze to the large emergency showerhead that hung from the ceiling just inside the doorway of this and every other chemical lab. Dangling next to it was a pull chain. In case of a fire, explosion, or chemical contamination, the victim could jerk the chain and be doused from a fifty-gallon reservoir of water. A large floor drain was underneath.

"You talking about the shower?" I asked. I was beginning to get an uneasy feeling.

He nodded. "You know those big … umm … eyebolts on top of the relay rack?"

My eyebrows raised. "Yeah.…?"

"Well, they got tangled with the … uh … shower chain." They were both gazing at me apprehensively.

"You mean—"

Barry finally spoke. "Yup, gave the computer a *bath*." A crooked grin followed the startling admission, and he pushed out a palm. "But, Doc, she's OK."

That's when John came to life. "You mean the computer got soaked in all that dirty, rusty water?" he exclaimed.

My thoughts, exactly. Those emergency showers were rarely, if ever, used. The water might have been there since World War I.

Barry replied, "We worked all night, Doc, cleaning it up, card by card."

Gerry added, "Yeah, Doc, we got all the rust and crap out and cleaned every contact with alcohol. Used a blow dryer, too."

My gaze wavered between the two culprits. "Did you fire it up?"

They looked at each other again. Barry answered, "Yeah. It's working fine."

I let out a breath. "Where is it?"

"Down in our lab," replied Gerry. "We'll bring it up now, if—"

"If you'd like to check it out," added Barry.

It was years later before Harry's students admitted they had agonized for hours before coming to tell me about the mishap. I probably still don't know the whole story. I do know that they were so concerned that I might discontinue the "computer on wheels" operation that they considered not telling me at all, except for one little problem.

Clearly visible in the lower right hand corner of the plastic front panel of the HP 2115A computer—perforated by dozens of blinking lights—was a colorful, permanent, crescent-shaped *watermark*.

They confessed to many anxious moments the night of the mishap, as they gingerly pulled out and cleaned stacks of circuit boards. I can't imagine how they screwed up the courage to put it back together and fire it up.

But they did. And thank goodness it worked. Otherwise our conversation that day might have taken a whole different turn.

The computer system returned to John's lab that day, and the "computer on wheels" operation continued as before. The survivability of the computer system was impressive—impressive enough that no one ever let Barry and Gerry forget that they had applied the "dunk test."

The legend of the "waterproof 2115" circulated for many years among the Hewlett-Packard reps. That front panel watermark became a badge of honor to proudly display at each of our computer courses.

At this point, it might seem that no noteworthy incidents occurred during this era that didn't involve student pranks or computers. To be sure, there were many of these, but they don't tell the whole story.

Not nearly.

# CHAPTER 51

# Football

Among my most enjoyable social interactions with grad students were the touch football games in the fall. The ready availability of guys who were eager to play was an unexpected and welcome fringe benefit of my early years at Purdue.

I was amazed at the number of chemistry grad students who had played college ball, the real thing, with pads and schedules and stands filled with people. My students informed me that my colleague and frequent touch football competitor—Harry Pardue—had played ball for Marshall. I could believe it. He was tough and fast and didn't really get the idea of a "touch" game.

Because we were invariably playing on opposite teams, Harry and I squared off frequently. When I asked him if he had learned his rushing techniques at Marshall, Harry assured me that he had not played college ball, but that he did play defensive end in high school. All I know is that he shot off the ball like a rocket, and I had the collection of bruises to show it.

One crisp, sunny Friday in October, 1969, Harry and I persuaded a dozen grad students to hike out to the intramural fields west of campus for a touch football game. Harry seemed to attract good athletes to his research group, and one of those was Jim Mieure, a veteran of premier Ohio high school football. I had heard that he played wide receiver for his college team.

Occasionally, I would pick up a research student that was also a good athlete. One of these was John Zipper, who had played high school ball in the tough Chicago Catholic league. "Zip" was a second-year grad student at this time. He had gotten off to a rocky start in one of my new research areas and had been somewhat disgruntled.

Zipper was a good athlete though—quick, hard and fearless.

Harry and I chose up opposing teams, and I was lucky enough to get the first pick. I didn't hesitate. I picked Jim Mieure. Jim had played receiver to my quarterbacking in the annual fall game at our division picnic. He had made me look like Johnny Unitas. It didn't take long to figure out that you only had to throw the ball up anywhere within ten yards of Jim, and he would float on air above every defender to pull the pass down. With feet on the ground, he ran like the wind.

Harry selected my student, John Zipper, as his first pick.

The stage was set. On my side was the finesse player who could turn any offensive play into a game-breaker. On the other side were the bruisers, Harry and Zip. Their strategy was simple—bust us up at every opportunity.

The opening kickoff set the tone for the game. We received, and Jim ran the ball back. I rumbled up the field looking for someone to shove one way or the other. Unfortunately, I found myself leading the ball carrier, with Harry steaming directly for me. Harry and I were about the same size. But he was solid as a tree trunk, and I was, well, a bit soft. We had collided many times, and I had taken the worst of it.

I saw that the ball carrier might find some running room to the right, if I could just manage to shove Harry to the left. To do that, I had to beat Harry to a spot on the field about ten yards ahead. Admittedly speed has never been one of my assets, but Harry was further from that spot. So I lumbered as fast as I could.

Everything happened in split seconds. My target spot came closer. I could cut Harry off. The beginnings of a smile formed around the labored wheezes that escaped my lips.

Suddenly, from out of nowhere, a body flew through the air and struck me about chest high. Despite my forward momentum, the blow blasted me backwards causing me to tumble awkwardly heels-over-head. The ground was hard from lack of rain, and the grass stung my elbows. I rolled uncontrollably into a patch of brown, and a cloud of dust puffed into the air. I tasted dirt.

When I regained my bearings, two sights struck me. The first was Harry grabbing Jim and "touching" him down. The second was my student, John Zipper, lying on the dirt next to me. He stared back at me with wide eyes and a white face. He cried out, "Jesus, I … I'm sorry, Doc. I … I didn't know that was *you.*" He bounced up and offered me a hand. "Damn! There goes my *Ph.D.,*" he grunted.

I squeezed out a chuckle and let him pull me up, despite the pain. "That's strike one," I jested. His face reddened.

"No, seriously, Zip, don't worry about it," I added hastily. "You should block me just like anybody else."

He eyed me curiously. "Well, OK, Doc. If you say so," he said, before trotting back to his teammates.

If this episode had intimidated him at all, he never showed it. Zipper continued to cream me whenever he got the chance.

I guess I should have seen what would come later, but I didn't; not that day.

Zipper never let me forget that episode. He would taunt me with it many times during our frequent, heated discussions over his research. He teased that I had passed judgment on him that day. We both knew that wasn't true, but that didn't matter.

Of all my students, Zipper would turn out to be the most outspoken and difficult. I always told my students that I would know that they were ready for the Ph.D. when they began to take charge of their thesis research and make good decisions. John decided he had reached that stage much earlier than I did. It made for some of the most contentious and intense advisor-student discussions I will ever remember.

It's an ironic truth that professors are rarely challenged intellectually by faculty colleagues at their own institution. Other faculty simply do not have adequate knowledge of a colleague's narrow specialty. With John Zipper I had someone around every day eager to challenge me intellectually. He was openly critical of my research ideas—not necessarily a bad thing. That is, healthy skepticism is something to be encouraged in a scientist. Unfortunately, Zipper's skepticism was in full bloom well before his depth of knowledge.

The good news was that Zipper forced me to justify my thinking like no other student ever did. We had heated discussions almost daily—discussions that often turned into *arguments.*

And these arguments exhausted me.

Strangely, though, these arguments also forged a genuine bond between us. There was little that we could not or had not said to one another. We came to treasure a very close friendship that would persist over time.

Not surprisingly, I was ecstatic when the day came that Zipper would get his Ph.D. and *leave* Purdue. I told him exactly that, the moment we walked together out of the room where he had just successfully defended his thesis research.

He chuckled. "I know, Doc. That was my strategy all along."

I guess I should have seen that coming on that bright, sunny October day on the football field.

# CHAPTER 52
## Family Affairs

The preceding chapters have painted the picture of a young man—with the help of many fortuitous events—moving toward a successful academic career and enjoying immensely the camaraderie of a special collection of students.

There is so much more to tell.

There is a bigger picture—another side of my life—where personal matters intertwined.

So I will step away briefly from the main story line and turn attention toward family affairs.

Working toward academic tenure at a top-tier university like Purdue is like living in a pressure cooker. A young un-tenured professor is focused twenty-four hours a day on jump-starting a career—doing whatever it takes during that four-year trial period to get promoted.

Besides teaching and committees that eat up much of every work week, a young professor must do research; publish a dozen papers; manage inexperienced research students; obtain funding; attend scientific meetings; and present research talks. Then, while striving desperately to get noticed and build a reputation, he or she must simultaneously avoid making enemies among tenured faculty.

Additionally for me, the first year at Purdue also involved striving desperately to complete a Ph.D. thesis.

It is hard to convey the devastating angst consuming an un-tenured professor. You've chosen an academic career and are seeking tenure at a

S. P. Perone

top university. The reward is great. Yet the bar is set very high and the penalty very deep. If you fail, your career will crash and burn. No other top school will look at you.

Industrial employers or schools that don't emphasize research might be interested in a Purdue reject. But neither of these options was what I had signed up for.

How did this play out with my family? First of all, Anita had no illusions about what would be required of me at Purdue, and she had supported my decision to take the job. She knew that I would be incredibly busy. She didn't understand technically what I was doing. Yet she knew that when I was working on a grant proposal or research paper, there was a race against time—that ever-present four-year tenure deadline.

Was there ever any conflict? Well, Anita was fond of saying, "Sam, even when you're here, you're not here." Positively true, of course, but that didn't make it less painful or prevent me from getting defensive.

Fact was, at home I was often consumed with reading, writing and planning. I was also spending more and more time away from home—working in the lab, meeting with students, attending out-of-town conferences.

There was one significant added complication. Anita was extremely close to her family in Illinois. Our earlier sixty-mile move to Madison had been traumatic. Most weekends we would drive to Rockford and stay at her parents' home, where I would reside in the attic, studying or preparing for tests.

Our move to "faraway" Lafayette had created even greater separation anxiety. The long, mostly two-lane highways to Illinois at that time were a formidable obstacle. We were rarely able to pack up the girls and embark on a 400-mile roundtrip.

For me, this was a relatively minor issue. For Anita, with my real and virtual absences, it was often more than she could handle. This was particularly true my first year at Purdue. The "Sword of Damocles" hanging over my head that first year because I hadn't completed my Ph.D. was incredibly threatening not only to me, but even more so for Anita. I at least could do something about it. Anita could do nothing

272

but watch and fret helplessly and silently, not knowing where we might be the following year.

Nothing brought this home to me more poignantly than Anita's near collapse from relief the week after I finally passed my Ph.D. exam at Wisconsin. I had no idea what she had been going through.

And this was just the beginning of our trials.

How did I deal with this? Not very well I'm afraid.

Did I make time to enjoy my growing family? I thought I did. After I made tenure, each year would include one long family getaway—always connected to some temporary job at another university, industry or government lab—usually to California and occasionally to places like Maryland and Texas. The girls enjoyed these travels, as their dad attempted to compensate for the distractions during the rest of the year.

During the early years, though, Vita and Amy would probably say that their memories of dad—when he wasn't away—were of him reading or writing, often with stereo headphones on, while they played in our large family room.

Buck and Eleanor Rogers were sensitive to Anita's silent anxiety and loneliness, and Eleanor did her best to take her under her wing. She visited our home often, and she introduced Anita to the unique world of faculty wives. It was a world incredibly foreign to her—afternoon teas; cocktail parties for visiting speakers; inane conversations; and all the time Anita wanting to be with her children and family.

Her escape from this alien atmosphere—and mine also—was with my students and our frequent parties. With them we found a comfort zone. Even more uplifting were the close friendships with Buck's postdoctoral students during those early years. The first of these were Jerry and Laura Fitzgerald. Following them were Mike and Jini Burke. We enjoyed their company—university staff who felt as out-of-place socially as we did.

Our friendship with the Burkes became deep and life-long. Their decision to find lodging near our residence in Lafayette was as fortuitous as were the similarities in our families—young, married, disenchanted Catholics, with daughters of similar age.

In Jini, Anita found someone equally uncomfortable with faculty wives' functions. With Mike, I found a wiser, more grounded version of myself. He became the confidant I needed so badly—someone who understood academic politics in a way that I never could. For Mike, I was someone going through something to which he aspired—working toward tenure at a top-tier university. He learned from my experiences; but I learned so much more from him.

*Left to right: Mike and Jini Burke; Anita and Sam Perone. 1966.*
*[Copyright, Mike Burke, Jr., Used with permission.]*

Not surprisingly, we found ourselves spending many evenings with the Burkes—playing bridge, sharing amusing observations on faculty elders, and wallowing in frustration over financial and spiritual struggles.

Why do I mention "spiritual" struggles? It was a difficult time for young Catholics. The Church was out of touch with modern times. Antiquated features—from the Latin Mass to male-dominant clergy—concerned us. For example, we were still bound to archaic notions of "family planning," where the basic tenets included the notoriously unreliable "Rhythm Method" or the very reliable but ridiculous notion of abstinence.

Yet this was now the era of the birth control pill—a mortal sin tempting the modern Catholic youth.

I believe most of the young Catholic school products of that day accepted the Church's doctrine on birth control. Many practiced the rhythm method faithfully, while remaining deeply frustrated with the Church's intransigence. But I was surprised to learn how many, like myself, were driven to ignore the doctrine. Every means of birth control—including the newly available birth control pill—was fair game.

Were we living in sin? I don't know. Did we believe we were sinning? Definitely. We were filled with guilt. We had knowingly cut ourselves off from the Church to which we had been attached at the hip from birth. It was a horrible feeling.

The young Burke and Perone couples, though, gained great comfort in sharing their frustration. We had become just worldly enough to recognize that the Church was still living in the Middle Ages. Whether or not we followed those archaic rules, we were angry and disillusioned.

This issue, along with so many other mutual concerns, brought the Perones and Burkes together as the closest of friends. During those mid-sixties we were virtually inseparable; and for all the following years our families remained close regardless of distances that separated us.

Other social relationships during those early years were important and telling. We were acquainted with other couples among young untenured chemistry faculty, primarily Harry and Ruby Pardue. Like most young Purdue faculty, they lived in West Lafayette and were much better connected to university couples from other departments.

They fit in well with that social group. We did not. There was a very distinct town and gown separation in the West Lafayette-Lafayette community. The Wabash River separated West Lafayette, the university, students, and most of the faculty from Lafayette and its mostly working class population. Although we were part of the university community, we were not part of the West Lafayette scene.

We had chosen to live in Lafayette originally because we couldn't find a rental elsewhere. Unexpectedly, we developed a kinship to local townspeople, perhaps because of their similarity to people in our Illinois hometown. We were determined to remain there.

From that decision evolved one of our most delightful social outlets—the Lafayette JayCees.

I may have been the only Purdue faculty member ever to become an honorary member of the Lafayette JayCees—the Junior Chamber of Commerce. JayCee membership in the 1960s was confined to men in their twenties or thirties. Dedicated to community service and providing a platform for business networking, these organizations included salesmen, businessmen, attorneys, technical reps, politicians, accountants, middle managers, etc., mostly with young families.

How did we fit in? We were the right age, and we had bought a home in a suburban neighborhood filled with a cross-section of these young up-and-coming families—a social segment that a couple decades later would be termed "yuppies."

What attracted us to this social group? At first it was that we all lived in the same neighborhood. More significantly, most were relative newcomers to Lafayette, married, often with small children, with stay-at-home wives, and husbands working hard to establish careers.

This social stratum hardly exists today, but it was the norm for Lafayette in the 1960s—from the all-male JayCees to the stay-at-home moms. Times were changing elsewhere, but we didn't know it yet.


At first, we had typical "welcome neighbors" kinds of engagements. Then we were invited to cocktail parties. Football season brought multiple parties for each Purdue home game.

At these parties we met other young Lafayette couples. Soon we were attending formal JayCee social events, dinners, and dances.

They realized there was no professional incentive for me to join their organization. They liked me and Anita though. And we liked them. Consequently, they made me an "honorary" JayCee and accepted us into the JayCee social world.

This social outlet filled a large void in our lives. We couldn't let our hair down at a faculty party. We were less constrained at student parties. Yet we could truly be ourselves with the JayCees.

A more significant factor was the extraordinary pressure both Anita and I were under during my pre-tenure days at the university. Blowing off steam with my students helped. But when we were with the JayCees, we could totally forget about our university lives, at least for a while.

Like the teen-ager sneaking out undetected to party with friends, it was our guilty pleasure—a secret life away from the university.

Anita became close friends with several of the JayCee wives, particularly those in the neighborhood with small children like ours. These relationships helped ease the pain of separation from her family in Rockford. She had much more in common with these women than the faculty wives. It was a good thing.

I interacted differently. Although none of the men had professions akin to mine, I found most of them to be refreshingly genuine and unpretentious. Surprisingly, they were keen to learn about my university life. To them, Purdue was that huge institution across the river that provided entertaining football games, attracting sixty thousand fans on a half-dozen fall Saturdays. The inner workings of the institution, however, and its people were a big mystery.

So I was a curiosity at first—that rare Purdue professor that wandered into JayCee circles and became an accepted member.

But there was a dark side.

Except for those few JayCees with political ambitions, these young couples were pretty uninhibited. Hard drinking and boisterous parties were the norm. Sixties music was the catalyst for unimaginable craziness. We exercised restraint at student parties, but not so much with the JayCees. It was at those events that I developed a taste for scotch, learned to do the Twist, the Pony and the Früg, and for the first time in my life became a "party animal." Anita had fun, too, but not as much as I did.

Throughout high school, college, graduate school and at Purdue, I had really been a "grinder." My first real social outlet had been with my graduate students. That was an awakening. When I entered the JayCee social circle, though, I really came unbent. Partying with these couples provided a release mechanism of seismic proportions.

Were we ready for this? Not really, although Anita handled it much better than I did.

Ordinarily, we would never mix our different social worlds. We didn't invite JayCees to our faculty or grad student parties and vice-versa.

However, it did happen one time.

Hal and Diana had moved into one of the ranch models on our street in 1964, not long after we had occupied our home. Hal was a pharmacist. Diana dabbled in interior design. Diana was tall, fair and blonde. Hal was black-haired, with an average build. They were about our age, childless, and regulars at JayCee events. We had a lot of similar interests, and we often went to Purdue events like Victory Varieties together.

Anita had arranged a surprise grad student party at our home to celebrate my birthday. It was another crazy event, with music blaring and couples gyrating in our huge lower-level family room.

Hal and Diana had dropped in to bring me a birthday present—a fine bottle of Stoly vodka. Of course we invited them to join the party. They slid right into the middle of a circle of dancers in our family room without missing a beat.

Well, the party carried on for quite a while that night, and we went through several punch bowls spiked with lab vodka. Unfortunately, I hadn't stocked up.

I ran out of booze.

And the party showed no signs of waning. What could I do? I ran upstairs, grabbed the new bottle of Stoly, and rushed back downstairs.

Unfortunately, Hal—dancing in the middle of the floor—saw me open the Stoly and pour it into the punch bowl. His eyes grew wide, and above the din of music he began to shout, "Noooo...."

I just grinned back. "It's OK," I shouted.

The wounded look on Hal's face is one I'll never forget. Could I blame him? I couldn't tell him I had run out of *lab* vodka. He knew nothing of that. So I just let him watch dumbfounded. I didn't know how he would process the fact that a great bottle of vodka—his birthday gift intended for nothing less than fine martinis—had just been dumped into a punchbowl filled with juice and soda.

There was one more-telling incident with Hal and Diana. We were sitting around a card table one evening in our lower-level family room, playing a rummy-type card game called "Euchre" that was popular in Indiana. Somehow we got into a discussion of our jobs, and Hal made a remark.

"I wish I had a job where I only worked three or four hours a week," he declared jokingly. Of course, like many others, he equated my work load to the hours when I actually met classes; and I was teaching only one that semester.

I probably should have laughed it off. But I didn't. I did something very rude. I interrupted the game, walked over to my desk in the corner, and stormed back with a stack of documents. Slamming them down on the card table, I stunned our guests and scattered four Euchre hands.

"What's this?" Hal asked in shock.

"This is what I've been doing with my time just this past month." I pulled out the top document and slapped it on the table. "This manuscript is a paper submitted for publication," I declared. Then I slapped down the next document. "This is a 20-page proposal to the National Science Foundation for a thirty-thousand dollar grant."

I continued this little tirade, storming through the rest of the pile. Then I bellowed, "This is what I do, Hal—including the weeks of research it took. This is what Purdue expects for me to keep my job. Teaching is just the tip of the iceberg."

Hal and Diana stared back at me open-mouthed and speechless. Finally, Hal spoke. "Jeez, Sam, I had no idea...."

I took a deep breath and calmed down. "I'm sorry, Hal. It's just that...." I paused, wagging my head slowly. "Nobody really understands."

Hal put a hand on my arm. "Do you want to talk about it?" he asked.

Diana affirmed Hal's request, while a glance at Anita revealed eyes begging me to let it go.

I shook my head in response and began picking up the papers. Before returning them to my desk, I paused to look at Hal. "I'm sure your job's crazy, too, and damned if I want to hear about it. What do you say we just play cards, have a drink, and forget about work?"

Hal laughed and added a heartfelt "Aaay-men."


Beth and Kent lived in the big bi-level home down the street from us at the end of Arapahoe Drive. There was no more handsome young couple in the JayCees. Charismatic Kent was a social magnet, drawing circles of both men and women at any event. Beautiful Beth, with movie star looks enriched with a sweet personality, suffered the unwanted attention of too many young JayCee males, while all the ladies sought her friendship.

With two young girls about the same age as ours, Beth and Kent became our close friends. It was because of this friendship—and their inclination to host frequent parties—that we had been drawn into the JayCee social circle.

Ultimately, this led to one of my most embarrassing episodes.

It was a hot August night. Another party at the house at the end of the street. A warm, humid Indiana evening welcomed dozens of young couples to a gathering that spread over both floors of the bi-level home and into the back yard, surrounded with strings of sparkling overhead lights. Music was everywhere, and couples danced on the grass.

Small clusters of party-goers gathered in every corner of the home, conversing, laughing, drinking and smoking. Some lounged in the upstairs living room, but most clustered in small standing groups.

Anita and I circulated separately, touching base with many acquaintances. The open bar resided in the back yard, and I had prepared drinks for us—a weak vodka/lemonade for Anita and a scotch on the rocks for me.

Before long, working on my second scotch, I found the rock music irresistible. Kent had an enviable collection of album selections that he had transferred to a reel-to-reel tape deck. The crowd favorites repeated frequently—*Wooly Booly, Satisfaction, Wild Thing, Hang on Sloopy,* and a healthy dose of the incredibly danceable early Beatles tunes—*I Wanna Hold Your Hand; Twist and Shout; Please, Please me* and a dozen others.

At first I danced with Anita. Working up a sweat and a thirst, I took on my third scotch and found other dance partners. After more dancing and another trip to the open bar, I didn't need a partner.

I lost count of drinks. Then I lost track of where I was. The next thing I knew it was the next day—Sunday, nearly noon, and I was sprawled out on the sofa in our downstairs family room. I had no recollection of anything that had transpired after finishing my third, fourth or whatever number of scotches.

I had a record-breaking hangover. It was aspirin, tomato juice and crackers for the next twenty-four hours.

Anita never told me what had happened beyond the fact that it had taken two or three of our burly friends to "persuade" me to leave the party and accompany me home. The cracked glass of the front storm/ screen door was testimony to my reluctance.

Before this episode, I had scoffed at people's accounts of "blacking out" from drinking. But that's exactly what happened to me. It was a scary experience. The outcome was so painful and embarrassing that I was determined not to ever let it happen again; and I never have.

Kent was too much a gentleman afterward to bring up my behavior. Others weren't so tactful. Fortunately, no one seemed offended, although I'm sure I must have been terribly offensive. A few good-natured jokes at my expense at our next gathering pretty much dismissed the matter. And I had at least learned one thing—never again use scotch to quench my thirst.

In fact, future JayCee events would far overshadow my trifling shenanigans.


Our acceptance into the inner circle of the JayCees found us frequenting smaller, more intimate gatherings of the organization's leaders and their wives. We valued the close relationships.

The subsequent implosion was a big shock.

It didn't happen all at once, and perhaps the way it began should have been a clue. I remember when, during one of the more raucous social events, someone in our group declared that dancing with spouses should be banned. Already alcohol-fueled by that time, everyone embraced an idea that quickly spread throughout the membership.

Another seemingly unrelated event that ultimately impacted the JayCees was the decision of our good friend and neighbor, Kent, to run for mayor of Lafayette. The JayCees embraced his candidacy enthusiastically. That made us optimistic.

We should have known better.

Kent's political platform took aim at an incumbent administration that hadn't paid much attention to the issues that concerned young professionals in Lafayette—like antiquated in-town traffic management. Lafayette had no easy cross-town routes. Roadways followed paths laid out in the horse-and-buggy era; there were an inordinate number of five-point intersections; turn lanes were unheard of; and two railways frequently blocked existing cross-town routes.

JayCees were very keenly aware of these kinds of municipal shortcomings, with many young professionals having recently arrived from other cities. Surely, we thought, local voters would embrace Kent's progressive ideas.

Well, we were wrong. Kent lost the election. Apparently, the long-time Lafayette residents were just fine with the antiquated traffic patterns. The Monon Railroad's right-of-way down the center of Fifth Street for its entire run through downtown Lafayette was heartily embraced.

Kent took the loss very hard, as did the JayCees. Clearly, the electorate preferred established politicians with Lafayette pedigrees over "out-of-towners" with a "to-do" list.

Of course, we were naïve to think it would turn out any other way.

But we didn't anticipate the toll the lost election would take on our friend, Kent. Within a year, after struggling to accept the verdict that left him and his progressive ideas out in the cold, Kent moved his family to Southern California.

Of course, Kent's departure only confirmed the Lafayette establishment's tagging him as a "carpetbagger." The departure of Kent and Beth also sent shock waves through the JayCee organization. They had been the social and spiritual hub, and there were no obvious successors.

The organization might survive that loss, but it would be devastated by the next big shock. This one came from a time bomb planted by its own members.

That "no-dancing with spouses" rule seemed innocent enough, especially because this group loved to dance. Naturally, this led to people getting to know each other better. Not necessarily a bad idea, it fostered many genuine friendships.

No one had been prepared, then, for the shock of learning that one of the JayCee officers was having an affair with the wife of another officer in that tight circle.

Some might expect this would be uncomfortable when the officers got together. Some might think that one of the men would resign. None of that happened. Instead, the new "partners" and their former mates began to show up at social events.

Was this uncomfortable? For some, yes. For most it was simply intriguing. Combined with the loss of Kent and Beth to California, however, it brought about the demise of the tight social circle to which we had been welcomed.

And that brought an end to our JayCee adventure.

Fortunately for us, our deep and lasting friendship with the Burkes blossomed about that same time. Later, when they left Purdue in the summer of 1967—as Mike took a position at the University of Arizona—a social void remained that would never really be filled. Yes, we developed good relationships with other postdoctoral visitors. And we even joined a social bridge group of four young chemistry faculty couples whose friendship we enjoyed and has endured over the years.

But, increasingly, in the late 1960s and beyond, my social outlets would intertwine with my travel and work away from Purdue. It isolated me from not only my colleagues and friends at Purdue, but from my own family.

That was a problem—one that would fester but would not be confronted for many years.

# CHAPTER 53

## End of an Era?

The late sixties and early seventies at Purdue—during my late twenties and early thirties—were filled with countless highlights, many of which have been shared here. Professionally, I was riding a wave of computer-fueled notoriety. Socially, I was surrounded by fun-loving students and associates close to my age. For me, it was a *golden era*—rich with gratifying highs, fond memories, and tangible rewards.

However, that era had to end. By the mid-seventies, I would be creeping toward forty, and I could already see that my primary career catalyst—computerized instrumentation—was no longer a novelty. I hoped that my contribution to this technological revolution had secured my next big career step—promotion to full professor.

Promotions notwithstanding, however, the imminent end of this era raised a new specter. What would I do next?

Many scientists build a reputation by staking out a narrow, previously-unexplored research area and then mining it forever. Analytical chemists don't generally do that. We tend to focus on developing novel measurement principles, and this draws us toward diverse and changing scientific problems.

For example, I earned a Ph.D. at Wisconsin by becoming, for a time, the world's foremost expert on a very narrow topic—electro-reductions of aromatic ketones. I might then have built a career with studies of countless other organic electro-reductions.

Instead, I chose to plunge into studies of very rapid photolytic reactions. In short, I had to learn the new-to-me fields of photochemistry and spectroscopy.

Later, when I fell into the embryonic computer instrumentation revolution at Livermore Lab, I had to develop expertise in digital electronics and machine language programming.

There is an obvious pattern here. It's one that I would follow for the rest of my career. It's a pattern followed by most research analytical chemists. In effect, we earn a Ph.D. by mastering principles of measurement science and solving a unique chemical measurement problem, but the subsequent career involves periodic excursions into new disciplines or technology. More so than for other chemists, to an *analytical* chemist, the Ph.D. is a "license to learn."

I believe this unique broadband perspective explains why many analytical chemists eventually find themselves in leadership roles. My major professor at Wisconsin, Irv Shain, for example, became chancellor there. My mentor at Livermore Lab, Jack Frazer—despite his lack of an advanced chemistry degree—led the entire chemistry program there.

It is also common to see analytical chemists making dramatic career changes. A number of my colleagues converted to business or law careers. My first chemistry Ph.D. student, Bill Kretlow, followed the business path, obtaining an MBA and becoming an accomplished professor of finance at the University of Houston.

In my case, this "analytical" trait undoubtedly pointed me toward long-term career choices. However, at the end of this "computer instrumentation era," I could only wonder where my career was going. Had I earned a full professorship at Purdue? What new research horizons should I pursue? Would I have the drive to seek higher levels of recognition? Would I stay at Purdue?

All of these questions haunted me even as I was enjoying the amazing highs of the late sixties and early seventies.

I didn't know then where I was going. And I wondered how it would all play out.

# PART 7
# Reaching for the Brass Ring

# CHAPTER 54

## What's It All About?

I never dreamed of being rich.

But after earning tenure at Purdue—a job many academics would kill for—I had begun asking myself what I really wanted from life.

Why had I chosen the academic life? Certainly not because I was a dedicated scientist or teacher. I had met both. I wasn't one of them.

So what was it?

With some introspection, I realized my choice of the academic life was because it gave me the opportunity to work at things I enjoyed most—doing as I pleased and getting well paid for it.

It wasn't that simple, of course. Academic freedom allows a scholar to pursue whatever research he or she perceives as worthwhile. Yet it doesn't provide the resources and doesn't guarantee results or rewards. The university might be obligated to provide the start-up resources for a new professor, but that's it.

Therefore, if I wanted to continue enjoying the benefits of the academic life, I had to find sufficient funding to keep my program alive. That, in turn, depended upon generating new and interesting research ideas. Not surprisingly, successful fund-raising was also tied to outside notoriety—as measured by publications, invited talks, awards, organized symposia, etc. Last but not least was the required ability to write compelling research proposals.

How much does it cost to keep a research program going at a university? That depends on many factors—instrumentation, operating costs, and personnel. Personnel costs are the easiest to quantify. My research group had rapidly attained a steady state of about ten or twelve graduate students and a postdoctoral associate. Because some held teaching assistantships, I would have to provide, on average, one full-time and six or eight half-time salaries.

I was also required to find funding for at least part of a clerical salary and for at least the nominal twenty percent of my time devoted to research. In addition, the funding would have to cover related overhead costs (typically twenty-five to fifty percent of salaries and wages).

In the 1960s, this would have required about $80,000 per year—just in salaries, wages and overhead. Adding in the costs of equipment, supplies and travel could push the total well over $100,000 per year. To put this in perspective, the average National Science Foundation chemistry grant at that time was around $30,000 per year.

Clearly, to sustain a vibrant research program, money had to be solicited from several funding agencies, every year. Compound that with the reality that, overall, four out of five requests were denied, and you can see that a research director would be continually submitting new or renewal proposals to a battery of funding agencies.

This required mastering the art of *grantsmanship*—combining good writing and creativity with the *politics* of research funding. That is, successful grant writing takes into account driving forces behind available funds. For example, after the Soviets launched Sputnik in the 1950s, U.S. science and engineering funding received big boosts. After the oil shortages of the early seventies, alternative energy research gained favor. Dozens of similar incidents and related federal funding bumps could be recounted. Successful grantsmanship requires understanding what kinds of proposals will satisfy those driving forces. That requires establishing effective contacts with federal funding managers. (Yes, sometimes it's not "what you know but who you know.")

Did I master the art of grantsmanship? That is, did I manage to bring in enough money to support my voracious research machine? Every year?

The simple answer was yes—though it was far from simple.

I did learn to write proposals that were in tune with the ever changing politics of funding. For example, when basic studies in computer instrumentation would no longer get traction with the National Science Foundation, I discovered—through connections with DOD research program managers—that the Department of Defense was interested in exploring specific advanced applications of computer instrumentation. I subsequently prepared proposals that matched their needs and received funding from the Office of Naval Research for many years.

When the National Institutes of Health decided that their cancer research program should no longer fund my work in photoelectrochemistry, I turned to the Department of Energy for new funding. Again, through conversations with one of the program managers, I learned that lawmakers were promoting solar energy research. I was then able to persuade DOE that my research fit well with their program goals—well enough to sustain long term funding.

Yes, I was able to bring in a lot of money—typically receiving funds from three or more federal agencies every year. However, other sources of financial support were needed. A number of my students received fellowships, and many earned salaries by teaching in the computer courses. Postdocs sometimes received outside funding. And my first-year students typically were supported by teaching assistantships.

Bottom line, my research time and my students, postdocs and secretary were completely funded every year that I was at Purdue from the mid-1960s on.

I can't say that I didn't spend many anxious moments awaiting funding agency decisions. When the salaries of a dozen people and the feeding of a hyperactive research program depend on persuading anonymous, skeptical, scientific peers, that is one very daunting responsibility.

*Doing as you please* has a price.

Now, what about the second part—*getting well paid for it?*

Not surprisingly, just like successful grantsmanship, the personal monetary benefits of the academic life are directly related to one's success at achieving outside scientific notoriety.

Other universities don't determine your salary. Not directly. Nevertheless, your reputation elsewhere is what sets your value at your university. The most direct impact is provided when you're offered a job elsewhere.

This is the problem:

Most universities have ill-defined salary levels for professors. Assistant professor starting salaries are competitive among universities, and their range is pretty narrow. But salary ranges for the various professorial steps are typically very broad and overlapping. In practice, what a tenured professor is paid is directly related to what the competition is willing to pay. The way to get that paycheck is to go out and get a hard offer from the competition.

Many professors have learned how to play that game very well. It takes a certain amount of brashness and courage.

This is how the game might be played:

A professor publishes several papers describing a new, exciting area—spawning invitations to present seminars at other schools. While speaking at one of those schools, the visitor expresses some discontent with things back at "the U" and hints that a change of scenery might be desirable. One thing leads to another, and the other school asks what it would take to get the professor to move.

Moving a research program from one school to another is not a trivial thing. Equipment purchased by federal grants can move, but anything purchased by the school doesn't. Grad students and postdocs may or may not move with you. Grants may or may not move. It will take a good year or more before the research program recovers. And it may cost the school offering the job a lot of money.

A professor would be foolish to consider moving unless the offering university is willing to provide at least the equivalent facilities and equipment and somewhat more. The salary improvement should also be substantial. Often, a promotion to associate or full professor—or perhaps an endowed chair—will be part of the deal.

Getting the offer requires brashness. Taking the deal requires courage. People who are sincerely looking to move will simply inform their department head that they are accepting the offer and give notice of their imminent departure. They know that they are looking at a one or two year drought in research productivity. That can be deadly.

Those who are playing this game to squeeze something from their current employer require even *more* courage. The courage comes in recognizing that if your university doesn't come up with a counter offer, you may be boxed into an unwanted move.

How does one *play* this game? I don't know. When I eventually left Purdue, it was only after I felt I had done all that I ever wanted there and would be going to a position that offered a new and exciting challenge. I wasn't trying to press for a better deal at Purdue—although it would have happened had I stayed. (See *Epilogue*.)

That doesn't mean I never considered other academic jobs. But I either rejected them or they passed on me without anything ever being brought to Purdue's attention.

How did I ever attain a substantial salary without playing games?

First, one has to understand *why* universities try to hire faculty away from other schools. It's all about money and prestige. Mostly money.

Bringing in an established researcher with a big name attracts attention; attracts good grad students; attracts other faculty; and attracts research funds. With research funding come overhead funds that the university can use—at their discretion. Putting up large amounts of money to bring in established faculty might be less risky and more rewarding than providing set-up funds for a neophyte assistant professor that might crash and burn in five years.

Because faculty poaching is an expected part of academic game-playing, universities can protect themselves by keeping their faculty "stars" happy—with high salaries and other perks.

Fortunately, the Purdue chemistry department leadership understood this game very well. In my case, they realized that my notoriety during the late sixties and early seventies made me ripe for poaching. The proliferation of research grants I was bringing in provided financial incentive. Bottom line, they voluntarily rewarded me with significant salary increases to actively discourage my interest in other schools.

Now that was competent salary management—seriously. In fact, it was Joe Foster—the biochemist that had succeeded E. T. McBee as department head—who called me in to award that first big salary bump and proclaim his desire to keep me at Purdue. He had gone begging to the dean for extra bucks to throw at someone who *wasn't* twisting his arm. Believe me, that doesn't happen often. That's why many professors have to play the offer/counter-offer games they do.

I'm so glad I didn't have to.

Well, not exactly....

# CHAPTER 55

## Playing Games—a Flashback

It was the 1965-66 academic year, my fourth year at Purdue.

Within the past year, Buck had enticed another well-known chemist to join the analytical division at Purdue. He had wooed Fred McLafferty away from his post as director of research at Dow Chemical Corporation to take a full professor position. With Purdue's historic commitment to analytical chemistry—enhanced by the newly-added "stars" of Buck and Fred, Dale Margerum's ascendance in both inorganic and analytical, and two up-and-coming, very visible youngsters like Harry Pardue and me—Purdue would soon be considered the top Analytical program in the country.

I didn't expect to get tenure that year, but it wasn't impossible either. My publication record was solid. I had gotten two outside grants from major funding agencies—NSF and NIH. My research program had turned the corner into the exciting area of photoelectrochemistry. And I hadn't totally screwed up my teaching and committee assignments.

However, Buck had recently pushed the department hard to hire Fred McLafferty, and I didn't see him wading into another campaign—to promote me early. Furthermore there was no compelling reason to do so.

That is, there was no other university knocking at my door.

I knew young faculty elsewhere that had played the game—getting offers from other schools to force their early promotion.

I was frustrated that I wasn't in a position to play.

But this was Harry Pardue's year—his fifth at Purdue. It was up or out for him.

There was no doubt in my mind that Harry should be promoted. He had done all the right things—publications, talks and grants. Most impressive to me, though, he *acted like* an established professor. He seemed to know the right things to say and when to say them. He mixed comfortably with academic colleagues. I was envious; and observant.

It was during one of our bridge nights at the Pardue's that year that Harry casually mentioned to me that he had recently visited Wayne State University.

"What do you think of the place?" he asked me.

"I was impressed when I interviewed there. Good chemistry department. A solid analytical program."

"Didn't they offer you a job?"

His wife, Ruby, at the kitchen counter slicing a pie, turned her head to throw Harry a puzzled glance.

"They made a nice offer," I replied. "But I'm glad Purdue came along."

"Would you have taken the Wayne State job?"

Ruby dropped the knife on the counter and turned around. "All right, Harry. Why don't you just tell him?"

I gave Harry my best vacant gaze. He was having a hard time forming words, but the body language was promising.

Finally, he blurted, "They offered me a job." He managed a tiny prideful grin.

I lost my voice while several questions vied for top billing in my mind. "With tenure?" I asked, finally. "Associate professor?"

A sheepish look, but a slight curl to the lips, as he replied, "*Full* professor, with tenure."

I whistled. "Wow! They must really want you."

Harry demurred while Ruby beamed. It was quiet for a few moments. Then I asked, "Does Buck know about it?"

He nodded. "Told him this morning."

"What did he say?"

"Not much. Congratulated me."

"What about your promotion?"

He shrugged. "You know Buck. He asked if I was planning to leave."

"What the hell is that? You wouldn't leave, would you?"

Harry cocked his head and seemed to think about it. "Well, I don't know—"

"C'mon, Harry," cried Ruby, "you're talking to Sam, not Buck." She gave up on dessert and returned to the bridge table.

Harry threw her a sharp look and then turned to me, "It's a good offer from a very good school. I like all the people there—Boltz, Rorabacher, Schenk. I think I'd fit in real well."

"You don't really think Purdue will let you go, do you?"

Harry shook his head. "This isn't a game, Sam. I'm dead serious about the opportunity at Wayne State."

I stuck out a palm. "I'm sorry. I didn't mean to imply—"

"—that he's using Wayne State as a ploy?" interjected Ruby.

"Yes … I mean, no," I stammered. "I don't know." I turned to Harry. "*Are* you?"

He wagged his head. "Not my intention," he replied. "I didn't go looking for it, you know. I've worked closely with the Wayne State people—on meetings and symposia—and, well, they decided they'd like to see me there."

I searched his face. "You're really serious about this? Moving?"

He nodded.

"Buck won't let it happen," I declared.

He shrugged. "I don't know. What can he do? He burned a lot of chips hiring McLafferty."

"Oh, Harry. Don't be silly," Ruby interjected. "Tell him, Sam."

I pulled back. "Wait a minute. I'm no expert on these things." The germ of an idea had struck me though—something worth exploring.

"What things?" asked Harry, interrupting my thoughts.

"Putting pressure on Purdue," I replied quickly, "to get your promotion."

Harry shook his head vigorously. "Not a game I want to play. Too risky. Miscalculate, and you're off to some place you really don't want to be."

I threw him a knowing grin. "Despite that, you're right in the middle of the game."

Harry shrugged. "Yes—although I'm actually serious about this other job. Which brings back my original question, what do *you* think about Wayne State?"

I looked at Harry for a moment, hesitant to throw out the wild idea hatching in my brain. "I think it would be … *great*," I offered tentatively, "if Wayne State had *both* of us."

Harry blinked. "What are you suggesting?"

"I mean, what if we *both* moved to Wayne State?"

Ruby stared at me. "I had no idea you weren't happy here."

My wife, Anita, hadn't said anything, but my professed idea had taken her by surprise. She glared at me and echoed Ruby's question. I felt a slight twinge of guilt—realizing abruptly how difficult it had been to share these ambiguous and personal career deliberations with my wife.

"I'm not unhappy," I insisted. "I'm thinking of how well Harry and I complement each other, scientifically, here, or at Wayne State."

"Oh, I get it," said Ruby, "Maybe you're thinking that Purdue might consider letting one of you go, but not *both*."

Ruby had put her finger on it. Harry might not want to play this risky game, but I was suddenly excited at the thought. "That's one factor," I admitted. "Like Harry said, though, you don't play the game unless you're really serious about the other job."

"So…." Harry drawled. "Would you welcome a move to Wayne State?"

"Well, yes, if it were *both* of us. Wayne State already has a strong analytical division. With *us* there, it would be one of the most complete, if not the best. I think we'd attract some good students."

"Hmmm, I see what you're getting at."

"What do *you* think?"

Harry looked away and appeared lost in thought for a few moments. Then he turned and said, "It's an intriguing idea, but…." He let the words hang.

I filled in the unspoken thought. "But it's not the deal on the table, right?"

He nodded. "I don't know if Wayne State could do it, even if they wanted to."

"Do you think it's worth exploring?"

This time Harry took a long time to reply. Finally, he said, "Sam, it means a lot to know that you would want to do this. Unfortunately, I don't think this is the way."

I dwelled on his words for a few moments and then shrugged. "You're right. It was a crazy idea; not very well thought out, I guess." I heard Anita breathe a sigh of relief.

Harry cocked his head and grinned. "I wouldn't have looked forward to dropping this one on Buck."

When I had time to think about it later, I realized what a dreadfully stupid and self-serving idea it was. It was Harry's party, and I had no business butting in. Thank God he was smart enough to ease me out and polite enough to spare my feelings.

And wise enough to realize he didn't need *me* to get what he wanted.

I learned later that Buck had done more than just congratulate Harry on the Wayne State job offer. He had asked Harry to postpone his decision until after Buck had had time to explore what Purdue might do. Harry and Ruby had taken off during a break to visit family in West Virginia when he got the call from Buck with Purdue's counter-offer.

Harry got his promotion that year. I wasn't privy to the negotiations, but I do know that he would have been promoted regardless of the outside offer. He turned down a very sweet deal at Wayne State, but I have no doubt it helped him get a good raise and a few perks for his research program. It was well-deserved.

I told Harry how glad I was that he had remained at Purdue, and I meant it. As Buck had predicted, Harry's successes would be my benchmarks.

I didn't get the chance to play the outside-offer game, this time. Nor did I ever play it like others did. But that's another story for a later chapter.

# CHAPTER 56

## A Bump in the Road

It was May, 1969. My academic career was going like gangbusters. Publications, research grants, invited talks; everything was humming. I was locked on to my ultimate goal—promotion to full professor. I was optimistic enough to think it could happen this next year, only three years after making tenure.

That was when the Indiana legislature decided to complicate my life. It wasn't their intention, of course. The target of their folly was the student population. Disturbed by student activism elsewhere—like California and Wisconsin—the legislators decided on a preemptive strike, causing the university to hike student fees.

What were they thinking? Did they think that chastised students would be afraid to speak up against an immoral war? Against social injustice? Against punitive acts by idiotic lawmakers?

If that's what they thought, they were wrong.

I was in charge of the trailer section of the mainstream freshman chemistry course with 1600 students enrolled. Four professors shared the lecture load. I managed a small army of teaching assistants and a Ph.D. lab supervisor. It was time for the final midterm exam.

The exam, as usual, was scheduled on a Wednesday evening in the 6000-seat Elliott Hall of Music, the only facility on campus large enough to give an exam to the entire class. There were three different versions of the same exam, with questions scrambled to hinder cheating by wandering eyes.

The legislature's punitive action hit the newspapers on the prior weekend. By Monday afternoon, students were staging a large protest in front of the main administration building. The minuscule core of campus activists opposed to the Vietnam War fanned the flames. The overwhelming show of force by Chicago police and National Guard at the Democratic national convention that past August had only increased the resolve. Purdue students threatened to shut down the university.

*Student protest outside executive building, May, 1969. [Courtesy of Purdue University Statistics Department (1950s – 60s Gallery, www.stat.purdue. edu), copyright, Lillian Cote, used with permission.]*

That was when I got the call.

The youthful male voice was raspy. "Dr. Perone, you need to cancel the exam in the Hall of Music tomorrow night."

"What? Who is this?" I asked in surprise.

"We're shutting down the campus. No classes Wednesday."

"This is an *exam*," I responded. "People have—"

"We don't care," the voice interrupted. "Everything gets shut down."

"I don't think I can do that."

The voice remained silent for a few moments. Then it remarked coldly, "Dr. Perone, you don't want to be *responsible* for what might happen to your students."

There was a click. And the voice was gone.

A dozen questions swirled in my head. Was this a hoax? Who should I tell? What should I do? How would students respond to a canceled exam?

But one thought emerged above all. *What might happen to my students?*

Would the students attending the exam have to run a gauntlet of protesters? Could someone plant a *bomb* in the Hall of Music?

I decided that the first person to call was the head of the general chemistry program, Derek Davenport.

"Derek, I just received a phone call—from a student, I think—telling me to cancel the freshman chem. exam Wednesday evening. They implied students would be harmed. I thought you should know."

With his typical British aplomb, Derek responded, "Congratulations. You've just gotten your first threatening phone call. Welcome to the club."

"Derek, this is serious. You know what's happening at the administration building, don't you?"

He remained silent for a moment. "Why don't you check with the Purdue police? See what they can tell you."

"What if they tell me to cancel the exam?"

"Then there's nothing you can do. Your students will be pissed—at least, most of them."

I thought about it. He was right. These were serious students for the most part, typical of the entire Purdue student body. Most of them would be irritated as hell that some militant minority was shutting down the campus. "So you think I should go ahead with the exam if the police tell me it's OK?"

"That's your call, Sam. You're in charge."


The call to the campus police had been put through to a captain whose name I had already forgotten. He had told me they would send someone to my office. Sporting a baggy gray linen suit, that man was now standing in my doorway.

"Dr. Perone? I'm George Crane, with the campus police," he said, extending a hand. He was sixtyish, paunchy, with short-cropped white hair. Beneath plain rimless glasses, the eyes were gray and tired.

For some reason I had expected someone younger and uniformed. I didn't know about plainclothes officers on campus. Then again, I thought, this might be a hired gun—some private Pinkerton brought in to deal with the crisis.

I stood and extended my hand in greeting, offering him the chair normally reserved for one-on-ones with students. He sat down with a sigh. His whole demeanor cried out for a return to that era when a student mob meant a football pep rally or a panty raid.

Crane listened patiently to the story of the telephone threat and my concerns for the safety of my students. He made notes on a small pad pulled from his jacket.

"What's your problem, Dr. Perone?" he asked when I had finished. "Why not re-schedule the exam?"

"Impossible. All the midterms for this course are evening exams—blocked out on students' schedules. There are no alternative dates."

"Give it during a lecture period."

"No way. This is a huge class. Four separate sections. It's impossible to prepare four different equivalent exams."

Crane's gray eyebrows arched above his spectacles. "You teach all four sections?"

"Yeah. Give the same lecture four times a day."

"Sounds brutal."

"It is. Good news is that four different professors divide the course into four-week segments."

Crane absorbed the information. "OK. I see. What do you want to do?"

"I want you to tell me it's safe to give the exam Wednesday night."

"Can't tell you that."

"Why not?"

"We're expecting thousands of protesters, nasty characters—Hippies, Yippies, SDS. They're looking to do some harm."

I shook my head. He was talking about the *Purdue* student body—probably the most conservative assembly of young people in the country. Sure, there was a smattering of activists, maybe a hundred on campus all told.

"Can't you at least protect the Hall of Music?" I protested. "I mean, set up some kind of perimeter—just let in my students?"

"That wouldn't guarantee anything."

"Why not?"

Crane sighed. "Let me count the ways. A fake ID lets in a troublemaker. Someone tosses tear gas into a ventilation shaft. Do you want me to go on?"

"Haven't you ever had to deal with this kind of threat before?"

*Students clash with police at the executive building, May, 1969. [Acc20130127_add16, courtesy of Purdue University Libraries, Virginia Kelly Karnes Archives and Special Collections. Used with permission.]*

Crane remained silent for a few moments. Then he replied slowly, "This is a whole new ball game. We may have to bust a few heads."

I frowned. "Sounds like you're telling me to cancel the exam."

"No. The administration wants business as usual on Wednesday."

I stared at him in disbelief. "You're telling me I should go ahead with the exam Wednesday night, even if the campus is in chaos?"

"I didn't say that. It's your call, Dr. Perone. I'm just saying we can't guarantee anything."

I just stared at him.

Abruptly, Crane stood to leave. He extended his hand and said, "Better think it over. Let me know by tomorrow noon."

I stood and took his hand. "How do I reach you?"

He pulled a card from his shirt pocket and handed it to me. I looked at it. It was a generic campus police card. Penciled on the face was his name and number.

Then suddenly the mysterious George Crane was gone.


The course staff meeting was scheduled for early Tuesday morning. The lab supervisor and all the teaching assistants were there. This was the first opportunity to inform them about the threat to the Wednesday night exam.

I announced that I would *cancel* the exam.

No sooner were the words out of my mouth than one of the T.A.'s shouted, "That's bullshit!" It was my own research student, John Zipper—never one to hold back.

I turned to John expectantly. He continued, "You're screwing all the good students because some asshole makes a phony threat?"

"I have to assume it's *real*, Zip."

Another T.A. spoke up. "The students will be mad as hell. They're prepared for this exam."

"Better mad than dead," I quipped. "The police can't guarantee safety."

Despite the grumbling, we hammered out the details. Students would be notified of the canceled exam in all lectures, labs, and recitations. Exam grades would be pro-rated.

The reason given for canceling the exam was that the campus police couldn't guarantee access to the Hall of Music because of the anticipated rally. That was sort-of true, but I knew the word would get out that a threat had been made.

I left the staff meeting dreading the groans and gripes that would greet my announcements during each of the day's four lectures.

But those would be nothing compared to the noises my faculty colleagues would make.


Before the staff meeting, I had informed my division head, Buck Rogers, about my decision to cancel the exam. He mouthed words of understanding, but steely eyes peering down that aristocratic nose delivered the real message.

Buck had volunteered to inform the department head. I had already informed the general chemistry head, Derek Davenport, by phone. Previous conversations with them had made it clear that canceling the exam would be my decision.

It wasn't until after the second lecture of the day that I was able to take a break. I needed the break like never before. The freshman chem. students had been testy and restless. A couple dozen of the nearly 400 in each of the first two lectures had left after I announced the exam cancellation. I suspected that some of the departing students were reporting to protest organizers.

I returned to my office for a sandwich and a little "quiet" time. Then I did something very rare. I locked the office door.

No sooner did I sit at my desk and grab my sack lunch than the phone began to ring. I sighed and picked up the black receiver.

"Sam? This is Harold Hansen," the gruff voice announced. "I heard about the general chem. exam." He paused and then growled, "Are you out of your mind?"

"Excuse me?" I replied, somewhat stunned by the blunt question. Hansen was one of the senior faculty in charge of some of the most difficult-to-teach general chemistry courses—like the one for agriculture majors. He had a very effective no-nonsense, intimidating style. I was one of his admirers. The feeling apparently was not reciprocated.

"You heard me!" he bellowed. "You backed down to those *hippies*. Who's running this goddam place—those filthy, long-haired freaks or *us*?"

I bit my tongue. "Do you know the whole story?" I asked. "The campus police said they couldn't protect my students in the Hall of Music. I didn't have any choice."

"Bullshit! That's not what I heard. You could've gone ahead with the exam."

"Is that what you would have done?" I asked.

"Damn right! Let the cops swing a few clubs. Students won't do this again."

I hesitated before responding. This wasn't going to get any better.

"Well," I said slowly, "I guess backing down means they *will* try it again. Then maybe you can do it *your* way."

Hansen sputtered for a second. But I didn't wait for more. I hung up.

To be fair, a number of faculty did call to tell me they understood my action. That was comforting. Yet that also meant that my dilemma and decision had been the hot topic of conversation in the hallways. Not good.

Whoever said, "There's no such thing as bad publicity," didn't have academic institutions in mind.

I never doubted that I had done the right thing. Nevertheless, I had to wonder if my chances for promotion to full professor hadn't just taken a big hit.

# CHAPTER 57

## Get a Ph.D. and See the World

As the 1960s came to a close, and despite apprehension regarding my future promotion to full professor, I considered embarking on one of the most treasured perks of a tenured professor—a sabbatical leave. I chose to spend the spring semester, 1970, back at the Lawrence Livermore Lab working with Jack Frazer again on developing human-computer interactive experimentation—an area where the Lab was again pushing the envelope.

My family thoroughly enjoyed the time in California, residing in a Livermore apartment, getting reacquainted with old friends, San Francisco, the beaches and Disneyland. Vita and Amy were enrolled in Livermore schools and made new friends.

I also applied for and received a NATO fellowship for a four-month stay in Zurich. Our young family had already become seasoned domestic travelers, accompanying me on extended business trips to both the east and west coasts. But going to live in Europe? The excitement reached record levels.

Accordingly, after the summer short course ended in late June of 1970, my family found itself waiting excitedly to board an overnight, overseas flight from O'Hare airport.

"You can't carry this on board, sir," she said sweetly.

My gaze snapped back and forth between the pretty red-headed flight attendant and the black leather flight bag in question. "But ...

but it says I can bring one carryon piece of luggage," I protested, waving the *Aer Lingus* boarding pass at her.

"Yes, but this bag is too large for overseas flights," she explained. The honey-like tone of her lilting Irish accent belied the firmness of her intent, as she literally barred us from boarding the plane.

"I don't understand. This bag is designed to be a carryon. It fits under the seat."

"I'm sorry, sir. It doesn't meet overseas standards."

"What does?"

She pointed to my wife's purse—a modest-sized shoulder bag. And she pointed to another passenger's Pan Am flight bag—about the size of a lunch box. "These are allowed," she said.

I began to panic. "What can I do? All of my important papers are in this bag."

That was an understatement. In preparing for a four-month stay, I had stuffed everything I would require for business and for managing family affairs into this one bag that I intended to keep within sight at all times.

"Perhaps you can re-pack your important items in the carryon pieces you're allowed," the young lady suggested. Her words were like honeysuckle vapors floating in the air and made me pause.

It took only a second's consideration, though, to realize the task was impossible. Beside my wife's bag, which had no room, we had a small flight bag with items for our three girls. The youngest, Renée, was only a year-and-a-half, and her needs pretty much filled that bag. I shook my head at the attendant. "That's not going to work."

"If you could step aside, sir, I'll call a manager to help you."

Reluctantly, our little family of five pulled out of the boarding queue. The man summoned by the flight attendant arrived quickly, and she explained the problem.

The manager was older, experienced and persuasive. "I assure you, sir, I will personally carry this bag on to the baggage compartment. It will be hand-carried off at Shannon Airport and will be waiting for you."

He tied a tag on the bag, gave me the stub, and carried the bag away.

I watched him disappear through a doorway leading to the tarmac below where other luggage was being loaded. I had nothing left but a luggage tag stub and an ominous feeling.

That long flight from Chicago O'Hare to Shannon in the western part of Ireland was filled with anxiety. This was only the first leg of our travel to Zurich. We would spend the first few days in Ireland and then catch a BEA flight to London. After a few days there, we would take a Swissair flight to Zurich.

Already I was regretting the travel agent's insistence that we book flights on each new country's airline. The *Aer Lingus* flight was on a Boeing 727—much smaller than the 707's or one of the new 747's we might have booked on TWA or Pan Am. With its limited range, the *Aer Lingus* flight required a refueling stopover in eastern Canada.

It seemed the only thing I could do was get off the plane quickly at Shannon airport and claim my flight bag. I wouldn't rest until it was back in my hands.

I was consumed with recounting all that I had placed in that bag: a complete set of slides for a month's lectures at the *Eidgenössische Technische Hochschule Zürich*; Larry Sybrandt's handwritten draft of his Ph.D. thesis; all correspondence related to the NATO fellowship; all correspondence with Professor Hans Günthard with whom I would be working at the ETH Zürich; my personal checkbook; a couple papers I was reviewing; drafts of a couple of my papers; a file folder containing all our travel arrangements; and our passports.

I had removed only the travel folder and passports to carry with us on board.

After an early morning approach and landing at an airport surrounded by stunningly lush vegetation extending to the horizon, I helped Anita and the girls off the plane and dashed madly to the baggage claim. I was quick, but not as quick as the more seasoned travelers. Much of the luggage had been picked up.

Frantically, I scanned the remaining scattered pieces until I saw it. The black flight bag sat by itself on a slowly moving belt. I ran to it and grabbed it off the track.

As always, I looked first for my ID tag. It was *missing*.

I started to panic. There was an *Aer Lingus* baggage tag. I compared it to my stub. They didn't match.

This wasn't my bag.

I tossed it back on the belt and quickly scanned the handful of remaining bags from our flight. Our other luggage was there, but no black flight bag.

I hurried to the clerk at the baggage counter and explained that my bag was missing. It didn't take a big IQ to figure out that someone had mistakenly taken my bag and left theirs behind.

Who? Where had they gone?

The baggage clerk had no answers. "They'll bring it back as soon as they realize they've got the wrong bag," he said. "Give us your hotel information, and we'll run it over to you."

The only thing I could think was, *why?* Why me? Why *this* bag? Why hadn't they checked the tag? I would gladly have traded any or all of our other bags for this one bag.

Having arrived early in the morning local time, we spent the day and night at a hotel near Shannon airport. Friends had advised us to fight jet lag by getting some sleep during that day as well as that night. But I couldn't. When I didn't get a call from *Aer Lingus*, I called them.

Nothing.

It wasn't until late that evening that I got a call. Yes, they had located the bag. A traveler had picked it up and brought it home with them before realizing it wasn't theirs. I was *ecstatic*.

Then I learned that the bag had been transported to the traveler's home in Donegal, Northern Ireland. That was a hell of long way from Shannon. Northern Ireland? I only knew about the civil unrest and bombings—the Protestant-Catholic thing that had been going on forever.

Of all places, why did my bag have to end up *there?*

The *Aer Lingus* people didn't seem concerned. They would have the bag forwarded to Dublin where we would be for the following few days. They provided me with the phone number of a contact at the airport. They were confident we would have the bag well before we flew on to London.

I breathed a tentative sigh of relief.

My Indiana driver's license was sufficient to prove that I was qualified to rent a car from Hertz for our drive to Dublin. That seemed awfully convenient.

Little did I know then that the joke was on *me*.

It was a compact, two-door British Ford—just barely enough room for our family, with much of the luggage strapped to a roof rack. It had a four-speed manual transmission.

I had driven a four-speed before, but not with the driver's seat on the *right*.

Left-handed shifting with everything mirror-imaged, including the oncoming traffic, was an unnerving experience. The good news was that the route we took between Shannon and Dublin was not heavily traveled. The bad news was that the sparse traffic made it easy to forget mirror-image driving rules.

By the time I began to feel comfortable behind the wheel, I started to realize that road markings in this part of Ireland in 1970 were nonexistent. There were no superhighways, just country roads. The road maps supplied by Hertz were useless. The only clues to location were the quaint crossroad signs along the way. These signs pointed to each of the little towns you might reach if you took the selected turn or fork. Rarely did one of these signs point to Dublin.

Needless to say, the trip to Dublin was an adventure. While Anita and the girls enjoyed the beautiful green countryside and the occasional tiny villages along the way, I struggled to maintain my mirror-image driving focus and put together a crude point-to-point navigating strategy. Of course, while I perspired in the driver's seat, the girls had great fun advising me which path to take at each crossroad.

I have no idea how we did it. An image of our dot-to-dot journey probably looked more like a pinwheel than a straightedge. Fortunately, we reached Dublin before dark. We were lucky to enter the city on a road that took us directly to our hotel. I didn't realize *how* lucky until the following day.

After checking in, my first call was to *Aer Lingus* baggage control at the airport. Going through the explanations and a couple of transfers, I finally got someone who might help. But, no, my bag hadn't yet shown up. He took my number at the hotel and assured me they would rush the bag over as soon as it arrived.

My next stop was to inquire with the hotel concierge regarding where I might cash a traveler's check. The travel agency had advised us to find a bank in each country for cashing checks, as we would get the best exchange rate there. Others had advised us to use a credit card for purchases. For this I had gotten a brand new American Express card— my very first credit card.

I had exchanged a hundred dollars for Irish currency before departing O'Hare airport. Good thing. We arrived in Ireland in the middle of a country-wide *bank strike*.

Hence, we were stuck with using the credit card—not always acceptable—or persuading Dublin shopkeepers to take American dollars, once our hundred dollars' worth of local currency expired.

Some fun.

Then there was the *city driving*.

We took off on a sightseeing excursion the following day in our rented Ford. What an experience *that* was. Driving a mirror-image car in an ancient city that never imagined roads laid out in straight lines was difficult enough. Add to that the heavy traffic of a metropolitan area and the introduction of a phenomenon I had never seen before— intersection rotaries.

All right, I could handle the left-handed, clockwise rotaries with a single lane and three or four entry/exits. But when they expanded to three or four or more rotary lanes with multiple entry/exits, I gave up.

Literally.

We found a quiet side street; parked the Ford; called Hertz to come and get it; and hailed a taxi.

That was the end of my rental car excursions. Done. Finished. Never again.

The good news was that we found a congenial taxi driver—a colorful, elderly gentleman who agreed to give us a guided tour of Dublin and environs. He drove us around for half the day for forty dollars American. Most relaxing time I had in Ireland.


It was a week later before we finally arrived in Zurich.

No, my flight bag hadn't yet appeared. Not in Dublin. Not in London. Not in Zurich.

By this time I had gotten to know a number of baggage handling managers. It was apparent to all that the bag was now completely lost. The party in Northern Ireland had gotten their bag back. Then they had forwarded my bag to Dublin as directed. That was the last anyone had seen or heard of it.

I was now resigned to the idea of making do without my flight bag. I wrote to my secretary, Connie, at Purdue and instructed her to provide Dave Jones with all the illustrations for my ETH lectures so he could get new slides made ASAP. I also told Connie to mail me another copy of Larry Sybrandt's draft Ph.D. thesis.

Also, because I had made arrangements with a Zurich bank to cash our personal checks during our stay, I had to write a Lafayette neighbor with our house key to mail me a replacement book of blank checks.

I would be just fine.

Or so I thought.

Ten days after Dave Jones got my request, I received an air express box full of slides. Inside the box was a sealed letter addressed to "The Wandering Italian who lost his to the Irish Revolution." For emphasis, the corners of the envelope were scorched.

The enclosed letter itemized all the slides Dave had produced. He finished by saying, "Next time hang on to the damn bag!" The corners were scorched for emphasis.

I got the message.

But I didn't get a copy of Larry Sybrandt's thesis draft. This time I sent a letter directly to Larry. If he wanted to finish up in a timely fashion, I wrote, he should get a copy to me quickly.

Eamon was the handsome, thirtyish, dark-haired Irishman managing the *Aer Lingus* office in downtown Zurich. Despite my nearly daily harassment, he politely and efficiently took up the search for my bag. In fact, he took on the mystery of the disappearing flight bag as if it were his own. He was determined to track it down.

Frustrated in that pursuit for two months, Eamon finally struck gold! By systematically pursuing all possible disappearance pathways, he got a report of a lonely little black flight bag sitting in the lost and found section of a Belfast bus station. How it got there was a mystery. It had been stripped of any I.D. tags but was otherwise intact. Without Eamon's persistence, that bag would have disappeared into the Land of the Lost.

I got the bag back and sent a letter off immediately to Connie so that she could calm down Dave and reassure Larry that I could now read his thesis.

In the meantime, even before the bag had been located, Eamon and his wife had befriended our entire family and begun showing us Zurich. All was well.

Except for one problem.

Connie wrote back to inform me that—contrary to what I had been led to believe—Larry's handwritten thesis draft in my bag was the *one and only* copy that existed.

Of course I never would have taken it if I had known it was the only copy. Larry had assured me that he had made a photocopy.

Only later did I learn how devastated he had been when he heard about the lost flight bag. Imagine writing your first and only novel—the all-consuming work of your life—and losing the only copy. He simply couldn't gather the courage to tell

*Larry Sybrandt, Purdue grad student days. [Copyright, S. P. Perone]*

me. Neither could he find the inspiration to write again what he had struggled to produce the first time.

So Larry did what anyone would do. He swore the group to secrecy and took up a Ping-Pong paddle and pool cue.

Larry spent his days in the Student Union, working out his depression. He got really good—with a trophy to prove it.

All of this came out, eventually— little by little—so that I knew the whole story by the time he finished his final oral exam.

However, the saga of the lost flight bag and Larry's emotional roller coaster journey paled by comparison to other events of that year.

# CHAPTER 58

## Zurich

We used Zurich as a hub for short excursions by rail to other European cities—Rome, Florence, Venice, Naples, Paris, Munich, Amsterdam, Copenhagen and Madrid.

Growing up in Rockford, Illinois, my wife and I had rarely seen the outskirts of town, much less another country. Conversely, our three young girls, in1970—at ten, eight, and one-and-a-half years—were becoming seasoned continental travelers. Renée, unfortunately, would remember very little of this experience, but—though she considers it little consolation—there is a delightful graphic record of her "backpacking" through Europe.

*Touring, 1970. Left, Amy in Venice; Center, Paris, Vita, S.P., Amy, Renée (in backpack); Right, S.P. and Renée surveying rooftops in Italy. [Copyright, S. P. Perone]*

In Zurich, we rented a lovely, furnished four-room apartment on the third floor of a vintage building owned by the mother of Professor Günthard's secretary. The octogenarian owner, Mrs. Einsele, occupied the fourth floor. She became a grandmother-substitute for our girls—who delighted visiting her for "tea and cookies" and listening to her piano playing. From our kitchen window we could see the tiny market where we did daily grocery shopping to fill our microscopic refrigerator. While we watched, the older girls, Vita and Amy, were allowed to run to the market and ask for items in their newly acquired German.

There was no crime to speak of and no unemployment. Everyone had a job, even if it were simply sweeping the streets. No one was idle.

We decided not to put the girls in school. Instead we transported their books and lesson plans for home schooling. It worked.

To help learn the local language, we rented a television set, quickly discovering that there were four official Swiss languages—German, French, Italian, and something called Swiss-Romaine that was closer to Latin. In Zurich they spoke German—really *Schweizerdeutsch,* the local dialect. Softer and more rhythmic, the speech was readily discernible from the more precise and harsh sounds uttered by Germans speaking the same words.

Most locals spoke two or more languages, including very good English, so we never felt pushed to learn more than a few words and phrases. When we traveled by train and had the rare encounter with someone who did not speak English, we could often find a common language to communicate on some level. I sometimes used broken French from my high school and college studies. Strangely, I was able to draw on the Italian (really Sicilian) that I had learned as a child. And that leads to a story that is probably the most memorable of our personal experiences in Zurich.

As a child I learned to speak in the Sicilian dialect of my grandparents because my parents worked and I spent most of my days and nights with my mother's parents—Giacamo (Jack) and Catherina (Tina). Jack was from Palermo; Tina was from Marsala. They had emigrated from Sicily as youngsters. Neither could read or write. Jack spoke only a few words of English. Tina spoke some broken English. Hence, as a child, I communicated with them in their own Sicilian dialect.

*Catherine (Licari) Parrinello, Giacamo (Jack) Parrinello.*
*November, 1942. [Copyright, S. P. Perone]*

Over the years, Tina kept in touch with her aunts, uncles, cousins, nieces and nephews back in Sicily. Although she couldn't read or write the letters, she found someone who could. When she learned that I was traveling to Europe, she let me know that one of my cousins—a young lady of my age by the name of Maria—was living near Zurich. Maria and her husband, Salvatore, were working in the little town of Olten, about 30 kilometers from Zurich. My grandmother told me in no uncertain terms that I *must* get together with Maria during my visit to Switzerland. She wrote Maria to tell her so.

Now, by the time I had reached the ripe old age of thirty-one and traveled to Europe, I had not used my childhood Sicilian language for a long, long time. If I recognized any written or spoken Italian words, it was due more to my experience with French or high school Latin than any conscious recollection of what I had understood as a child. Although I had the address of my cousin in Olten, I knew that they did not speak English. So I didn't really have a good idea about how to get in touch with them.

Nevertheless, I knew that I had better do something or face my grandmother's wrath. And none of Tina's grandchildren cherished that idea.

But the issue was taken out of my hands.

On one lazy Sunday afternoon in Zurich—a rare excursion-free weekend for our family—we were startled by a knock on the apartment door. My attention was diverted abruptly from the historical novel I was reading about *The Arms of Krupp*, and I walked apprehensively to the door. No one had come to our door uninvited since the day we had moved in. My former student, Bill Kretlow, had come to visit us briefly as he toured Europe. Eamon and his wife had been invited over. Doctor Urs Wild, who I worked with at the ETH, and his wife, Eve, had visited. Our upstairs landlord, Mrs. Einsele, did not come to our apartment. Our girls went up to visit her.

I opened the door tentatively, peering through the widening crack. What I saw looking back at me was the face of pretty young dark-haired lady with fair skin and a smile that would melt an iceberg. Behind her was a handsome, brown-haired young man, grinning broadly. Another young couple stood behind them.

No one spoke. They just stood there, all smiles. "Hello?" I offered tentatively.

Although I didn't think it possible, the young lady's smile brightened. She pulled something from her purse and showed it to me.

It was a picture. It was a picture of *me*.

Finally, she spoke to me. "*Tu*," she said, pointing first to the picture and then at me. "*Tina*," she added, making a funny waving motion with her hand and then pointing to the picture.

I could feel the frown creasing my brow. Then, suddenly, I got it!

She was talking about my grandmother, sending the picture. I knew right then that this was my cousin, *Maria*.

She saw the light in my eyes. I spoke out. "Maria?"

That was when she reached out her arms, and we embraced as if we had known each other our entire lives. It was a moment I will never forget.


They spoke no English. We spoke no Italian. That didn't matter. Within moments we had embraced all of them and they all of us. Salvatore hugged and kissed me on the cheeks like a long-lost brother. We embraced their dear friends, Pietro and Catherina. They were all about my age. Catherina had sandy, curly hair, and a girlish giggle that found humor in everything. Pietro was a darker, thinner version of Salvatore.

We visited that entire afternoon and made plans for a train trip to Olten the following weekend. We learned that they all worked in Olten at the Bally shoe company and that they had moved to Switzerland from Sicily because there was no work back home. They had temporary work visas and would have to return to Sicily someday. They sent much of their earnings home. They had a good life in Olten, much better than in Sicily. They were happy. They were best friends.

Salvatore and Pietro found it amusing that I identified with their jobs—having worked my way through high school and college by shining and repairing shoes.

How did we manage all of this communication? It was an amazing experience. At first we used sign language and props. Soon I realized that I was able to understand much of what they said—especially if they kept it simple. Then I began to use a word or two from my long lost Sicilian vocabulary. I remembered the Italian-English dictionary I had brought along. When we were stuck, I looked up the words.

By the end of the afternoon, enough of my childhood Sicilian had mysteriously surfaced, and we were able to carry on crude conversations.

*Sicilian cousins in Zurich apartment, 1970. From left: Amy, Anita, Maria, Salvatore, Vita, Pietro, Catherina. [Copyright, S. P. Perone]*

I also discovered something I had never suspected.

It happened when Catherina asked to use the bathroom. I responded by referring to the bathroom in the Sicilian dialect I had learned as a child. That brought a spontaneous burst of wild laughter from our guests. I thought Catherina was going to wet her pants.

I had no idea what was so funny.

Finally—interrupted by frequent snickers—Salvatore attempted to explain it to me. It took a while, but I finally understood that I was using an antiquated form of the language. Of course! I had learned the dialect and idioms that existed when my grandparents had emigrated in the early 1900s. The language had changed. The world had changed. Radio and television had brought people and language together. Now, even Sicilians used the more polite forms of the language—what Salvatore referred to as the "Roman" form. But, to their boisterous amusement, they all recognized the term I had used.

In short, I had referred to the bathroom as—in English translation—"the shit-house."

# CHAPTER 59

## Options

Upon returning to Purdue after four months in Europe, my thoughts naturally turned to resuming my domestic travels. One of my first trips was to Tucson where I would give a talk at the University of Arizona and, most importantly to me, visit with my old friend, Mike Burke.

Naturally, Mike laughed at my story.

"Drink your tequila and *forget* it," he quipped. Over a gin and tonic, he shot a rebuking glance across the cocktail table. It was late. We were in a deserted hotel bar in the heart of Tucson on the night before my scheduled talk at the university.

"I *can't* forget it," I shot back. "It's just too damned important—this promotion." I swirled the gold tequila in my glass, causing the ice cubes to crackle, but didn't drink.

Mike leaned forward. "Look, those student protests and the canceled exam fiasco, that incident is a non-issue. Forget it. Buck would tell you if there was *any* kind of problem."

"No. He won't talk about it."

Mike sniffed. "That's just Buck being cagey."

I shrugged my shoulders. "You're probably right. All I know is, if I don't make full professor this year, I'm leaving."

Mike glared at me. "Come on, S.P. Where would you go?"

"I've had some nibbles. University of Colorado had me out. And I hear some California schools are discovering analytical chemistry. Maybe I'll trade my snow shovel for a surf board."

Mike chuckled. He had gladly left behind the snow and cornfields of Indiana for a faculty position at Arizona. "Come on, be serious," he chided. "I know people that would sell their first-born to get your job at Purdue."

I flashed a quick smile and shook my head, recalling what had happened during the previous academic year when I had foolishly expected promotion. "Look, Mike. They promoted Harry to full professor *last year*. Buck told *me* to wait my turn." I glared expectantly at Mike. Surely he understood.

I took a sip of the icy tequila mixed with a splash of tonic. The cool liquid soothed my parched mouth.

Mike sat back and gave me a long curious stare. His keen mind was fully engaged. No one had better insight to faculty politics.

"You didn't *really* think Buck could get *both* you and Harry past the promotions committee last year?" he asked.

"I had just as good a shot as Harry," I protested. "Publications; invited talks; hell, the committee knew that I would get the NATO Fellowship."

Mike nodded slowly. "All good, S.P. With the recognition from the short course...." He paused, and his eyes narrowed. "I hope you didn't push it."

I shrugged and began to reply, "I had hoped—"

"For what?" he interrupted. "Haven't you learned *anything* about academic politics?"

I stared back blankly.

"Look. The promotions committee meets once a year, yet horse-trading goes on all the time in hallways and cocktail parties. By the time the full professors walk into the meeting in November...." He let the words hang.

I shrugged. "What are you getting at?"

Mike sighed. "Do I have to paint a picture? Harry was promoted to full professor four years after tenure. That's pretty fast. Buck wouldn't have put him up without testing the water first. Now try to push Harry *and* you for early promotions—and yours even earlier? You and Harry *both* would have gone down in flames. He knew that."

I wagged my head. "All right, Professor Burke. You made your point." I stared at Mike for a few moments, debating whether I should tell him what I had done. "I ... I guess I shouldn't have complained to Buck."

"You did *what?*"

"Last spring, when I was on leave at Livermore, after Harry's promotion, I wrote to Buck—telling him I was disappointed at not getting promoted."

Mike wagged his head. "That's when Buck told you to wait your turn?"

I nodded.

"He was right."

After a long pause, I asked, "You think Buck's pissed at me?"

He grimaced. "I don't think it matters. He won't screw up your promotion."

"What do you think will happen?"

He shrugged. "I think you'll be promoted."

"Oh, c'mon, Mike. Play devil's advocate."

He leaned back and squinted. "OK, S.P. You play Buck, and I'll be one of the, say, unfriendly organic professors."

"All right. Let's say I—Buck—just finished making a pitch for my promotion."

Mike gave me a mock-serious look. "Well, 'Buck,' I've been looking over Perone's list of invited lectures. Very impressive. But—"

"Oh, sure, there's always a—"

"Are you going to let me do this, or not?" Mike threw me a sharp glance.

Smiling back at him, I said, "I'm sorry." I took a sip of my drink, scooted back in the chair, and listened.

"As I was saying, Professor Rogers, about Perone's invited lectures, it seems most people want to hear about his work with computers."

Mike paused and glared at me.

"Oh, sorry," I said. "Missed my cue. Umm ... yes, that's true. Do you have a problem with that?"

"I certainly do. This is a *chemistry* department, not computer science. Our *full professors* should be outstanding *chemists.*" Mike threw me another anticipatory glance.

"Well," I countered, "take a look at his other publications— electrochemical studies with flash photolysis. Damn good work, and well-funded by NIH."

Mike grew a sardonic smile at the self-serving words I was putting into Buck's mouth. "True, perhaps," he declared, "but where's the outside recognition? He's rarely invited to talk about the other work. He's a *curiosity. Not* an exceptional chemist."

I scowled at Mike and contrived Buck's reply. "What's *your* definition of a *chemist*—a pot-boiler turning crude oil into nylon or—"

He pushed out a palm. "Hold on, Professor Rogers. Don't put words in my mouth. I recognize the breadth of the chemical field. My *point* is that Perone is doing computer science, *not* chemistry."

"No. Your point is that he is most *recognized* for bringing computer science *into* chemistry. That's why other schools want to hear him talk. It doesn't diminish the other work he's doing."

Mike shook his head and laughed. "Christ, S.P., quit beating your drum. I give up already."

I gazed at him for a moment. "You really think this issue will come up?"

He nodded. "Some professors are downright obstinate when it comes to expanding their exclusive club. *Let me in,* they say, *but then shut the door.*"

I wagged my head. "That's pretty depressing."

"Hey, you *asked* me to play devil's advocate. Don't worry, you're going to be promoted, S.P. Buck can handle the *prima donnas.* Let them puff up their chests and condescend. Then he'll cut 'em down to size."

I took another sip of tequila. "Well, I guess I'll find out next week. Only thing I know is, no promotion, and I'm *out* of there."

# CHAPTER 60

## Finish Line

It was early March, 1971. I had carefully avoided passing by Buck's office. It had been awkward for both of us. The list of Purdue promotions hadn't hit the local newspaper yet. He knew what was on my mind. And I knew that he knew. I didn't want to see him.

Did I mention that it was awkward?

Buck handled it in his own inimitable way. He parked himself outside his office, chatting with two of his students.

Too late, I caught a glimpse of him, standing tall in his gray suit, one hand in a side pocket, the other pointing at a student. He leaned into the conversation, probably delivering one of his golden quips.

"Hey, Sam," I heard suddenly, as he shouted over the students' heads. "Got a minute?"

I cringed, but I gave him a wave and sauntered in his direction—thinking, *Oh, Crap! I really don't want this.*

As I approached, he sent his students on their way and motioned me into his office. I slid inside. He followed and closed the door.

"Sit down," he said. "We need to talk."

*Oh, shit!* I moaned to myself. *This is it.* I sat down in a chair off to the side of his desk and waited for Buck to get comfortable. He crossed one leg over the other and rotated his chair to face me.

He must have seen the color draining from my face. "Relax!" he decreed. "I'm not giving you bad news."

I breathed an audible sigh but said nothing.

He took a few seconds to examine the fingernails of one hand. Then he shoved the hand in a side pocket and stared me down. "You didn't hear this from me," he declared. "You'll get the official word tomorrow."

He paused, and my heart pounded.

A rare grin came over Buck's face. "Congratulations!" he announced. "You've been promoted to full professor."

I caught my breath. I thought my heart would beat itself out of my chest. "Th … thank you," I stammered. I felt my face flushing. "I … I'm really pleased to hear that."

He reached out to shake my hand. "Well done, Sam."

I took his hand and pumped it until he had to pull back. He dialed back the grin to expose his usual poker face. "I know you've been concerned about this."

I nodded, putting on my own poker face. "Yeah, it … it's been on my mind."

His head turned slightly and he gave me a crooked look. "You understand that I couldn't say anything?" It was more a declaration than a question.

I nodded. "I understand." At that moment I really did. As much as I would have wanted the misery ended sooner, I would have been disappointed if Buck had broken with protocol. Knowing the good news now made me very, very understanding.

"I really don't need to tell you more," he continued, "but I will."

I felt my eyebrows climb a bit.

He explained. "I know you've been a little nervous—and perhaps a bit impatient—about this promotion."

I felt my face redden. "I … I'm sorry about that letter, last year."

No more needed to be said. Buck knew what "letter" I meant.

He nodded solemnly, still eyeing me askance. "I don't know what might have happened last year. You'll just have to trust me on that decision. But…." His face turned so he could gaze directly into my eyes. "Your promotion *sailed through* this year. I've never seen such solid support—from *everybody*—even the hard-asses."

I attempted to visualize the contrary characters of Buck's allusion when, suddenly, I realized they would surely reveal themselves at my first sitting on the full professors' committee in the fall.

I wagged my head as the significance of Buck's statement sank in. "Thank you for sharing that with me," I said. "I ... I take it that's privileged information."

He shrugged. "It's supposed to be. Please don't repeat it."

We both remained silent for a few moments. Then Buck continued, "Everyone on the promotions committee understands that discussions don't get outside that room. Yet somehow, every year, there's a 'leak' or two that circulate, and that's disturbing.

"That's why I'm asking you to say nothing. I'm not in the habit of spilling secrets, but I'm making an exception."

My face must have been a question mark, as he quickly added, "I know you've been *concerned*. Maybe a little ... umm ... *angry?*"

"I'm not—"

He shoved out a palm. "It's OK. You're entitled. I just wanted you to know that I never doubted you would get here."

I gave him a shaky smile. "I don't know what ... well ... thank you."

He threw me a nodding grin. "Well, you—you and Harry—are *my guys*. I brought you here, and you've *both* done well and done me proud. So, let me thank *you*, Sam. Now...." He paused, and I thought he was about to tear up. But he kept his composure, sat back, and gave me that patented down-the-nose look. "Don't you guys begin to *slow down*. I expect great things from both of you, and don't you dare disappoint me."

I took that as his parting shot, and rightly so, as he began to rise and shove out his hand. I rose and grasped it warmly, "I don't think either of us would ever want to let you down, Buck."

I strode out of Buck's office on a cloud. I was a *full professor. Damn!*

I hadn't expected to hear the news from Buck, but I understood why he had broken the silence. He had shown a rare glimpse of his inner feelings. It wasn't the first, nor the last, time that Buck would refer to Harry and me as *his guys*. He had revealed also how personally engaged he was with our welfare and how sensitive he was to our feelings—or at least to my pathetic paranoia.

It struck me then that Buck had always had my back, even and especially when I was totally unaware. How many times had he done battle on my behalf behind the scenes—to get me more lab space; to help me pick up students; to get me invited to Livermore Lab; to win a research grant? What else?

I flashed back to that moment in 1962, when I first met him—standing on the front porch of that charming old bungalow in West Lafayette's faculty row, probably wearing the same gray suit that he wore today. Tall and thin, with a crooked grin and piercing eyes. Renowned professor, but down-to-earth and straight as an arrow.

That early April spring in central Indiana was the siren call that had brought me to Purdue. Buck had made that possible. In that flashback moment, it became clear to me that Buck had been more than just a mentor to me. I remembered then the words he had uttered during that first meeting when I had casually asked him about the key to success.

*Just do the things you know you should be doing,* he explained.

*Too simple,* I had thought. Yet I never forgot those words. It took me a while to fully appreciate their meaning. With each new challenge, I began to realize that it really was *just that simple.*

At this climactic moment, it struck me that—despite the turbulent personal, cultural, political and scientific changes that had rocked the sixties, and despite my own shortcomings and insecurities—adhering to that simple rule of Buck's had brought me through.

It has been my guide ever since.

# EPILOGUE

## The Rest of the Story

*Be careful what you wish for,* they say.

I had begun my academic career in 1962 with one goal in mind—to become a full professor at Purdue University. In March, 1971, I reached that goal. I was thirty-two years old and at that time—I was told—the youngest to ever achieve that rank in Purdue's chemistry department.

Was I happy? For a guy who, as a kid, hadn't even expected to go to college—I was *ecstatic*.

But that gratified feeling soon gave way to a strange malaise—a new quandary, the likes of which I had never experienced. It took a while—years—before I understood or appreciated the impact.

For as long as I could remember, I had awakened each day with a single thought—*where am I?*

No, I wasn't lost, physically. This was my way of making sure I stayed on course, professionally. Answering this question always led to the day's agenda—running an experiment; writing this; reading that; making a contact; planning a trip. Whatever.

Buried within that daily question, though, was the larger issue of progress toward my long-range professional goal. I didn't consciously address that larger issue every day, but sub-consciously my daily agenda adhered to its constraints.

Now, suddenly, this daily ritual lost its larger meaning. I didn't stop the daily ritual. I just didn't realize for a long time that I wasn't going anywhere. More accurately, I had no idea *where* I was going.

Perhaps I should have thought about the subsequent thirty or forty years before I achieved that full professorship. I hadn't.

Looking around at my colleagues—other full professors—I wondered: *What are they doing? What are their aspirations? Are they happy? Fulfilled?*

There was no single answer. Yes, there were further professional goals—awards, distinguished professorships, election to honorary societies, national and international recognition, and so on.

To achieve these goals, the full professor's pursuit of new scientific knowledge would have to continue unabated after promotion. In fact, for the goals mentioned above, the bar would be quite high.

The 1960s provided one avenue of activity that I couldn't ignore. Along with the notoriety of my role in the computer instrumentation revolution came a quantum leap in professional opportunities.

I received frequent invitations to spend time away from Purdue—presenting talks, organizing symposia, lecturing at universities here and abroad, serving on science panels, and consulting. Dave Jones and I organized a "road version" of the intensive computer instrumentation short course that we presented at Eli Lilly, Amoco Research, Hewlett-Packard and other sites.

Industrial scientists wanted computers dedicated to their instruments—collecting and analyzing data. Yet hardly anyone was prepared for it. Knowing that they had to adapt quickly prompted companies to develop computerization plans for their labs. That was when I got called in.

For the decade following 1968, I was swept up into a whirlwind of professional activities that threatened to take over my life. I was traveling somewhere an average of once a week. Some weeks—like when I was on speaking tours for the American Chemical Society—involved as many as five different stops. My list of invited talks would climb up into the hundreds.

I was having a great time. And I was getting paid for it. I learned enough about airlines, flight schedules, connection times, hotels, motels, restaurants, and rental cars to write a travel book. I had a canned talk for every audience—from novices to experts.

Did I mention that I was getting paid for it?

In fact, my consulting income began to approach my professor's salary—a situation ripe for distorting one's perspective. (Of course, my total annual income still wasn't enough to pay the service contract on a Wall Street broker's Lamborghini. But it seemed a lot to me—a guy who had hustled fifteen-cent shoe shines to finance college.)

With so much of my time devoted to business and professional travel, people might wonder if that violated university rules. It didn't. Travel to meetings was considered part of research time, paid by research grants. Most universities also allowed professors to do off-campus consulting during school breaks and perhaps one day a week during school sessions, as long as teaching obligations were met.

I had bought a ticket for a crazy merry-go-round and was having so much fun that I didn't realize I couldn't get off.

What was so tantalizing about that state of affairs?

First of all, air travel was still *fun* at that time. I rarely traveled first class, but even economy passengers were treated with TLC. In-flight meals might include a shrimp salad or a filet mignon. Flight attendants were young, friendly and attractive—and they still called themselves "stewardesses."

Then there were the restaurants. Experiencing fine dining in New York, Las Vegas, Washington, Boston, San Francisco, Chicago, New Orleans, Miami Beach, Philadelphia and Honolulu was doable, often within the same calendar year. Per diem allowances might not cover the cost of fine dining, but I could skimp on two meals to enjoy one great one. More often than not, some client was picking up the tab.

I never cared for hotels in convention cities. Lodging allowances didn't cover the cost of swanky places, and the others were pretty bad. A typical affordable big city single room at that time was probably built in the 1920s and was just big enough for one person and a suitcase.

One time, though, I made a tardy decision to attend the American Chemical Society meeting in New York City. All the lower cost hotels were filled, so I got a room at the Waldorf-Astoria. Now that was a *nice room*. The cost was more than triple my lodging allowance, and I had to take it on the chin. But it was worth it.

What really got me hooked, though, was meeting new and interesting professionals. Networks were being created that would benefit me— from getting papers published to getting proposals funded. Many of my grad students got jobs through these networks; future students came to me through these networks.

A surprising benefit of these professional interactions was the boost to my scientific creativity. During dozens of trips each year, I would come face to face with excellent scientists in my field. They would ask insightful questions; questions that made me think. Many times these inspired new research ideas that I wouldn't have conceived otherwise.

There's another intriguing aspect of professional travel—the purely social. I developed interesting and stimulating personal relationships with individuals all over the world. For a guy who had had practically no social life before arriving at Purdue, this was intoxicating.

Professional travel had a dark side though. It was like an addiction that I couldn't shake. I can't remember turning down a single opportunity. Subconsciously, I must have considered it compensation for the social repression of my high school and college years. It was an exciting ride, and—for better or worse—I was hooked.

My students saw the problem before I did, and they let me know about it. John Zipper speared me with barbed remarks at every opportunity. The most memorable skewering took another form.

It was at Frank Pater's farewell party at The Pub in the mid-seventies. After an evening of pizza, beer and tequila, Rick Baldwin took the floor to roast Frank and deliver a royal blue tee shirt with gold lettering, proclaiming Frank as a "Charismatic Avatar." Rick's dry humor left little doubt about the appropriateness of the descriptor, and at the time it made a lot of sense. Today, absent the beer and tequila, I haven't a clue.

After giving out Frank's tee shirt, though, Rick indicated he wasn't finished. He reached into his bag and brought out a second shirt. It was a Purdue gold tee shirt with black trim. He held it up backwards so that no one could see the lettering on the front.

"We have another gift," Rick announced, "for someone who spends a lot of time on the road, often in strange surroundings. We thought this might help."

Rick held up the tee shirt and nodded in my direction. "Doc, this is for you."

Flipping it around, he exposed the lettering, highlighting **Purdue University**. Above those letters was inscribed:

**If found,**
**return to:**

*S.P., in San Francisco, 1970s . [Copyright, S. P. Perone]*

The exposed words were met with an unprecedented round of hoots and guffaws. For the price of a tee shirt and a handful of black letters, Rick had captured the group's growing frustration with my constant travel.

It was then that I recalled the conversation I had had with Buck's students during my first year at Purdue. After listening to them complain about Buck's habitual absences from Purdue, I had remarked that I could never see myself abandoning my group like that. One of Buck's students—the wise, old Don Guran—had assured me it would happen to me, too.

He had been right.

My group's fondness for capturing truth with tee shirts was always entertaining.

For example, at a party in 1976, celebrating Rick Baldwin's Ph.D. oral exam and his upcoming professorship at the University of Louisville, he was awarded a tee shirt in Purdue gold with black lettering proclaiming him as "Doctor Grabber"—a dubious honor that Rick *claimed* alluded to his ball-hawking prowess on the championship intramural touch football team that he and other chemistry grad students had formed.

Rick then turned around and handed out a series of tee shirts of his own design. The white lettering on my shirt spelled, simply, "Ph.D." The others brilliantly captured the current dynamic of the Perone research group:

*From left: S.P.; Betty Hatfield (secretary); Rick Baldwin (new Ph.D.); Betty Hall, Phil Gaarenstroom (grad students); John Bixler (visiting professor). Summer, 1976. [Copyright, Keith Dahnke, used with permission]*

Clearly, my group's penchant for fun and pranks continued unabated in the 1970s.

Moving into the new wing of the chemistry building in spring, 1973, was a catalyst for such mischief. The moving boxes had barely been unpacked before my students hatched a devious strategy to stir up chaos.

That was the day a six-and-a-half foot Easter bunny visited my computer instrumentation lecture.

The bunny popped up from the shallow stairwell at the back of the large, tiered lecture room. Naturally, I was the only one that saw him. When students realized that I had halted in mid-sentence, they turned toward the back of the room to see what had captured my stunned gaze. Of course, the rabbit had disappeared down the stairwell and out the back door. The students saw nothing.

They returned attention to me, awaiting an explanation.

"You're not going to believe this, but...." I paused to examine the students' faces. Blank stares. I made a quick decision. Pointing to the wall clock showing ten minutes remaining, I said, "We've covered enough today. Let's pick it up next time."

I gathered up my lecture materials quickly, fending off questions from students, and prepared to run back to my office as quickly as possible.

*What mischief are they up to now?* I asked myself.

I rushed out of the lecture room and down the hallway connecting to the new wing. I scurried up two levels of stairs to the fourth floor. Bursting into the corridor, I caught a glimpse of the giant bunny at the other end, just as he slipped into the doorway to my office and labs.

Then I noticed the sign, "Hall Closed. Egg Hunt."

After hurrying down the corridor and ducking into my labs, I came face-to-face with the lanky Easter bunny—with my secretary, Sandra, perched on his lap. Neither spoke a word, but simply pointed to my office door.

I rushed into my office and noticed immediately a freshly drawn colorful Easter egg adorning my blackboard. In the middle of my cluttered desk was an old empty scotch bottle that had previously occupied a spot on my bookshelf. Inside the bottle was a sheet of notepaper containing the cryptic message:

> *Find the six Easter eggs hidden in your office, or else...*

*Or else what?* I wondered. I turned to see a small crowd of my graduate students observing me from the door connecting to my secretary's office. I voiced my query to them.

After proclaiming ignorance for a while, Rick Baldwin finally suggested that "perhaps" the Easter bunny had planted *raw* eggs in my office.

With my students mocking every move, I launched into a search, finding five eggs in short order. To their delight, the last eluded me. Despite my suspicion that the sixth egg did not really exist, I kept on looking.

In the meantime, the giant Easter bunny continued making mischief throughout our new building, while one of my students documented every move.

I'm happy to report that I did find that sixth raw Easter egg in my office, after a day or so, with no help and plenty of commentary from my students. It didn't take a genius to figure out, also, that my grad student, Terry Berger, had donned the Easter bunny outfit. He was the only one tall enough.

*Spring, 1973. Easter Bunny spreads cheer through the new chemistry building. Notable among the recipients: Upper right, Perone students (L to R) Marty Pichler, Sam Fratoni, Nobiyuki Kamiya (Postdoc from Japan), Rick Baldwin; lower right, Dr. Zara Welch (affectionately dubbed "Zorro" by students), Grad Student Administrator; middle left, Prof. Dale Margerum. Easter Bunny: Terry Berger. [Copyright, S. P. Perone]*

As evidenced by this uninhibited mischief making, social interactions with my students remained close throughout the early- and mid-seventies. Touch football games were replaced by handball tourneys. Crazy parties at the Perone's and rowdy gatherings at The Pub became less frequent. By the late seventies—with the age gap growing—I realized the student-professor relationship would never again be as it had in the sixties.

Successful research became its own reward. Financing a large research group became a full-time job, while I continued to maintain a brutal travel schedule.

That's when I began to realize that I was lost.

I was still young, but I had been at Purdue for nearly twenty years, and I was looking at another thirty years of doing what I was doing.

And I didn't like that idea at all.

Without a compass pointing to a higher professional goal, I had been sucked into a whirlpool that carried me past the same scenery over and over while I paddled as fast as I could to keep afloat. I didn't cherish the thought of spending another thirty years in that same vortex.

That was when I realized I had to make some drastic choices.


I'm not suggesting that the seventies were a waste.

I continued to get excellent research students. The group's personality changed, reflecting cultural shifts from the sixties to the post-Vietnam era. The group's productivity continued to generate publications, invited lectures, and research grants for me.

The analytical division at Purdue grew in size and stature. Fred McLafferty left for a position at Cornell, but we brought in John Beynon, a world-class mass spectroscopist, who split his time between England and Purdue. We expanded the division in the early seventies by adding two crackerjack young assistant professors, Fred Lytle and Nick Winograd. And we lured Peter Kissinger away from Michigan State to a tenured position at Purdue.

Buck Rogers left Purdue in the mid-seventies to join the University of Georgia. I hated to see him go. He had been an incomparable mentor to me. Under his direction, Purdue's analytical chemistry division had become the acknowledged leader in the world.

I took a turn as division head from 1975 to 1979, and I'm pleased to say I was a party to making two key tenure-track additions to the division—Ben Freiser and Graham Cooks. Both of these turned out to be great hires for Purdue and did me proud, as Buck would have said.

A number of postdoctoral associates and visiting professors joined my group from overseas in the seventies. They came to me from

England, Spain, Czechoslovakia, Denmark and Japan, and contributed enormously to my program.

My federal funding changed. As Mike Burke had predicted, NIH realized eventually that my photoelectrochemical research was good for measurement science but hadn't done much for cancer-related photochemistry. Fortunately, two other agencies—the Department of Energy and Office of Naval Research—saw value in my research for exploring solar-energy-related processes.

My funding for computer-related research from NSF petered out also. Again, I was fortunate that the Office of Naval Research was interested in picking up that part of my research program.

By the end of the seventies, thirty students had completed their Ph.D.s with me at Purdue—twenty-eight men and two women. There were also a number of masters and senior research students.

Four secretaries were part of the group during that period—Judy Snyder, Connie Dowty, Sandra Lawton, and Betty Hatfield. Today, we would call them "administrative assistants," which more accurately describes what they did. The last was Betty, who worked with me the longest. Holding now one of the top departmental administrative posts, she continues to be my liaison to Purdue.

So many of the good things that happened for me—and the bad things that were avoided—could be attributed to the competent oversight of these four women.

*Partial Group Photo, 1974. Standing, left to right: Dave Burgard, Quent Thomas, Rick Baldwin, Marty Pichler, Phil Gaarenstroom, Betty Hall, Keith Dahnke, Sandra Lawton (Secretary). Seated. John Zipper, Sam Fratoni, S.P. [Copyright, S. P. Perone]*

*Partial Group Photo, 1976. Standing, left to right: Betty Hall, Marty Pichler, Rick Baldwin, Bill Farrell, Dave Burgard, Betty Hatfield (secretary), Sam Fratoni, S.P. Seated: Lilly Lai-Miaw, Phil Gaarenstroom, Quent Thomas. [Copyright, S. P. Perone]*

Earlier, I listed a number of higher professional aspirations for full professors and noted that I hadn't adopted any. I failed to mention, however, that, sadly, some full professors lose their edge and *coast* toward retirement. Research productivity drops off; higher teaching loads or administrative jobs are taken on; research students become scarce.

That didn't happen to me.

But I did make a few mistakes. One of these was to get so wrapped up in outside professional activities that I would sometimes forge ahead blindly into new research areas. Inevitably, I slipped up.

The mistakes only happened a couple times, but they haunt me to this day. More than the thousands of flawless seminars, I recall vividly the two occasions when I really screwed up. One was a lecture at U.C. Riverside and the other at the University of Arizona. In each case I was asked a question pertaining to a collaborator's expertise, and I should have replied that I didn't know. Instead, I tried to answer and knew immediately—by the looks of those in the audience—that it was a mistake.

One mistake was bad. The second was unforgivable. I never did that again.

Fortunately, the seventies provided a number of ego-boosting events. I've already mentioned the NATO fellowship study in Zurich.

In 1975, the National Science Foundation invited me—along with four other American professors—to travel to Japan for a series of lectures on computer instrumentation. The University of Texas invited me to be a visiting lecturer for a month in 1976. Aarhus University in Denmark invited me to present two weeks of lectures; the British Chemical Society asked me to do a one-week lecture tour of several British universities; the American Chemical Society asked me to do several one-week lecture tours of American colleges and universities; I presented an invited paper at the International Conference on Photochemical Conversion and Storage of Solar Energy, at Oxford University, UK; and gave a plenary lecture at the J. Heyrovsky Memorial Congress on Polarography in Prague.

The ground-breaking book that Dave Jones and I had written, *Digital Computers in Scientific Instrumentation*, was published by McGraw-Hill in 1973. By graduate textbook standards, it was a "best-seller" and directed a lot of attention my way. One consequence of that notoriety was an intriguing foray into high-profile academic politics.

Shortly after the book was published I received a phone call from David Harris, an acquaintance in the chemistry department at the University of California Santa Barbara. "Sam, what are the chances you might consider leaving Purdue?" he asked.

Knowing that most U. C. chemistry programs spurned analytical, I expressed myself accordingly. "You're establishing a chair for me?" I quipped.

"Not exactly," he replied evenly. "Do you recall my telling you about setting up a Computational Chemistry Institute here?"

"You finally got it approved?"

"Yeah. U. C. San Diego blind-sided us with their proposal, but the chancellor picked us."

"When do you get started?"

"Soon as we pick a director."

"You have someone in mind?"

"We'd like you to come out for a visit."

"What does that mean?"

"I'm on the search committee. I think you're a great candidate."

"Anyone else thinking that way?"

He chuckled. "A few of us here know what you've done. We've got copies of your book."

My turn to chuckle. "Do they know it was an *analytical* chemist that wrote it?"

"Don't get chippy. We're more enlightened than our colleagues up in Berkeley."

"Good to hear. Tell me more."

Harris went on to describe the U. C. concept for a research institute, including the fact that seed money for salaries and a bare-bones computer hardware budget would be provided. Clearly, it would be a "soft-money" institute, surviving only with grants from outside agencies. The director would be people manager, part-time researcher, and full-time fund-raiser.

I had some serious reservations.

"I'm not sure I want to move into management," I said.

"We envision an *assistant* director to do the management. We need a director with a reputation and track record for getting federal funding."

"Hmm. What about moving my research group? Or teaching?"

"We would get you a joint appointment as professor of chemistry."

"With tenure?"

"That's the idea."

"Idea?"

"It's not in the job description. But to attract someone like you...."

"Have you considered getting someone from computer science?"

"You know the answer. Computer scientists aren't interested in chemistry."

"I'll bet most of your chemists aren't interested in my kind of computer applications either."

Harris paused. "Yeeesss," he drawled. "That's true. Most, like myself, are interested in theoretical computations."

"Why would you want *me*?"

"Two reasons. Your computerized instrumentation work is making a bigger splash. You've proven yourself as a director and fund raiser."

"Directing a computer short course is not the same as directing an institute."

"Playing college ball is not the same as the NFL, but the pros draft college players every year."

He had a point.

Well, long story short, I went on the interview trip. I had long ago fallen in love with California, and Santa Barbara was beautiful. Although I had serious reservations about the job, I had found that sun, surf, palm trees and year-round warm weather could be very persuasive. I let the hiring committee know that I would consider an offer.

The interview went well. My research talk was warmly received, although I seriously doubted any of the faculty appreciated the measurement science. When addressing the proposed institute, I talked about potential federal funding sources. They talked about how little the university planned to contribute.

Clearly, they wanted someone to come in and build something to attract outside money and be useful to chemistry professors—something they could tout as a resource while poaching some reputable physical chemist from Stanford or Harvard. I thought I could be that guy.

But there was a problem.

My conversation with David Harris several weeks after my interview trip was classic. Officially, he could only tell me that I hadn't gotten the job. The agony of the experience, though, prompted him to say more.

"It was a disaster," he declared. I sensed the despair in his voice. "We met with the dean—the committee did—and told him you were our choice. We asked about the joint appointment with chemistry."

"And?"

"He had no problem with it."

"What happened?"

"The chemistry department had to buy into the joint appointment, too. We made our pitch, but they shot us down. It was a pretty bloody battle. I'll spare you the details."

"I can guess."

"Let's be kind and say that some of the full professors didn't think you'd feel very comfortable here. It got pretty testy. Some of the younger committee members got beaten up pretty badly."

"My God, Dave, I'm sorry."

He sighed. "The young guys get what you're doing. They just didn't have any clout."

"Hope there's no permanent damage."

"Don't know. I'm glad I already made tenure."

It was disappointing to not get an offer. I had nearly convinced myself it would work out, pending the tenured appointment in the chemistry department. If the research institute didn't succeed, I could always retreat to a full-time position on the chemistry faculty.

Unfortunately, the UCSB chemistry department didn't want to let an analytical chemist into their club. I felt bad for Dave Harris. He had badly misjudged the openness of his senior colleagues there.

On a positive note, I had learned a very valuable lesson about academic elitism, and that would serve me well later on.

Perhaps the most significant activities I undertook in the seventies involved consulting. I had a long-term consulting agreement with Lawrence Livermore Lab. Most summers saw my family motoring to California, where I worked at the Lab for a few weeks. I would also fly to Livermore several times each year to engage in ongoing projects, often classified work. As previously mentioned, I spent part of a sabbatical leave there in spring, 1970.

During this time I also entered into a long-term consulting agreement with the Electric Power Research Institute in Palo Alto. In 1978, I spent a sabbatical leave there.

It was during the late seventies that I finally recognized my ambivalent feelings about what I was doing at Purdue. Admittedly, consulting was providing my most challenging and gratifying activity.

Before long I realized that I would have to make a choice.

Should I continue in a good and comfortable life at Purdue—albeit at the cost of continuing to do over and over what I had already been doing for nearly two decades? Or should I choose a more challenging—but potentially more gratifying—move to another area?

People might not be surprised to learn that my marriage also fell apart during this period. I take full responsibility for that. The seeds of disintegration had been sown decades earlier, but my rudderless navigation of an increasingly active professional life created strains that would test even the most solid marriage.

Undoubtedly, the turmoil in my personal life propelled me toward career decisions that I might have put off literally for decades. After considering several academic options, I decided that I would go off in a new direction. I chose the Livermore Lab.

Moving from the top academic analytical program to one of the most highly regarded non-academic analytical programs was a professional move that made sense to me. Nevertheless, it rarely happens. Academicians almost never abandon a hard-won university position for anything else but a better position at another university.

My colleagues at Purdue realized that my decision was driven by more than professional reasons, but they didn't understand the inner turmoil that was driving me toward this dramatic career change. Dale Margerum, who was the chemistry department head at the time, persuaded me to postpone leaving Purdue and to take a one-year leave of absence. He tried hard to make my return to Purdue as attractive as possible.

I did take the leave of absence at Livermore Lab for the 1980-1981 academic year. In the end, though, I chose to take a permanent position there. I left Purdue on good terms and retained an appointment as adjunct professor there for the next decade.

My colleagues everywhere were stunned to learn of my decision to move to Livermore Lab. They could not fathom how this would benefit me professionally. For me, however, it was a no-brainer. I needed a new challenge to turn me on again like I had been *turned on* in the 1960s. Livermore Lab—with its wealth of scientific talent tackling thorny national security issues—offered me an exciting new challenge, in spades. Years of consulting there alerted me to the pressing skirmishes both technical and political that would challenge me daily.

Would my professional reputation suffer? I didn't know. But if Jack Frazer's Lab career had set an example, I shouldn't worry. Jack's professional stature in analytical chemistry set a standard that I could emulate.

Not surprisingly, the dramatic changes in my personal life during this same period contributed significantly to the timing of this career move. My divorce was final in June, 1980. One year later, toward the end of my leave-of-absence from Purdue, I married my present wife,

Sylvia, a California native who then lived in Pleasanton, California. She and her two young girls, Stephanie and Melanie, were prepared to move east with me on my return to Purdue.

Moving back to Indiana, however, would mean that I had turned down the career-changing job opportunity at Livermore Lab.

And I really *wanted* that opportunity.

The most gut-wrenching part would be moving away from my children. Long discussions with them and my ex-wife, however, convinced me that the distance would not be an impediment to sustaining a close relationship. My children were eager to spend time with me in California. And I would make frequent visits back to Lafayette as part of my continuing position as adjunct professor at Purdue.

After much soul-searching, I concluded that the timing was ideal not only to make a career move to Livermore Lab, but also to make a "fresh start" in my personal life. The personal trauma of this move was mitigated greatly by the fact that, over the years, I had acquired a large circle of friends and colleagues in the San Francisco Bay Area—including former students, like Jim Birk who worked for the Electric Power Research Institute in Palo Alto. My consulting at E.P.R.I. had garnered a close friendship with my project manager, Bill Spindler, and his family. My close friends at Livermore Lab included not only Jack Frazer, Roger Anderson, Jack Harrar and their families, but many others. I already felt very comfortable in the Bay Area.

The decision was made. On July 1, 1981, I began my Lawrence Livermore National Lab career as a senior scientist.

Concerns about leaving my family back in Indiana and Illinois were allayed by our mutual desire to remain connected. Sylvia and I were also committed to embrace each other's as our own. My middle daughter, Amy—just nineteen and just out of high school—spent the summer of 1981 with us. She got a job as a waitress at Bellina's Ristorante in Pleasanton and helped with our wedding.

*Pleasanton, summer, 1981. S.P., Stephanie (11), Amy (19), Sylvia. [Copyright, S. P. Perone]*

Vita, Renée, and Sammy came for extended periods. My dad and my sister Nora's family from Illinois flew out for the wedding and a long

visit. The extended family visits would be characteristic of every subsequent summer for many years. I would travel frequently back to Illinois and Indiana. Sammy would come to live with us in 1988 when his mom passed away. Over the years, all of my children—and my sister's family—would establish residence, at least temporarily, in Pleasanton or nearby.

*Clockwise from upper left: Amy, Sylvia, Renee (Carmel, 1981); Melanie, Renée, Sylvia, Stephanie (Golden Gate Park, 1981); Sammy, Renée, S.P., Vita, Amy (CA, 1987); Vita, Stephanie (Pleasanton, 1981). [Copyright, S. P. Perone]*

I was both excited and apprehensive about my new position at Livermore Lab. It was a unique kind of professional environment—one where academic credentials might get you hired but were practically meaningless afterward. Your value to the organization depended on what you could contribute, not your title. The Ph.D. provided no safety net; neither did the lack of one exclude you from the director's chair.

I was grateful that I would not have to give up any of my professional activities. The Lab was operated by the University of California, and Lab scientists enjoyed many of the same perks as U.C. professors— like professional travel, sabbaticals and consulting. Lab scientists could pursue their own research interests, if they could obtain funding from outside agencies.

I was able to sustain research funding from the Office of Naval Research after joining the Lab. And I was able to continue my consulting relationships with E.P.R.I. and other organizations. In short, I had resources independent of the Lab, allowing me to continue personal research—although on a much smaller scale than at Purdue. But I could continue publishing, attending meetings, and other professional activities.

In fact, the 1980s were, in many ways, my most active, professionally—particularly regarding foreign travel. One or more European trips were scheduled each year—for consulting, attending meetings, and presenting lectures. My wife, Sylvia, was able to join me on many of these trips.

After a couple years of learning the ropes at Livermore Lab—a *matrix* organization filled with some of the sharpest scientists and engineers I would ever meet—I became the analytical chemistry section leader there. It was to become one of the most challenging, gratifying, successful—and ultimately the most frustrating—professional experiences of my career. Before it came to an end, my role had expanded to become manager of the analytical chemistry and materials characterization sections that included seventy scientists, engineers and technicians.

*European Travels, 1980s. Clockwise from upper left: S.P., Windsor, 1982; S.P. and Sylvia, Munich, 1980; S.P., Sylvia, Bill Jorgensen (Professor, Purdue), Henry Freiser (Professor, U. Arizona), I.U.P.A.C. Conference, Leuven, Belgium, 1981; Sylvia, London, 1982. [Copyright, S. P. Perone]*

Managing these numbers of exceptionally talented professionals—in an environment where our part of the Lab matrix was considered a *service* organization—was the single most challenging thing I've ever done. And I *loved* every minute of it.

Not surprisingly, this exciting challenge came with a price.

Lab programs were incredibly demanding. Weapons programs—with "national security" as a wedge—wanted our exclusive attention. Energy programs—in perpetual competition with Los Alamos National Lab—were even more persistent. Needless to say, expectations were high and patience low.

Daily engagement in programmatic crises was exhilarating, and success provided instant gratification. Yet looking to program managers for respect was usually met with some version of "what have you done for me lately?"

Stress levels were so great for middle managers at the Lab that in 1985 the Lab directors instituted a "stress management program" for us. About two dozen Lab middle managers, identified as "future leaders," were selected to participate in a six-month program that brought in a series of experts to work on everything from diet and exercise to psychotherapy and meditation. We met as a group every week. One week was spent on a retreat at Pajaro Dunes on the Monterey Peninsula. We began and ended the course with a complete physical. It was a very serious program.

And it probably saved my life.

Going into the program, I didn't think I was in bad physical shape. I found out differently. I wasn't obese, but a water-submersion test told me that a whole lot was fat—thirty percent of my body weight. Wow! That was a shock.

My blood pressure was elevated. I wasn't getting regular exercise. I wasn't getting enough sleep. The only word to describe my diet was "eclectic."

When we did our first psychological profile to measure the stressful elements in our lives, mine were off the charts. Divorce, remarriage, relocation, career change, blended family, economic dependents, workplace responsibilities, business travel and more—they added up to someone headed for a heart attack or worse.

By the end of the program, I had learned to recognize and manage mental and physical stress triggers; acquired a life-long addiction to jogging; and developed a taste for healthy foods. I had dropped over twenty pounds and lowered body fat below fifteen percent.


The biggest challenge of managing analytical sciences was convincing Lab programs that my scientists and engineers could not respond competently to their daily crises if the programs didn't provide for their professional growth. For various reasons the programs were unsympathetic. Some of these reasons were historical.

Jack Frazer—the gifted leader of the Livermore Lab analytical and chemistry programs for many years—had ceased being the analytical section leader in 1975. By the time I took over in 1983, Frazer had left the Laboratory. Despite the competent leadership of Frazer's successors, I inherited an organization whose political clout at the Lab was slipping. Financial support and employee morale were waning.

Program managers had become hypercritical of analytical services. Valid or not, the criticism excused their developing their own analytical facilities or turning to outside commercial labs. Rightly or wrongly, I concluded that analytical had to take responsibility for whatever the programs perceived as wrong with the system and *fix* it.

What was *wrong* with analytical at the Lab? Similarly to other national labs, analytical had evolved as a collection of independent high-level practitioners of analytical chemistry. Some were pursuing independently funded research. This kind of organization was perfect for addressing the challenging one-of-a-kind analytical problems delivered by the programs. But it was not easily managed. Nor was it well-suited to large numbers of repetitive samples coming in the door—an increasingly common scenario.

Even with well-trained technicians, the responsiveness of the Lab's analytical operation did not resemble that of commercial service labs—because it hadn't been built that way. As much as program managers might wish that it were, they wouldn't want to give up the skilled, but time-consuming, attention to their non-routine problems.

The key to resolving this dilemma, I concluded, was to introduce operational procedures comparable to outside commercial laboratories for the increasing volume of repetitive samples, while at the same time bolstering the expertise that had made Livermore's analytical facility intrinsically resourceful for one-of-a-kind problems.

The fact that these two goals were inherently incompatible—given a finite budget—was not lost on me or anyone else.

Somehow I sold my department head, Charlie Bender, on the idea. Then I persuaded my group leaders that we could do it.


My group leaders and I pulled together a five-year plan to turn things around. The plan included a number of new-hire Ph.D.s and technicians; new equipment; a state-of-the-art quality assurance program; and, above all, a commitment by everyone that responsiveness to program needs was our highest priority.

Getting that commitment required convincing our people that the programmatic support that had been elusive in the past would actually be realized through our efforts. They bought it. And that's what made it all work.

We quickly improved our sample turn-around times, quality control, and interfaces with all of the Lab programs. Program financial support improved. New scientists and new research came our way. Outsiders were eager to join our division. We achieved our five-year goals in three.

Once again, analytical became a thriving, energetic organization.

Then the sky fell.


The previous Chemistry and Materials Science department head, Charlie Bender, had hired me with the expectation that I would eventually lead the analytical program and he would advance to the associate director level. Unfortunately, Charlie got cross-threaded with upper Lab management and left.

After some re-organization in 1985, the department came under the direction of a new laboratory associate director, Chris Gatrousis. Unfortunately for me, he believed that all chemistry was a sub-set of physics—not an uncommon perspective at Livermore Lab, with Teller, Lawrence and Oppenheimer in its history.

In any event, Gatrousis had no place in his scientific universe for "analytical chemistry" or "measurement science." He never told me that. He just let me keep doing my job. I thought things would be OK.

Did I ever mention I was naïve?

After a few years of banging my head against the wall, vainly competing for financial and moral support, I gave up and resigned my post.

Strangely, I was asked to help find my replacement. A number of qualified candidates emerged, including a couple of my lieutenants. However, the biggest buzz came from a program manager from another department whose interview consisted of telling the hiring committee how poorly the analytical organization had been managed—exactly what the boss man wanted to hear.

Other interviewees—and the formally reported success of our five-year plan—distinctly repudiated the critique. So, of course, they hired the one who had told them what they wanted to hear.

A year later the analytical organization was in ruins, and their new hire had been exiled to another department. Talk about self-fulfilling prophecies. Very sad.

Fortunately, I had moved on. I took a position as a senior scientist in the ultra-secret Z-Division that worked closely with various intelligence agencies. It was fascinating work, but I could talk about none of it to practically anybody. This work, exciting as it was, came at the most awkward moment for me, professionally, as I was also the chairman of the analytical division of the nationwide American Chemical Society. This was possibly my most visible professional position ever, and I couldn't even tell people what I was doing. The work I was doing was stimulating, challenging and important, but continuing there would scuttle my outside professional presence. I didn't want that.

I had come to the Lab with the idea that I would be there until I retired. For seven or eight years I did things that gave me great satisfaction. I knew that I was doing what very few had ever done—moving successfully between high-level academic and non-academic positions. I had learned a whole new set of rules of survival and success, and turned them into a thriving operation, only to realize ultimately that nobody in "middle-management" is safe in any organization.

That's when I realized I had developed something valuable to offer to my old profession—academia. I had now experienced the best of both worlds—academic and non-academic—and I could relate that experience to a student body in a way that very few academicians could. The old saying—*those who can, do; those who can't, teach*—had been proven wrong by at least one person, and I believed I had something to sell.

The chemistry department at San Jose State University felt the same way. They asked me to join the department as a full professor. However—having been burned once at U.C. Santa Barbara and more recently sold out at Livermore Lab—I insisted on being appointed *with tenure.*

Turns out that had *never* been done at SJSU. They assured me that granting of tenure would be a *formality* after a year or two. However, having observed cutthroat academic politics first-hand at Purdue and having been dissed once by the myopic view of UCSB academic elitists, I held my ground.

So it happened. In September, 1989, I began my third career—at SJSU, as a *tenured* full professor. I know I made immediate enemies, but I had developed a thick skin.

Did my move to SJSU suggest that I considered my Livermore Lab career a failure? Far from it. At the very least, I had had a lasting impact at the Lab by recruiting a flock of competent, new, young scientists and technicians that were the future and now the present heart of analytical science there. For myself, I had acquired expertise in areas that practically no analytical professor ever had—managing a real analytical laboratory.

I considered the move to San Jose State a big positive, professionally. First of all, I was eager to develop a graduate course that featured the kinds of concerns peculiar to industrial environments, like quality assurance and good laboratory practices. Most academics couldn't do this, but my Lab experience qualified me. It would be a unique course.

Secondly, while California State Universities are not ordinarily chartered to offer Ph.D.s, San Jose State was lobbying with some success to get the chemistry department certified to do just that. With my previous experience in a highly-regarded Ph.D. program at Purdue, SJSU saw my hiring as a big boost to their campaign. I was excited to contribute.

Finally, I had been developing a new graduate level course combining my old computer instrumentation topics from Purdue with advanced data processing applications like multivariate analysis and artificial neural networks. I didn't know of a similar course being offered anywhere.

I wasn't eager to re-kindle a research program—grooming students, getting research grants, etc. Been there, done that. And, frankly, I didn't think I would get competent graduate students at SJSU like I had at Purdue.

Well, I was wrong about the students. I discovered that many of the chemistry graduate students were already fully employed in Silicon Valley industries. They were competent and motivated. The only drawback was the university wasn't their full-time occupation. Progress might be slower, but the talent was there.

Unfortunately, the Ph.D. program never materialized at SJSU. Like so many other things at the California State Universities, it succumbed to repeated budget crunches. On the other hand, the other things I had aimed to do did bear fruit. I introduced the two new graduate courses I described above. To my knowledge, they were not offered anywhere else.

I obtained research funding and directed a dozen successful master's projects. I also obtained NSF grants to up-grade the undergraduate analytical labs and develop an innovative undergraduate analytical curriculum based on my unique academic-industrial experience. This work was extended to a number of other universities and written up in the *Journal of Chemical Education.*[3]

For a few years I also served as Associate Dean for Science Research and worked at fostering good grantsmanship.

Ultimately, though, I saw the handwriting on the wall. The CSU system had once been the national flagship of higher education for the masses, but was rapidly becoming the neglected stepsister to the more prestigious, but similarly deteriorating, U.C. system. After a few years of zero to minimal raises and a misguided new policy of so-called "merit" raises—i.e., rewarding a select few without correcting the inherent problem of a noncompetitive salary scale—that was the last straw.

I left SJSU in 1999 to do full-time consulting. The consulting was great fun, challenging and rewarding. In addition to working with E.P.R.I, I had become involved with LifeScan, a Johnson & Johnson company, working on noninvasive blood sugar monitoring technology. I could consult two days a week and make *more* than I had made as a full professor at SJSU.

However, fiction writing soon became my new passion. My restrained consulting schedule allowed me to devote considerable time to this pursuit. I published my first novel in 2002, and completed six more in the subsequent decade. (Check out my website, www.samperone.com.)

---

[3]  "Transforming Traditional Quantitative Analysis into a Course on Modern Analytical Science", Perone, S.P.; Pesek, J.; Englert, P.; Stone, C., J. Chem. Educ., 1998, 75, 1444-1452.

What made me think I could write novels? I didn't know that I could. But I had always wanted to. From that day in seventh grade when I read my first novel—Robert Heinlein's *Red Planet*—I was hooked. I read everything he would ever write and expanded to other science fiction authors, like Asimov, Clarke and many more. Eventually my tastes expanded to other genres. Irving Wallace, Michael Crichton, John Grisham, Tom Clancy, David Baldacci, Alistair Maclean, and so many others fed my need to read. For some, like Heinlein and Wallace, I so loved their stories and style that I have read and re-read their novels many times.

From the beginning I knew I wanted to write. For literally decades I accumulated files of ideas and outlines for novels that I would write some day.

That day finally arrived.

In 1999, after nearly four decades of publishing technical work—constrained to reporting facts and observations—I looked forward to writing *fiction*. How delightful it would be to just *make it up*.

My first three novels were published in 2002, 2003, and 2004. These were a futuristic trilogy in the science fiction/time travel genre, featuring a main character, Tony Shane, who was a computer science professor at a large Midwestern university and also a government consultant doing classified research.

Sound familiar?

Friends and family assumed that the Tony Shane character was really Sam Perone. I wish. In fact, all the characters in this trilogy were composites of real people that I knew. The situations and settings—universities, government labs, Washington, California, San Francisco, New Orleans, Switzerland, Denmark, etc.—were very familiar to me. Using these helped give the books an air of authenticity.

Did I have any writing talent? I don't know. I'll let others be the judge.

Did I have writing credentials? I certainly thought so. Writing two textbooks, well over a hundred technical articles, numerous book chapters, and countless research proposals at least taught me how to organize thoughts and construct readable prose. In fact, I compare writing *novels* to writing *research proposals*. In both cases one conceives a new idea, does the fact-finding to give it some credibility, writes it up in the most compelling manner, and tries to convince someone to buy it.

The experience of technical writing doesn't translate directly to creative writing. I knew that. Nevertheless, in the summer of 1999, I just plunged ahead—first digging out from my dusty, decades-old files of possible story lines the idea that would become my first novel, *The StarSight Project*.

*The StarSight Project* was about university professor, Tony Shane, consulting for the CIA and developing a pattern recognition program that could predict terrorist attacks. My personal experience with pattern recognition programs—examining enormous amounts of seemingly unrelated data to pull out previously unsuspected correlations—gave the premise some credibility. The novel became a futuristic mystery-thriller about a race to develop the program before a bold Al Qa'eda attack might bring down countless commercial aircraft simultaneously in flight over the Northeastern United States.

Does that terrorist scenario sound familiar? Does the government data mining project sound familiar? Did I think at the time that these things would come to pass? Certainly not as quickly as they did.

I completed the novel and sent it off to a New York literary agent on September 6, 2001. A week later—after the eerily similar terrorist attack of September 11—I contacted the New York agent and asked for my manuscript to be withdrawn.

Those friends and colleagues who had reviewed the original manuscript were spooked by the uncanny similarity between my novel and reality. So was I. It's one thing to write about fictional disasters; it's another thing when that scenario turns into reality.

I revised my novel, opening instead with the September 11 terrorist attack, and ultimately got the book published with an independent publisher, iUniverse, in 2002.

Was it any good? Looking back, I can find lots of fault with it. It was too long, too wordy, too little dialogue, too linearly organized, too technical, etc., etc.

I wrote the second and third books of the trilogy using a completely different approach—one that I have used ever since. I write the most essential chapters first, even if they are in the middle or end, and write subsequent chapters according to plot priorities. I keep chapters short, keep sentences concise, keep the action moving, and assume my audience is smart enough to connect the dots. Finally, I write as if I were creating a screenplay—that is, moving from scene to scene with graphic descriptions of each setting.

Am I doing any good at this? I can only say that it's a good thing I don't have to do this for a living. I publish independently and sell my print and e-books online. It's a good business model if you can crack into a big market. I haven't done that, yet.

My goal has been to sharpen my writing skills until I reach the point of producing a knock-your-socks-off book that gets national attention. I'm still working on it.

There is one good objective appraisal of my novels. *Five* of the seven have been recognized in award competitions. *Youthanasia* (2009), in fact, was cited in *three* different competitions—as runner-up to the Book of the Year for young-adult fiction by Forward Reviews, Next Generation Indie, and National Indie Excellence Awards. My illustrated children's book, *Star of the Future* (2010), was a finalist for the National Indie Excellence Book of the Year Award in Juvenile Fiction.

I've taken time away from writing novels recently to put together this memoir. It's been great fun tripping down memory lane. I hope that every reader will enjoy it, too. But I'm ready to get back to writing *fiction*.

I have this great idea for a new Tony Shane novel....

# Author's Notes

While early reviewers have enjoyed this accounting of my experiences as a young professor in the 1960s and beyond, nearly all have wanted to hear more than the brief glimpses of family life that I've provided. I understand that the picture remains incomplete, but my intent was to tell a story primarily of my journey through the academic minefield, with the turbulence of that era as a background. These provide more than enough material. My personal family history is colorful enough to fill a separate volume someday.

Those who were at Purdue in those early years know that there are many more stories to be told than could possibly fit into this volume. Some reviewers have added input to the stories I have told.

It may be obvious to some that I have tried to stick to the terminology that was prevalent during the time periods described. For example, the Livermore Lab has been called "Lawrence Livermore National Laboratory (LLNL)" for many years now, but in 1967, when I first went there, it was called Lawrence Radiation Laboratory (LRL). Some "antiquated" technical terms were also used, like "core memory" rather than "RAM"; memory "words" rather than "bytes"; and "megacycles" rather than "megahertz" ("megahertz" became the official term in 1960, but did not fully replace "megacycles" in common usage until the seventies).

Unfortunately, I didn't anticipate in the early 1960s that I would someday write a memoir. I didn't begin to collect photos until the late sixties when the summer computer course evolved, and that fact is reflected in the selection of photos in this book. Hopefully, the verbal descriptions of early students and events are adequate for reader visualization.

Sadly, my long-time friend and confidant, Mike Burke, and the individual most responsible for encouraging this memoir, Jim ("J.R.") Birk, both passed away before the book's completion. It is to their memories and the memories of many of the book's characters that are no longer with us—Buck Rogers, Dave Jones, Larry Sybrandt, and John ("Zip") Zipper—that this book is dedicated.

Sam Perone
July, 2014

# ABOUT THE AUTHOR

Sam Perone was born in Rockford, Illinois. He received a B.A. from Rockford College, where he was elected to Phi Beta Kappa and won a Woodrow Wilson Fellowship to attend graduate school at the University of Wisconsin. He completed his Ph.D. in analytical chemistry with Irving Shain in 1962 and then joined the faculty of Purdue University. After rising to the rank of full professor in 1971, and serving as analytical chemistry division head from 1975-79, Perone moved, in 1981, to the Lawrence Livermore National Laboratory, where he subsequently became Associate Division Leader for Analytical Sciences. In 1989, Perone joined the chemistry faculty of San Jose State University, serving for a time as Associate Dean for Research in the College of Science.

Perone has published well over 100 research articles in electrochemistry, chemical instrumentation, photoelectrochemistry, chemometrics, and chemical education; and he has co-authored two textbooks, *Digital Computers in Scientific Instrumentation* (1973), and *Digital Electronics and Laboratory Computer Experiments* (1975).

After taking early retirement in 1999, Perone has been an independent consultant in the San Francisco Bay Area and has devoted

his spare time to the writing of fiction. To date, he has published seven novels: *The StarSight Project* (2002), *Crisis on Flight 101* (2003), *Einstein's Tunnel* (2004), *Murder Almighty* (2005), *Judgment Day* (2006), *Youthanasia* (2009), and an illustrated children's novel, *Star of the Future* (2010). Five of his novels have been honored in Book of the Year competitions. (See www.samperone.com)

Sam Perone and his wife, Sylvia, live in the Sierra Foothills of Northern California.